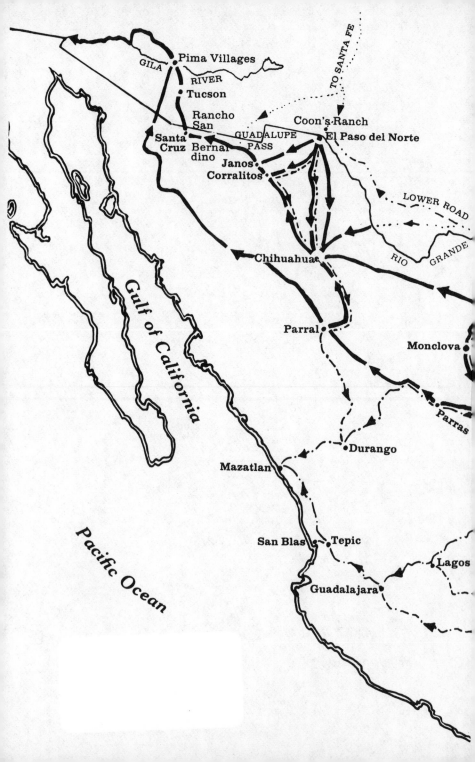

# The El Dorado Trail

# The
# El Dorado

*The Story of the*

# Trail

*Gold Rush Routes*
*across Mexico*

## BY FEROL EGAN

University of Nebraska Press
Lincoln and London

First Bison Book printing: 1984
Most recent printing indicated by the first digit below:
1    2    3    4    5    6    7    8    9    10


Library of Congress Cataloging in Publication Data
Egan Ferol.
    The El Dorado trail.
    Reprint. Originally published: New York : McGraw-
Hill, 1970.
    Bibliography: p.
    Includes index.
    1. California—Gold discoveries. 2. Overland
journeys to the Pacific. 3. Mexico—Description and
travel. 4. El Dorado. I. Title
F865.E35 1984      917.2'04      83-16708
ISBN 0-8032-6706-1 (pbk.)

Reprinted by arrangement with the author

**FOR MARTY,**
my wife and companion
of the trail

Gaily bedight,
A gallant knight,
In sunshine and in shadow,
Had journeyed long,
Singing a song,
In search of Eldorado.

But he grew old—
This knight so bold—
And o'er his heart a shadow
Fell as he found
No spot of ground
That looked like Eldorado.

And, as his strength
Failed him at length,
He met a pilgrim shadow—
"Shadow," said he,
"Where can it be—
This land of Eldorado?"

"Over the Mountains
Of the Moon,
Down the Valley of the Shadow,
Ride, boldly ride,"
The shade replied,—
"If you seek for Eldorado!"

Edgar Allan Poe

*1849*

# CONTENTS

# CONTENTS

# Contents

# ACKNOWLEDGMENTS

The sources for this book are listed in the notes and bibliography. Because of the nature of the gold rush, there is some overlapping of citations. The overall purpose of such documentation is twofold: to provide leads for the general reader on a given topic, and to provide leads to unworked veins for other historians.

The book is based upon primary sources, *i.e.*, diaries, reminiscences, and letters. Other source materials are government documents, newspapers, and a few important biographies and historical introductions to primary sources.

Another very important source for this book was the country itself. For in Mexico, it is still possible to follow the routes the Argonauts took as they traveled *The El Dorado Trail*.

Most of the research for this book was done in the Bancroft Library at the University of California, and I wish to thank Assistant Director Mr. Robert Becker and all the members of the staff, who were extremely helpful. I especially wish to thank Dr. John Barr Tompkins, who gave his time freely in the search for leads and who was exceedingly helpful in locating illustrations and maps for me. Two other members of the Bancroft Library who gave me advice and shared their considerable knowledge of the American West and the history of Mexico were Mr. Dale L. Morgan and Director Emeritus Dr. George P. Hammond.

Among friends and mentors, the following persons deserve a special thanks: Mr. A. B. Guthrie, Jr., who took an early interest in this project and saw it as a part of *The American Trails Series;* Dr. George R. Stewart, who encouraged me to become a writer; Dr. Charles L. Camp, who suggested journals and diaries that were of help; and Mr. Richard Dillon, author-librarian and friend, who sent me obscure references and took time from his own busy life to answer many technical questions.

Finally, my greatest debt of thanks is to my wife Marty. She retraced

# ACKNOWLEDGMENTS

*The El Dorado Trail* with me, photographed it, kept me going at the low moments, and typed the manuscript.

Ferol Egan

*Berkeley, California*
*July 9, 1968*

# PROLOGUE

The voyage had been very long, and it was only the second day ashore for the men. They were not yet accustomed to walking on the non-rolling ground, and they didn't really know which island their ships had reached. But they were thankful to God and the Admiral, for they had not sailed off the end of the world.

Using sign language, the Admiral tried very hard to communicate with the natives. In his journal he described these people and their manner of living. He also stated he had been "... attentive and worked hard to know if there was any gold ..."[1] He noted some of these people wore little pieces of gold as nose decorations. He asked them where they got this gold, and they told him that somewhere to the southwest lived a great king who had lots of the yellow metal.

Here, then, was the beginning: an Italian sailor from Genoa; Spanish caravels; the Caribbean island of San Salvador which the Admiral believed to be close to Japan; and a story about a golden kingdom. Unknown to Christopher Columbus on that second day of landfall in 1492, what took place was to become the pattern for all gold rushes in the New World. First, there would be a legend or rumor; second, a piece of real gold to give credence; and finally, the gold fever that made men willing to believe and to seek.

Though Columbus failed to discover a golden kingdom in his four voyages to the New World, he brought back enough gold and enough tales of gold to be found to cause tremendous excitement. The wildest dreams seemed within reach for men willing to run the risk, and many men were awaiting the opportunity. For the men who followed in the wake of Columbus were true questers. They believed in the existence of Atlantis, the Holy Grail, the Fountain of Youth, the Amazons of Queen Califia, and the Island of Antilia, that refuge from the Moors where a Christian archbishop and six bishops had built Seven Cities near beaches of golden sand. And even if all these questers were not readers, they at least knew about the travels of Marco Polo. So the effect of the golden artifacts carried to Spain by Columbus was the beginning of a search for New World gold that continued into the twentieth century.

Then when Cortés and Pizarro carried out their golden conquests, nothing seemed impossible or implausible. No matter how wild the tale, men were willing to believe another Aztec or Inca nation was waiting to be plundered if only it could be found. To add to this belief, descriptions of Spanish treasure fleets were circulated throughout Europe in newsletters and broadsides by the great financial House of Fugger. After all, a man could tell himself, it had happened in Mexico and Peru. Why couldn't it happen again?

By 1535 that story of a rich king to the south—the story first heard by Columbus—began to assume a fuller shape. It went like this: somewhere on a plateau in the high mountains of what is now the Republic of Colombia lived a king whose wealth was even greater than that of the Aztecs or Incas. The king's name was *el hombre dorado*, or El Dorado: the gilded man of Cundinamarca. Once a year El Dorado was the central figure in a ceremony that required the covering of his body with gold dust. To accomplish this, his body was coated with resinous gums. Then it was liberally dusted with gold. When this was done, El Dorado was carried in a litter decorated with discs of gold. The first part of this procession consisted of men whose bodies were painted with red ochre, as this was a mourning ceremony for the wife of an earlier chief who had drowned herself in Lake Guatavitá and became the goddess of the lake. To pay tribute to the goddess, all those following the men painted with red ochre were dressed in richly adorned costumes of jaguar skins, bright feather headdresses, and all were decorated with gold and emeralds. Songs and music accompanied the procession; and when it reached the shores of the mountain lake, El Dorado and his nobles got into a canoe and paddled to the center of the lake. There the gilded king threw offerings of gold and emeralds into the icy water. Finally, at the close of the ceremony, El Dorado jumped from the canoe and washed the gold dust from his body.

# Prologue

The story of El Dorado touched off a series of expeditions from both sides of the Andes. Spaniards, Germans, and Sir Walter Raleigh tried to find the kingdom of the gilded man; and some expeditions did find the plateau and the lake. They even found a few golden artifacts, but they did not find a golden kingdom. But such legends are hard to kill. Some men tried draining Lake Guatavitá in order to find the gold that El Dorado had tossed into it. Other men began to search elsewhere as they thought the land of El Dorado had not been found. Then to add to their ideas of another location, a strange event took place just inland from the Sea of Cortés and less than 100 miles from the northern Mexico outpost of Culiacán. Here, in March of 1536, only one year after Sebastián de Belalcázar coined the name El Dorado for the gilded man, four ragged, gaunt, and weatherbeaten men—followed by Indian friends—came out of the arid brushland and stumbled into a party of Spanish soldiers commanded by Diego de Alcáraz. No one could have been more amazed than Alcáraz and his soldiers; and no men could have been happier than the bearded Núñez Cabeza de Vaca, the tall Negro Moor Estevánico, and the two other survivors of the 300 men of the Narváez Expedition that had set out to conquer Florida.

In the eight years since their shipwreck off the Florida coast in 1528, these men had wandered from one Indian tribe to another as they walked westward in their attempt to get back to Mexico. During their incredible journey, the men had heard Indians tell of the Seven Cities of Cíbola. The story of these golden kingdoms somewhere in the north tied in neatly with the Seven Cities of Antilia, and once Cabeza de Vaca told other Spaniards this story the rush was on. Expedition after expedition rode northward in search of the golden cities, and found mud huts and the endless horizon of the Great Plains. The most famous of these expeditions was led by Coronado, who got as far north as present-day Kansas before he killed his Indian guide, gave up his dream, and returned to die in peace at Cuernavaca.

True enough, gold and silver mines were being worked in Mexico, and were producing a considerable fortune. Still, many Spaniards could not accept the fact that there wasn't an El Dorado in the south, or Seven Cities of gold in the north. Myths kept turning up to carry the golden dream along. As late as 1844 a scholarly New Yorker, J. A. Van Heuvel, published *El Dorado,* in which he argued that the gilded king's country had to be somewhere in South America. What

Van Heuvel did not know and what the people of Mexico did not know was that the golden land had already been occupied by the Spanish and the Mexicans, and was about to be taken over by the Americans. Within four years the fabled Seven Cities of Cíbola and the fabulous El Dorado were destined to merge and become one place called California after Califia, Queen of the Amazons.

After all the questing, the discovery of the golden kingdom took place on January 24, 1848, as the result of Captain John Sutter's prosaic project—the building of a sawmill on the south fork of the American River in the foothills of the Sierra Nevada at Coloma, California. As the news of this discovery traveled to the east coast of the United States, the first reports referred to this discovery as the *real* El Dorado. Once again the quest for El Dorado began, as there were pieces of real gold from this land; and there were stories of what was there by men who had *really* seen it. So, while there was no gilded man, there was a golden land.

The ways to El Dorado were many, but one of the first routes led across Mexico—the land of that first golden kingdom plundered by Cortés and his army. This, then, is the story of the trails across and up and down the *barrancas* and plateaus of Mexico: the trails that led to the Pacific Coast ports where Manila galleons once were anchored; the trails that followed in the footsteps of Coronado and all the others who trekked into the deserts of northern Mexico and the American Southwest. For while there were many branches to the El Dorado Trail, all were bound for the golden land of El Dorado.

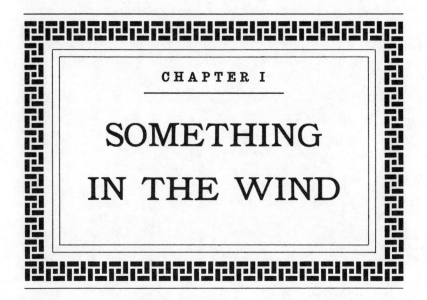

CHAPTER I

# SOMETHING
# IN THE WIND

# A PERUVIAN HARVEST?

That unpopular war with Mexico was over, and the troops were coming home. The first arrivals had already been home long enough to begin to bore hometowners with their stories about the country south of the Río Grande. In political circles all the talk centered around the hero of Buena Vista—"Old Rough and Ready" Zachary Taylor, who was about to become the Whig candidate in the Presidential race of 1848. Along with speculation about a transcontinental railroad, the business world watched the movements of the Pacific Mail Steamship Company. It had received a Federal subsidy to deliver mail to the Pacific Coast, and Howland and Aspinwall were building steamships that would be ready to sail round the Horn and up the coast of South America to California by early 1849. And there was something in the wind about gold in California.

The prospects of gold were dubious at best. California was a long way off, and the Americans living there were a bit prone to stretching the truth. Furthermore, nobody had really offered any definite proof of the existence of gold. Still there was that news story in the New York *Herald* on August 19, 1848—the one that mentioned the discovery of a gold mine "... on the south branch of the American fork ...," and ended with the prediction that "... a Peruvian harvest of the precious metals ..."[1] awaited only enough miners. But the San Franciscan who had mailed this news to the *Herald* had posted it on April Fool's day, and frontier people were noted for tall tales. A wise man would do well to take care of things at home until there was some solid news concerning California gold.

## THE TEA CADDY OF GOLD

What skeptical Easterners did not know was that solid news of the affair at Sutter's Mill was on its way. At Monterey, the military governor, Richard B. Mason, had just returned from a tour of the gold country. On this trip he had been accompanied by his Negro servant Aaron, young Lieutenant William T. Sherman, Captain Joseph Folsom, four other soldiers, and two civilians. Colonel Mason had visited the placer mines to verify the gold strike. This he had accomplished, but even more, he had had Captain Folsom buy "... an oystercan full ..."[2] of gold. In addition, various persons—including Captain John A. Sutter—had contributed gold specimens to be sent to Washington. Altogether, Colonel Mason had enough gold to fill a tea caddy with 230 ounces, 15 pennyweights, and 9 grains.

Governor Mason then selected Lieutenant Loeser of Company F, 3rd United States Artillery, as the courier to carry the tea caddy of gold and a long letter to Adjutant General Roger Jones. Within his letter Mason gave a full description of the richness of the goldfields, the problems of the Army and Navy as more and more men deserted and headed for the gold country, the rising cost of living in California, and the early rush of tradesmen, merchants, and professional men to the Mother Lode—a rush that had almost made other California settlements into ghost towns.

At the end of August, 1848, Lieutenant Loeser boarded a schooner that was southward bound. When the ship put into port at Payta, Peru, Loeser left her and caught a British steamer sailing northward. He left this vessel at Panama, crossed the Isthmus, and caught another ship to Jamaica. From there he sailed aboard the schooner *Desdemona* to New Orleans, where he had his first opportunity to send a telegraph message to Washington about the discovery. He then continued on his way and arrived in Washington with the tea caddy of gold in the early part of December. Only then did he learn that a Navy lieutenant had arrived there ahead of him with official letters about the strike and small samples of California gold.

8

Something in the Wind

## SAILOR ON HORSEBACK

While Lieutenant Loeser was still in Monterey during July of 1848, Naval Lieutenant Edward Fitzgerald Beale was stationed aboard the flagship *Ohio* in the port of La Paz, Mexico. Here the Commander-in-Chief of the U. S. Naval forces in the Pacific Ocean, Thomas ap Catesby Jones, notified his officers that he needed a courier to carry dispatches across Mexico and on to Washington. These dispatches from Consul Thomas Oliver Larkin and Commodore Jones described in detail the great wealth to be picked up in California and pointed out the strain this discovery was placing upon normal activities. With his letters to Secretary of State James Buchanan, Larkin enclosed a small amount of placer gold, and wrote that the yearly yield of gold would equal ". . . the whole price our country pays for all the acquired territory."[3] In letters to the Secretary of the Navy, John M. Mason, Commodore Jones stated that here was the ". . . real *Eldorado.* . . ."[4] Jones also made it quite clear that ". . . Beale [had] volunteered to cross the country [Mexico] *at his own expense* to be the bearer of my communications to you."[5] And nowhere in his communication did Jones say anything about an Army-Navy contest to get the news to Washington. In fact, all documents indicate neither Commodore Jones nor Lieutenant Beale had any knowledge of the plan to send Army Lieutenant Loeser to Washington.

In addition to dispatches and Larkin's samples of gold, Beale carried a small amount of his own gold. With this very solid news of the California discovery, young Beale left the *Ohio* at La Paz on July 29 and boarded the *Congress,* which was bound for Mazatlán. Outside the Gulf of California the *Congress* sailed smack into the beginning of a summer storm front. By the time Mazatlán came in sight, heavy waves were breaking along the curved, white beach named Olas Altas, or high waves, and dashing white foam and spray over the rocky promontories extending from the coastline.

On shore Beale hired a small Mexican *goleta,* or schooner, to take him south to San Blas. The voyage was quite stormy and rough, and

9

it took five days for the battered vessel to sail a little over 100 miles to the old Spanish port. When Beale arrived, the wind was whipping the tall palms lining the long white beach; but the weather was warm, and the handsome lieutenant quickly learned he was in the northern edge of the tropics. Every move seemed to require effort, and the heat was like a steam bath. Even periods of clear sky in between squalls made no difference. The sun only made the moisture-filled air that much muggier. Beale's clothes stuck to his skin, and he found it difficult to breathe. To make matters worse, he felt as though he were being consumed alive by every gnat, mosquito, and chigger that thrived in the decay of dead vegetation, dead animals, and deadly heat. As he swatted and cursed his tormentors, he saw he had landed in an insect paradise—a marshy jungle village where the small population of human beings burned punk inside their houses during the rainy season and lived in a cloud of smoke in order to combat the swarms of buzzing, hopping, and crawling insects.

Beyond the beach and San Blas itself, Beale saw a squared-off bluff which the Mexicans called Cerro de Basilio. On this hill, named after the crested iguana lizards that lived in this lush country, were the remains of old San Blas. This was Spanish San Blas left over from the time when Manila galleons were built and repaired there, and when it was a thriving port with shipping offices located in Tepic—that mountain town some 50 miles above and away from the heat, insects, snakes, and lizards. Even from the beach town, Beale saw that the old Spanish settlement was being taken over by the jungle. The chapel built of lava boulders, the nearby *contaduría,* or customs and storage house, and the fort overlooking the beach with its cannons pointing out to sea still had firm walls. Yet the jungle was closing in on them, as it had on the rest of the old town, so that it was hard to see it from the beach. Banana trees, mangroves, and avocados intertwined the pillars, walls, and foundations of other buildings, making the dark lava boulders seem like parts of trees.

Fine-featured "Ned" Beale was a long way from the District of Columbia, where he had been born on his father's estate not more than a mile from the White House. Standing in San Blas in front of the Mexican governor, this brown-haired, dark-eyed *gringo* hardly looked the type to ride across Mexico. He had a thin moustache that was more like the hair above the lips of an unfortunate girl, and his beard was a pleasant outline that made his face appear to be resting on a wiry buggy robe. True, his face was tanned, and he was dressed in an outfit which he fancied would be a disguise. But all it would tell a bandit was that here was a lone man from another class, a man who might have a jingle in his pocket and no taste for violence. Even as Beale talked to the governor in more than passable Spanish, the governor was shaking his head in disbelief at what this young man planned to do.

To travel from San Blas to Mexico City required preparations, required a large force of guards who would not hesitate to shoot or slash with the machete. To make this trip alone or even with one or two others was to bid this world good-by. "*Señor*," the governor told Beale, "an American like yourself could not travel a dozen miles in Mexico without being robbed and murdered." [6]

With the Mexican War just over, this could not have been a surprise to Beale; but he was not afraid to try what the governor considered suicidal. He had been in tough situations before as a courier. It had not been easy to crawl through the Mexican lines at the battle of San Pascual and run to San Diego for reinforcements to save Kearny's Army of the West. Still, Beale wanted to know what dangers he should expect, and he asked the governor why the road out of San Blas was so dangerous.

The governor pointed out that since the end of the war Mexico's roads and trails had become the lifeline of the lawless. He said that many soldiers from the forces of General Mariano Paredes had deserted and become bandits. "These *ladrones*," he said, "are desperate, *señor*, and would not hesitate to kill you for the horse you ride." [7]

Lieutenant Beale thanked the governor for his warning. He secured the services of a guide, purchased a horse, and got ready for his trip. When he was prepared to leave San Blas, he was wearing a ". . . sombrero, a red flannel shirt, leather breeches and boots." [8] For protection against the *ladrones* he had armed himself with four revolvers and a bowie knife. He had not taken the governor's warning lightly, and believed he was ready for the *gente de camino*.

It was August 12, 1848, when Beale thanked the governor of San Blas, said *adiós*, and headed for Mexico City. The beginning of his journey was not fast, but it was not made difficult by bandits. The first obstacle was the area of low swamplands between San Blas and the beginning of the foothills at La Puerta, or the gateway. Beyond this point were the villages of Guaristempa and Navarrete, and be-

yond them the trail led upward to Tepic. But as Beale and his guide
passed the tall coconut palms at the northern edge of Cerro de Basilio and looked across the swollen estuary—the Río Santiago just to
the north, and the miles of swampland between them and La Puerta
—they wondered if they would ever reach the foothill gateway leading out of San Blas.

Just beyond the northern base of Cerro de Basilio they caught a
raft ferry and crossed the estuary. Beale looked south and saw the
thick line of mangrove trees crowding the banks; the huge mud-
dauber nests of parrots in the forks of trees—the size of a hundred
hornets' nests stuck together—the color and movement of parrots,
egrets, macaws, and more tropical birds than he knew existed. Add-
ing to the color were the wild orchids festooning the shaded mangrove limbs; and on the river the dugout canoes of silent fishermen
skimmed the water—fishermen who held spears aloft and watched
the water for the movement of fish. To the northeast and northwest
Beale saw the swampland, the water country: the home of alligators,
water snakes, an occasional shark that drifted in on a high tide at the
Río Santiago's mouth, and dazzling flights of water birds.

Across the estuary they headed into the swamp country and began
their trek to La Puerta. Yet even though their horses walked through
water most of the way, Beale's guide was following a road the Spanish had built in 1768. The roadbed was made of stones and San Blas
oyster shells the size of small abalones. Not far beyond the ferry
landing the men passed large salt beds where the Spanish government once had royal warehouses and charged their obligated customers one *real* (about 12 cents) per load for storage. They walked
their horses past the salt beds, carefully followed the old Spanish
road, and in the distance saw the tall palms that marked the beginning of the foothills and La Puerta. Beyond the foothills, beyond the
first ridge of higher mountains, away in the distance was the dark
purple shape of the Sierra Madre Occidental.

As they neared the end of the oyster-shell road, they began to
climb out of the level swampland and into the thick green forest of
banana, fig, and palm trees intertwined with a network of wild vines.
Through this stretch there was no chance for direct sunlight even
when the sun was shining; for they were underneath a green umbrella that allowed only filtered light to reach the forest floor.

When the men emerged from this forest, they had passed through

La Puerta. Next they entered a short stretch of almost treeless plain where it was impossible to escape the burning sun during the dry season. But they only crossed a short section of this country before they started their upward climb toward Tepic. Very soon their tired horses were in a country of steep hillsides, bluffs, *arroyos*, and *barrancas*. The hot country was now behind them. They climbed upward through the temperate land and into the territory of the *ladrones*. As they rode along, they watched carefully for any movement above or below the road and for the approach of strangers who might be bandits. Nearing Tepic, they passed tobacco fields and just as they seemed beyond the point of danger, three bandits rode toward them and shouted for their surrender. Beale and his guide drew their guns and aimed them at the *ladrones*. Not expecting this, the highwaymen were caught off guard. They decided the adventure was not worth the risk, and rode away.

Because of this experience with *ladrones*, Beale decided that before leaving Tepic he had better make copies of the dispatches and send them on by mail to the American Minister, Nathan Clifford, in Mexico City. So, in the mercantile city for the port of San Blas, Beale copied the dispatches. He also looked about the city and noticed the wide, clean streets; the columns and arches of the covered sidewalks in the area of the shipping firms, and the non-Spanish atmosphere of much of Tepic—an atmosphere influenced by the many French, English, German, and American businessmen involved in the import and export trade.

From Tepic to Guadalajara, Beale and his guide rode night and day, taking no chances of being caught off guard by bandits. At wayside stops they picked up fresh horses, and the only rest they got was during the changing of saddles from jaded mounts to fresh ones. At these stops Beale flopped on the ground for a few moments' rest before climbing back into the saddle and riding on. Between Tepic and Tequila they rode by hillsides covered with *maguey* plants with long, sharp leaves extending into the air like a silent army of green bayonets. At one point they carefully crossed an outcropping of obsidian—an area that must have been a true mother lode for makers of arrowheads and sacrificial knives. Beyond the slippery, black volcanic glass, just before nightfall what they had feared most happened. Almost from out of nowhere, as though the mouth of Hell had smiled and let them free, a gang of bandits appeared. The chase was on. Beale and his guide knew they would be murdered as well as robbed if they were caught. They whipped their horses, crouched low and forward in their saddles, and raced for their lives. Beale felt the heavy Mexican saddle horn pressing against his stomach. His whole body was jarred whenever his horse ran into a rough stretch of road, and he heard and felt the wind that made his eyes water. Mile after mile the *ladrones* galloped behind them, calling for them to halt, telling them they would not harm them, then cursing and threatening to kill them slowly—inch by inch—if they did not stop. After a few hours of this chase Beale heard the bandit leader call a halt. This was followed by the whistling of lead hornets close to him and the delayed noise of rifle shots. With this Beale spurred his horse, and with a final burst of speed the tired animal bore his rider out of rifle range. Outriding the *ladrones* had exhausted the horses. Covered with a white lather of sweat, they slowed to a trot when Beale reached a post where fresh mounts were available.

At this stop, station keepers told Beale he would have added protection and travel in greater safety if he could catch up to a party of eleven Mexican travelers who were not too far ahead. But even before he neared the party it had been ambushed. And if Beale had ever doubted the dangerous conditions of travel on Mexico's roads, the sight that greeted him erased any such notion. All eleven members of the party had been robbed and murdered. The blood of these innocent travelers had not yet been washed away from the muddy ground.

Not knowing whether or not the killers were close by, Beale didn't stop to bury the bodies. He and his guide passed the bloody ground, sickened at the sight of this brutal slaughter. They rode their horses at full gallop from this scene, and slowed the animals to a trot only when they had passed every area where they could have been surprised and ambushed. Ironically, the travelers had died very close to safety: a few miles beyond the death trap the large city of Guadalajara came into sight.

Soon Beale and his guide were in the midst of life. They slowed their horses to a walk, passed by the large, clean plaza, the cathedral and government buildings. Beale noticed everything was clean and that the streets were lined with trees. They found an open *mesón*, and had a large meal of eggs smothered with tomato and pepper sauce, *frijoles* and *tortillas*. They drank hot, thick black coffee that helped take the chill from their bodies. While they ate their worn horses were replaced with fresh ones. When they had finished eating they rode east, in a gathering storm, out of the city toward the last ridge of mountains before they reached Mexico's great Central Plateau and the fastest route to Mexico City.

Hours later they topped a ridge and slowly rode the switchback road into a deep valley surrounded by high hills. At the floor of the valley they passed through a small village the guide called San Juan de los Lagos. The intensity of the storm increased, and very quickly small streams became rushing torrents which they had to swim their horses across. Once they had crossed the valley and its floodwaters, they began to work their way up the eastern ridge beyond San Juan de los Lagos. As they did, the road became almost impassable because of mud slides and uprooted trees. But late that night they reached the top of the ridge and descended to the Central Plateau and entered Ciudad Lagos. Again they changed horses, and headed south toward Mexico City. Beyond Lagos they rode the same horses to the iron-manufacturing town of León, where they again changed to fresh mounts. The storm was extremely violent, and Beale later reported that they found their way by flashes of lightning. On and on they rode, passing through *poblado* after *poblado,* and changing horses wherever they could. It was all they could do to keep from falling asleep in their saddles. At times they were half awake, and the landscape passed by as though it were part of a wild dream. Then on the eighth day after leaving San Blas, August 20, 1848, they entered the City of Mexico. Caked with mud, bone-tired from their long ride, exhausted from the constant threat of death, they rode past the old Cathedral and up the straight, wide streets. After traveling 725 impossible miles, they savored their accomplishment with a sudden wave of weariness and an intense feeling of relief.

---

## MEXICO CITY INTERLUDE

---

In Mexico City Lieutenant Beale had his first chance to relax since he had ridden out of San Blas. Nathan Clifford, the American Minister, congratulated him and opened the mud-and-water-soaked saddlebag that held the dispatch case. He quickly glanced at the

contents, looked at the weary Beale, and told him to get a few days'
rest while he prepared other dispatches for him to carry on to Washington. Beale was grateful for the chance to rest, but he discovered
he was too keyed up to relax completely. He took a warm bath, put
on clean dry clothing, and looked at this city still occupied by American troops.

"Ned" Beale saw the long, wide streets; the tree-shaded *alameda*;
the five- and six-story buildings in the center of the city where bache-
lors had their garrets on the flat roofs; the large stone calendar of the
Aztecs, which he heard Americans lightly refer to as "Montezuma's
watch"; and rode in a carriage on ancient Aztec causeways that
crossed ". . . the half-marshy soil that once formed the bottom of the
lake." [9] In the few days he had to look at the capital of Mexico,
Beale also saw the heights of Chapultepec—standing some 200 feet
above the floor of the valley—where the students of the military college fought bravely against General Winfield Scott's troops.

He also saw the Mexican people. He saw the Mexican women,
really looked at them for the first time: the women of the upper class
with their beautiful *mantillas* and lace shawls, and the women of the
very poor class with their *rebozos* and brightly colored dresses. He
saw the upper-class men wearing broad-brimmed hats that were
bordered along the rim with lace, tight-fitting jackets with silver
buttons, trousers that hugged the hips and legs and flared out in
bell-bottoms to flap back and forth against well-polished boots, with
polished silver buttons forming a rich line down the side of the
trousers, and finally a wide silk sash—tightened just so around the
waist. In contrast, the men of the poorer class wore white cotton
trousers and shirts, *serapes* that covered the upper part of the body
and extended below the hips, straw sandals on bare and dirty feet,
and broad-brimmed sombreros that appeared to be almost too heavy
for the head.

Across from the Plaza, Lieutenant Beale walked into the headquarters for Americans in Mexico City. This was a two-story building. The upper story was called the Gran Sociedad and used as a
hotel, while the lower story housed a gambling casino called the
Astor House. In the Astor House, where monte and faro games were
in full action, Lieutenant Beale met a young Army officer, Ulysses S.
Grant, who was to become a very close friend for the rest of Beale's
life. Another American he talked to at this place, an American old

enough to be his father, was Daniel Wadsworth Coit. Coit was a business representative for the firm of Howland & Aspinwall, and he was extremely interested in Beale's information about the California gold discovery. As he wrote to his wife:

> The accounts which this gentleman brings in regard to these discoveries are truly marvelous and one would think if they are in any considerable degree to be credited that we may soon have gold in such abundance as to be overstocked with it.[10]

All too quickly Beale's Mexico City interlude came to an end. Once again they were back in the saddle and on their way. To Beale the end of his Mexican journey was in sight, but between the Valley of Mexico and the port of Vera Cruz he faced a hard and dangerous trip. He had to cross the Sierra Madre Oriental, drop through the temperate zone into the tropical, and, worst of all, run the constant threat of *ladrones* once again. Knowing all this, Beale pushed his horse, his guide, and himself to the limit of endurance and then beyond it for that extra amount of effort he demanded of himself and asked of others.

## THE WILD RIDE TO THE GULF OF MEXICO

They rode out of Mexico City, crossed a long causeway over the remains of Lake Texcoco, rode through the *poblados* of Los Reyes, Ayotla, and Santa Bárbara, and climbed to the foothill *poblado* of Zoquiapan. At this point they were out of the basin-shaped Valley of Mexico and heading southeast on the National Road to Puebla.

The road zigzagged upgrade. The horses slowed to a walk, grunting and groaning, and Beale looked at the nearby pine forests and at the fantastic view of Mounts Popocatépetl and Ixtaccíhuatl—their peaks only partially visible as the shifting winds blew a clearing in the banks of clouds. The temperature began to drop, and Beale felt the cold wind blowing down from the snowy heights of the volcanoes as they rode toward the summit and Continental Divide, some 10,500 feet above sea level.

Beyond the summit, the men rode downgrade past roadside crosses marking the graves of travelers who had been killed by *ladrones.* They paused for a short stop at the Río Frío to water their horses. Then they continued on their way, and passed through the *poblados* of San Martín Texmelucan and Huejotzingo. Not far from Huejotzingo, they rode by the Toltec Pyramid of Cholula, but Beale only saw its gigantic outline in the darkening twilight.

Early that evening the men entered Puebla, and even in the darkness Beale saw the beauty of the Grand Plaza and the Cathedral of the Immaculate Conception. While their horses were being changed, Beale and his guide stretched their legs and walked around awhile. They drank some brandy and hot coffee, and visited narrow streets full of shops and stalls "... tenanted by old ladies selling dulces [sweetmeats] ... and all manner of nicnacs." [11] They bought and ate some of the famous *dulces* as Beale looked at "... booths and stalls, belonging to crowds of half-naked Indians, each having his own fire of pine-wood chips, blazing like gas, and giving out a most delicious odour." [12]

Beale rode out of Puebla in the dark and was unable to see more than the jagged outline of the four tall volcanoes towering above the valley. His guide was beginning to appear more and more exhausted, and Beale worried that the man might not make it. But they continued their rapid pace through the *poblados* of Amozoc and Acajete. Then at Nopalucan they changed horses again and started into a stretch of country known as Las Derrumbadas, the Precipices. Throughout this leg of their journey the traveling was extremely difficult, for most of the bridges spanning the *barrancas* had been blown up during the Mexican War, and they had to ride down makeshift roads to the bottoms, ford rivers, then climb to the top on the other side.

Once they had passed Las Derrumbadas they skirted along the edge of a large, arid mesa as well as Lago Alchichica—a lake in the crater of an extinct volcano. From this lake it was a 12-mile ride to Perote. They passed this battleground of the Mexican War in the early hours of dawn, and Beale saw cannon balls scattered in all directions. Then a dozen miles east of Perote the riders came to the small and poor *poblado* of Las Vigas. Outside this village the Na-

tional Road became a series of switchbacks that wound in and out
of an area of moss-covered pines, junipers, and oak trees as it
descended to Jalapa. Somewhere in this isolated country the men
were attacked by *ladrones* once more. They quickly spurred their
horses, and Beale led the way in a wild ride ". . . down an almost
precipitous mountainside." [13]

Escaping from the bandits, the men crossed a bumpy stretch of
lava flow about 10 miles west of the walled city of Jalapa. In Jalapa
Beale saw gardens of ". . . oranges, limes, coconuts, bananas . . . ," [14]
and other tropical fruits. As he rode through the narrow cobblestone
streets of this colonial city he noticed the clean houses with their
tiled roofs, iron-grilled windows, thick, heavy wooden doors, and
iron-grilled balconies well away from the reach of walkers or horsemen. He felt the change in temperature from the mountain heights
and welcomed its mildness. Almost automatically, he became aware
of the similarity in location and appearance of Jalapa to Tepic.

After Jalapa the National Road very quickly dropped into the
tropics as the riders neared Vera Cruz. Not far away, they passed
along the base of Cerro Gordo. Even in his haste, Beale looked up
at the steep, conical hill where ". . . Colonel Harney's dismounted
dragoons worked their way with the help of bushes and props, and
to which they clung in the face of a sweeping fire from the Mexican
batteries on its summit. . . ." [15] By this time his guide was almost falling off his saddle with fatigue. Yet they were not in a safe enough
place to call a halt. But with Beale's encouragement and the guide's
own fear of being left to the whim of the *ladrones* the exhausted man
found the added strength to continue riding.

Twenty miles beyond Cerro Gordo they rode their horses across
the cement and limestone National Bridge. Not many miles east of
here the men dropped down from the foothills and onto the sandy
plain at the base of the Sierra Madre Oriental. Now they were in the
tropics again, and Beale felt as though he were suddenly back in
San Blas. The odor and taste of salt water was in the breeze, and
the humid air was warm and filled with moisture. The distance to
Vera Cruz was not great, but the sand-covered road made the going
tougher and slower. Next to the road Beale saw the vine and cactus-
covered sand dunes, chaparral brush, and tall coconut palms. The
sky was alive with colorful movement as flights of parrots and other
brightly colored, tropical birds flew by.

As the men drew nearer to Vera Cruz they passed mule trains headed for the city. Some of the animals were loaded with oranges, limes, papayas, avocados, and mangos; others carried high loads of thin tree limbs not much larger than those on a fair-sized bush, but this was the kind of wood Beale had seen stacked high in pack saddles of burros and mules during his whole journey. For what must have seemed like the longest part of the trip they rode along this route between high sand hills that furnished the breeze with an endless supply of material to blow into their faces. Finally they were free of the hills. Two or three miles ahead Beale saw the outline of Vera Cruz upon the sandy plain. Opposite the center of the city and about a thousand yards offshore and in the harbor was the Castillo de San Juan de Ulúa on Gallega Island—the fortress which had been shelled into submission ". . . by the big guns landed from Matthew Perry's fleet . . ." [16] and put into an excellent firing position by a young Army officer named Robert E. Lee.

As the two men rode into Vera Cruz their bodies were a solid mass of weariness, for they had covered the 280 miles from Mexico City to Vera Cruz in sixty hours. This remarkable ride plus the strain of their trip from San Blas to Mexico City was more than Beale's guide could take. This unknown, unnamed hero collapsed in Vera Cruz, breaking down both physically and mentally. Lieutenant Beale and the Mexican authorities placed the unfortunate man aboard a stagecoach, and sent him back to Mexico City. When this was done, Beale learned it would be four days before he would have passage to the United States aboard the sloop-of-war U.S.S. *Germantown*. Then, and only then, did he allow himself the luxury of rest.

## VERA CRUZ: PORT OF EMBARKATION

Tired as he was after his 1,000-mile ride across Mexico, Beale found Vera Cruz quite uncomfortable after his first exhausted sleep. In this month of August the temperature was in the sultry eighties. There was rain every day, and mosquitoes and other insects were a constant plague. The coolest time was in the evening, after sundown, and after the rain. At that time Beale strolled along the *alameda* and watched the evening promenade.

Having had short rations—except for his brief stop in Mexico City —he took time for a full schedule of meals. In the early morning, at six or seven, he was awakened and served a cup of thick, hot chocolate. Then at ten or eleven o'clock he ate breakfast. This, as an English tourist described it, consisted ". . . of fish, often soup, and hot meats of all kinds, tea and coffee being introduced only into Anglicised houses, the natives always drinking wine—mostly bad Bordeaux." [17] With hardly enough time to digest breakfast, Beale was served a large dinner between three and four in the afternoon. The principal dishes on the table were seafood from the Gulf of Mexico. Except for a possible late supper after having watched the evening promenade, the dinner was his last meal for the day.

After the dinner hour Beale tried to siesta, but was too keyed up and tense from his wild ride to sleep. So he walked the cobblestone streets of Vera Cruz. He saw reminders of the American invasion in the many buildings riddled with shellholes from the bombardment of American artillery during the war. He also saw the scattered debris and wreckage of battle that made the beach and port into a junkyard. Along with the aftermath of battle, Beale saw the many churches, thick adobe-walled commercial houses—the sidewalks in front of them covered by the balcony floor of the second story that was supported by columns with arches in between them. Most of the houses had flat tiled roofs, and the entrances to these homes were through large iron gates that allowed the passage of a carriage. Where he was able to peer into the patios, he saw that the houses were built around gardens. As in the commercial buildings, he noticed that the walls were of thick adobe, and that the doors were made of beautifully carved hardwood. And as in Jalapa, windows were protected with iron grilles. Attached to these houses were stables and barns for the horses and carriages.

Even though he had crossed Mexico and had seen many turkey buzzards, Beale was amazed at their number in Vera Cruz. Like other first visitors, he was duly impressed by the efficient scavenger service. One traveler was so astounded by the ability of these birds to clean the streets that he wrote, "I have seen a horse give his last gasp at three or four o'clock in the afternoon, and when I passed the same way . . . the next morning, nothing was left but bones, and those disjointed and flung in every direction." [18] Everywhere Beale looked were the big black birds. They perched on roofs, walls, and trees. They watched and waited for some animal to die or for some scrap of garbage to be tossed into the open.

Four days in Vera Cruz was quite enough for Beale. Not only did it give him time to view the town but also time to visit the Castillo de San Juan de Ulúa, which was to have been Mexico's equivalent to Gibraltar when the Navy of the United States tried to enter the harbor. But the old fort had been built for another time, and for another kind of war.

Finally, Beale went to Isla de los Sacrificios where the Aztecs once performed human sacrifices. Here at this island some miles to the south of the city was the best anchorage for larger vessels, and this was where he boarded the sloop-of-war U.S.S. *Germantown*. This was the place where Aztecs sent souls on dark voyages, and this was the place where the young officer with his dispatches and golden secret set sail for Mobile Point, Alabama.

## THE PRICE OF FAME

When Lieutenant Beale landed at Mobile, Alabama, in early September, 1848, he was not as tired as when he had boarded the *Germantown* at Vera Cruz. During the voyage he had been issued a new uniform to replace his dirty and odd-looking outfit. Also, he had rested and had a regular diet. Even so, he was totally unprepared for the reception he received.

His first inkling of things to come occurred during his stagecoach ride from Mobile to Washington, D.C. On the final leg of his trip Beale became involved in a lengthy conversation with a fellow passenger. As it turned out, the companion was Senator Foote of Mississippi. He pumped the young naval officer with a series of questions. There seemed to be no end to the Senator's curiosity once Beale told him the nature of his mission. It was as though Foote were a child hearing a great adventure tale for the first time; and with the same excitement he plied Beale with question after question regarding all the details.

## Something in the Wind

Before the swaying stagecoach reached its destination, Senator Foote told Beale that he would see to it that he got a chance to relate his information to the Senate of the United States. Even as the excited Foote said this, Beale probably thought that if anybody were to bring him before the Senate it would be Senator Thomas Hart Benton of Missouri, an old family friend. But Beale was politically naive. He didn't realize that Senator Benton would not be in a position to exclude Senator Foote now that Beale had introduced him "to the elephant." °

Senator Foote's constant questioning during their trip was only the beginning. Beale quickly learned that to be the bearer of golden tidings is to be the recipient of mixed opinions polarized in two directions. Either he was one of the damnedest liars to have come out of the West in many a moon, or he really was telling the truth—there was an El Dorado, and it was in California!

By the time Lieutenant Beale arrived in Washington on September 16, 1848, he had traveled 4,000 miles via ship, horse, and stagecoach. He had dodged Mexican bandits, watched his guide lose his sanity, and carried saddlebags and a small amount of gold across a large portion of Mexico and on to Washington in less than two months. What Beale did not know was that he had left more than distance, a sick guide, and broken-down horses behind. The news he was carrying had already spread in his wake. In New Orleans the *Daily Picayune* had received a letter from Mexico, which it published on September 12, 1848. Along with other items, this letter brought out two important factors. It indicated that Beale carried news about men earning as much as $70 a day without using more than an ordinary shovel. It referred to California as the *new* El Dorado. Within the framework of this letter was the outline of things to come: there was gold, and Beale carried proof of it. The christening of California as El Dorado had taken place, and one of the most plausible ways to get there was to cross Mexico. After all, one could say to doubters, wasn't that the way Beale had come to Washington in less than two months?

Nevertheless, there were doubters; and they, too, expressed themselves in print. In St. Louis, the *Daily Missouri Republican* took the attitude, "I'll believe it when I see it." The newspaper stressed the possibility that land speculators in the Far West were trying to get

° "Seeing the elephant" meant reaching out for the impossible and hoping you could get it. The expression is part of gold-rush lore.

people to go to California so that they could sell land to them. The newspaper saw no reason for people to go rushing off to California when there was so much good land available right in Missouri. The editor cynically suggested that owners of gold mines weren't apt to invite other men to share with them.

The combination of Beale's incredible trip and his news of a golden California made him an overnight hero. Newspapers and magazines published stories about him. Senator Thomas Hart Benton and the non-deniable Senator Foote introduced the young lieutenant to the Senate, and Beale told the Senators that California faced the danger of starvation because the farmers had fallen victim to gold fever.

Further confirmation of the gold discovery reached Washington in November when Lieutenant Loeser of the United States Army finally arrived in New Orleans and telegraphed the news to Washington. On the day of his arrival, November 23, 1848, Loeser was interviewed by reporters; and the New Orleans *Mercury* printed the following story:

> We to-day had the pleasure of a personal interview with Lieutenant Loeser, just arrived from California, which land of gold he left on the 1st of September. He fully confirms the most glowing accounts heretofore received in the States, of the richness and extent of the gold region. He says the whole truth cannot be told with any prospect of being believed—that the gold is found from the tops of the highest mountains to the bottom of the rivers . . . Lieut. L. showed us specimens of the gold: it is found pure or mixed from the size of wheat to that of the fist. All other business is neglected—wheat left standing in the field, houses and farms deserted, etc. The citizens are rejoicing in the annexation to the United States. Lieut. L. has seen the mines, and knows what he says to be a fact.[19]

With this added information brought by Lieutenant Lucien Loeser, what Beale had called gold fever began to show signs of becoming a plague. When President James Knox Polk stepped to the speaker's rostrum before Congress on December 5, 1848, the plague was given an official blessing. "The accounts of the abundance of gold in that territory," the President said, " are of such an extraordinary character as would scarcely command belief were they not corroborated by the authentic reports of officers in the public service. . . ."[20]

There it was. By God, there was gold in California! Beale had brought samples of it. Loeser had brought a whole tea caddy full of gold, and President Polk had said California was full of gold! Even the greatest showman of them all, P. T. Barnum, couldn't resist this. As Lieutenant Beale had brought the first official news of the gold strike, Barnum wrote to him and tried to get his sample of gold—a sample which had quite suddenly grown to a solid eight-pound chunk:

Barnum's Museum, Philadelphia
May 29, 1849

Lieutenant Beale:
Dear Sir:

Mr. Harding of the Inquirer has just informed me that you have in your possession an 8 lb. lump of California gold. As I am always anxious to procure novelties for public gratification I write this to say that I should be glad to purchase the lump at its valuation if you will dispose of it and if not that I should like to procure it for exhibition for a few weeks.

A line in reply will much oblige.

Your obt. servant,
P. T. BARNUM.[21]

All this publicity and attention was much more than Lieutenant Beale wished to endure. He had not been involved in a race to deliver the news of the gold discovery—contrary to popular belief. He did not wish to sell any gold—contrary to what P. T. Barnum wished to believe; and he did not wish to be interviewed by more reporters—contrary to what the newspaper publishers might believe. Trying to scotch all the snakes was more than even a hero of Beale's stature could accomplish, but he did try. He asked a reporter friend, William Carey Jones, to write a restrained account of his trip across Mexico for the *National Intelligencer*, but this sober account could not halt the first true believers; and it certainly could do nothing to slow things down after the President's message. To avoid the problem of being pursued by P. T. Barnum and the press, Beale gave half his gold to the Patent Office in Washington. The other half he had fashioned into an engagement ring for Mary Edwards, ". . . his childhood sweetheart and fiancée. . . ."[22] But Beale did not have to worry about much more attention, for while the population was eager to hear the first stories of El Dorado, once the news was official the important thing was to get there.

# CHAPTER II

# SELLERS
# OF THE DREAM

# DRUMMERS AND THE MYTH

The salesmen for the new El Dorado were a different breed from the windmill tilters from Spain. These were the cash-on-the-barrelhead, no-nonsense Yankees. They had a background for the job, the proper credentials to show if need be. They'd made a living on the cold Atlantic coast in those first years of settlement. They'd endured the fever summers of Southern deltas. They'd told the British to go to hell and made it stick. They'd trapped for beaver in the Rocky Mountains and fought the Blackfeet and the Sioux. They'd sailed the South Pacific for years at a time and brought back shiploads of whale oil. They'd been Santa Fé traders when the trail to Chihuahua was a good place to get an Apache or Comanche lance between the ribs; and they'd high-tailed it to the Oregon country to do a little farming when they'd heard the soil was as fresh and new as a baby's bottom. In short, they'd been there and back and had the calluses, scars, and memories to prove it. To put it plain, simple, and clean—the way they liked it—these Yankees were a damned practical lot, or so they'd have you believe.

Nevertheless these practical men, these down-to-earth Yankees, were dreamers of the wildest sort. After all, these were men who had tilted the greatest windmill of them all. For they were the inheritors of the dream of individual freedom, and they'd come a long way, stayed a long time, and buried many of their friends. They believed in the royalty of the common man, the kingdom of the individual. To make all this a reality they had learned to endure, to survive, to strike out and then duck behind rock walls or the nearest tree or buffalo wallow. They knew how to win when the odds had already proved they would lose and leave their bleached bones as a warning to others who might get notions. These were the new sellers of the golden dream, these crazy Yankees with their cocksureness. And they knew they could be sure. Nobody knew their customers any better than they did, for they had grown up with the knowledge of what it took to make another horse trader overlook the flaws for the sake of one big, winning purse.

## DID YOU HEAR ABOUT . . .

The word spreads far and wide if given enough time, if given enough talkers, and man has never been noted for keeping his mouth shut. But the word spreads even faster when it is printed. Those who knew how to read told the non-readers that the story heard in the local tavern was a bit more than a yarn. This way the news about the gold strike in California got all over the country and then all over the world in a very short time.

Letter writers started it. Of course, there were the official letters from Consul Thomas Oliver Larkin, Military Governor Colonel Richard B. Mason, and Commander of the Pacific Squadron Commodore Thomas ap Catesby Jones. But there were unofficial letters as well. Larkin took time to drop a line to his old friend Stephen Reynolds in Honolulu, and invited him to ". . . come to California, bring 100 Kanakas, 100 spades, shovels & picks with 100 wooden dishes and bowls . . ." [1] and make a fortune on the American River.

And even the official letters received a much wider circulation than usual, as they were released to the newspapers. From Washington, D.C., Larkin's half-brother, Ebenezer Childs, wrote to Larkin, "Your letters & those of others have been running thro' the papers all over the country, creating wonder and amazement in every mind." [2]

Childs had sized up the situation perfectly, and he tagged it quite properly. "Already I see indications of the prevalence of a California fever which will spread itself thro'out the States, & pour upon you a tide of population by no means desirable." [3]

The fourth estate published everything that came along about this *real* El Dorado. President Polk's message to Congress on Decem-

ber 5, 1848, about the discovery of gold, appeared in all the major
newspapers in the United States and in many newspapers in other
parts of the world. The long letter from California's Military Governor Richard B. Mason was printed in whole or in part by many of
the country's principal newspapers. And if ever a final impetus was
needed to start the gold rush, that happened when the *Daily Union*
of Washington, D.C., printed a letter from the director of the mint at
Philadelphia to the Secretary of the Treasury. The director stressed
the purity of California's gold, and casually mentioned that it was
". . . extraordinary, the gold dust yielding 982/3 pure gold . . ." [4]

Before the first month of 1849 ended, the newspapers had shifted
from stories about the gold strike to stories about parties bound for
the *new* El Dorado, and advice on how to prepare for the journey
and which route to take. On January 25, 1849, the *Democratic Telegraph and Texas Register* of Houston neatly ruled out any crossing
through Panama or Mexico by stressing their expense: "No emigrant
should attempt to travel to California by these routes with a less sum
than $250 or $360," [5] and by indicating that emigrants might be delayed ". . . at the sickly ports of the Pacific for weeks, perhaps months,
waiting for vessels to transport them to California." [6] The newspaper
did not even mention the overland route across the central plains in
this article, nor did it indicate it was possible to sail around the Horn.
The paper made it quite clear that the only sensible trail for any
man to follow was to go to El Paso del Norte (now Juárez), though
the writer neglected to map this trail. From El Paso del Norte all
anybody had to do was to drive his wagon to where the Gila River
emptied into the Gulf of California (the paper did not mention the
existence of the Colorado River), and from there it would be an easy
trip to San Diego (the paper failed to mention the Colorado Desert).
The route referred to was Lieutenant Colonel Philip St. George
Cooke's wagon trail south into Mexico; northwest to Corralitos,
Janos, and across the Sierra Madre Occidental at Guadalupe Pass to
Rancho San Bernardino; then on to the Sonora outpost of Santa
Cruz, and from there to the Gila River. On paper it all sounded so
simple. It was simple, too, if you were *not* going to make the trip; if
you were only trying to get customers for Texas towns; and if you
didn't really understand the difficulties of such a journey. For the
paper did not indicate the scarcity of water or grass for the animals
along this route, made no mention of the ruggedness of the Sierra

Madre, overlooked the roving bands of Apaches and Comanches, and ignored the Colorado Desert—one of the deadliest areas in the Southwest.

Another Texas newspaper, the Corpus Christi *Star,* suggested a variation of the same route. It had a little better concept of the geography involved, but it did not bother to give the prospective emigrant anything more than the names of places he should pass through. Without going into detail at all, the article in the *Star* referred to the route south from Corpus Christi across the border and then north to the Guadalupe Pass as the best way to go. And the whole trip was devilishly simple. All the traveler had to do was to go southwest of Corpus Christi to a point north of Río Grande City, cross the Río Grande into Mexico, go to Mier, ". . . thence to Monterrey, Saltillo, Parras, and through the states of Chihuahua and Sonora to the junction of the Gila and Colorado rivers, emptying into the Gulf of California. . . ." [7] Then, in a classic of understatement, the writer of this chamber-of-commerce plug added: "This route passes through no wilderness—all of it is thickly settled country." [8] In contrast to the glib optimism of the Corpus Christi *Star,* the Santa Fé Trader Josiah Gregg pointed out the existence of Los Médanos, the shifting sand hills not too far south of El Paso del Norte, ". . . huge hillocks and ridges of pure sand, in many places without a vestige of vegetation." [9] And even though Gregg mentioned it was possible to skirt Los Médanos, he also pointed out the danger of Apache raids, and the shortage of water between El Paso del Norte and Chihuahua. Putting it quite bluntly, Gregg wrote that as far as water was concerned, "All that is to be found on the road for the distance of more than sixty miles after leaving El Paso, consists in two fetid springs or pools, whose water is only rendered tolerable by necessity." [10]

## THE GUIDEBOOK MEN

Newspapers were not the only dream merchants who offered advice and oh, so easy directions to El Dorado. The excitement touched off by President James Knox Polk's message and the follow-up by newspapers had created a built-in market for authors and publishers of guidebooks. There was "... an army of potential readers eager for any scrap of information about the West and mining, yet so uninformed that they would buy anything that would feed their enthusiasm."[11] Between official confirmation of the discovery and the spring of 1849, over thirty guidebooks were published and put on the market for eager buyers.

In general, these books fell into two categories. Either they were reprints of older volumes such as John C. Fremont's *The California Guide* and Lansford W. Hastings' *The Emigrants' Guide to Oregon and California,* or they were slapdash publications containing a hodgepodge of newspaper stories, copies of official documents which had already been printed, and a considerable amount of fiction concocted from rumors, other volumes of false data, and descriptions of routes that possessed as much value as a map of Alice's Wonderland.

Not content with the re-issuing of *The Emigrants' Guide to Oregon and California,* a book which had the notorious stigma of having helped to create the Donner Party disaster by making the Great Basin and Sierra Nevada crossing appear easier than it was, Lansford W. Hastings quickly put together another guidebook in which he described the various routes to the gold fields, what to expect in the way of hardships, what to take along for supplies, what to figure with regard to cash outlay; and if the emigrant was going to cross Mexico, Hastings included a blend of factual data and outright prejudice. His statements concerning cost, distance, accommodations, and the danger of being attacked by bandits were fairly reliable. But his view of the Mexican people was colored by an attitude that pictured all Mexicans as cowards and thieves, and which belittled the Catholic faith with calculated bigotry. Then, running true to form, Hastings pictured a very difficult journey as a trip that sounded like a spring outing any normal Yankee family could take. His estimate for the total traveling time from New Orleans to Mexico to California amounted to a maximum of thirty-six days! Hastings broke this trip into the following stages:

> The emigrant who travels by this route, ships at New Orleans for Vera Cruz, where, if he sails from New Orleans, he arrives in seven or eight days; thence by stage, three days, to the city of Mexico; thence by stage, six days to Guadalaxara; thence on horseback, five days, to Tepic; thence on horseback, two days, to St. Blas; thence, by water, twelve days, to California. . . .[12]

A careful examination of the time schedule Hastings outlined for California emigrants indicates that either he was not too clear about how difficult the journey across Mexico could be or he simply did not care what happened to persons who followed his guidebook. If Hastings was aware of Beale's crossing and what it had been like, he completely ignored it. Instead he was quite specific that the journey took only sixteen days from Vera Cruz to San Blas. The implausibility of this becomes very clear when compared to Beale's wild and incredible ten-day ride, as a courier, to cover the same distance. In order to accomplish this, Beale rode day and night, fought off bandits, played out horses, and pushed his guide to a physical and mental breakdown.

Hastings apparently never considered the fact that the men who would buy his guidebook were not of Lieutenant Beale's stamp. A good many of them simply did not have the know-how, stamina, and courage of a man who was able to keep up with Kit Carson on courier missions from the Pacific Coast to Washington, D.C. Finally, Hastings assumed that all any Argonaut had to do was to arrive at San Blas, and there would be a ship at anchor in the harbor, awaiting his arrival, all ready to take him to San Francisco in twelve days. No consideration was given to the fact that a man might have to wait as long as thirty-six days or more before a ship put into port, and that there was always the possibility that the anxious Argonaut might have great difficulty in securing so much as deck passage on a northbound ship.

The best that can be said for Lansford W. Hastings and others like him is that they were uninformed men who wrote their guidebooks with a minimum amount of knowledge and a maximum amount of ignorance and carelessness. The worst that can be said about Hastings and his ilk is that they were out for the fast and easy dollar, did not care that they were passing on sketchy or wrong information to greenhorns, and never considered the fact that human suffering and tragedy might be the end result of a slapdash guidebook complete with a useless map.

All guidebooks, though, were not of this variety. Some gave fairly useful information. Such books tried to give an accurate estimate of distances involved; of the geographical and climatic conditions emigrants should expect; of the supplies necessary for the journey; of the dangers of the trail from disease, bandits, or Indians; of the ex-

penses involved; and of the various routes that were both practical
and possible between the States and California.

One of the best guidebooks was Joseph Ware's *The Emigrants'
Guide to California, Containing Every Point of Information for the
Emigrant.* This was published in St. Louis in 1849, and ". . . com-
piled by a newpaperman who tried to sift the truth from a wide
variety of travel information." [13] Ware listed four routes in his
guidebook, and he told his readers that the distance was ". . . great,
and in some respects, perilous." [14] In order of preference, Ware listed
the following routes: first, the central trail across the plains, the
Rocky Mountains, the Great Basin, and the Sierra Nevada; second,
across the Isthmus of Panama; third, the long voyage around Cape
Horn; and fourth, across Mexico from Vera Cruz to the Pacific ports.
He also stated that the expenses for any routes other than the central overland crossing would be in excess of $300. The major flaw
in this book, which Ware dedicated to Senator Thomas Hart Benton, was that it did not explain or map the route through Mexico.
However, it was the best guidebook for the other routes. Ironically,
though, when Ware set out for California, he came down with cholera ". . . on the first leg of the journey, was abandoned by his companions, and perished miserably." [15]

For the Mexico crossing most of the guidebooks were much too
sketchy once the trails went beyond areas that had been penetrated
by the Army during the Mexican War. Joseph Hutchins Colton's
guidebook gave a fair breakdown on the time, distance, and cost of
a journey from Vera Cruz to Mazatlán; J. Ely Sherwood's book did
the same for the Corpus Christi to Mazatlán route; and Robert
Creuzbaur's guidebook was not too bad for the route across northern
Mexico and the southwestern United States. But for an over-all view
of the various branches of the El Dorado Trail, the best guidebook
was one put together by J. Disturnell—a mapmaker by profession.
Disturnell's guidebook gave a mileage and place-name breakdown
on the routes through northern Mexico; Vera Cruz to San Blas and
Mazatlán; and Corpus Christi to Mazatlán. In addition to a mileage
chart, Disturnell included such things as the cost of food and lodging; stagecoach fares; schedules; stopover points; the cost of mules
and mustangs; the kind and quality of food; and the scenery to be
seen as the traveler made his way through Mexico. Oddly enough,
the principal flaw in Disturnell's guidebook was that his map was

not completely accurate. This later caused a considerable amount of difficulty for the team of American and Mexican surveyors who were given the task of establishing the boundary between both countries. According to the Treaty of Guadalupe Hidalgo, the surveyors *had* to use Disturnell's map, and they discovered that it was off by a half degree in latitude and a half degree in longitude. This was enough of an error to place El Paso "... thirty-four miles too far north and well over a hundred miles too far east." [16]

Guidebook writers, letter writers, zestful newspaper reporters, government report writers who saw to it that their documents circulated freely in the interests of Manifest Destiny, and countless tales told by men who had talked to somebody, knew somebody, or had simply heard about somebody who had been to El Dorado—all these creators of news were instrumental in sending the Forty-Niner on his way. Even songwriters reached out for some of the easy money to be made from the gold fever. [17] Yet writers, talkers, and songwriters were not the only persons making a business out of convincing others to strike out for California. Individual promoters also played an important role. Such men were sometimes half-confidence man and half-hero who tried to help the emigrants while making as much of a profit as they could from them. Other promoters were colorful swindlers in the true fashion of nineteenth-century American flim-flam men. Both types contributed to the rush for El Dorado. The flim-flam man did so because of his ability to deceive. The man who dreamed of building his own personal empire did so because he picked up an immediate profit by selling goods and services to the Forty-Niners and drew fellow empire builders to his home territory.

## THE EMPIRE BUILDER

He was tall, lean, extremely handsome, and spoke Spanish as well as he did English. His hair was dark but he had a slight, distinguishing touch of gray at the temples. His father had been a Pennsylvania lawyer—a practical man well designed for pragmatic America. But Henry Lawrence Kinney was a romantic adventurer who had once courted Daniel Webster's daughter. Yet this man of vision, a man many called a dreamer, was a shrewd Yankee trader who spoke gently but was quite capable of shooting another man's head off if the man asked for violence.

Kinney's restless nature, coupled with his unsuccessful courtship of Miss Webster, had sent him from the settled and stable North to Texas and the Gulf of Mexico. Here in a wild land that represented the extreme opposite of Kinney's Pennsylvania home, the tall man from the North had established a trading post on the wind-swept and barren shores of Corpus Christi Bay in 1840.

By the time of the Mexican War Kinney held more than 400 square miles of territory, most of which he had actually stolen from the grant of Señor Enrique de Villareal of Matamoros. However, Kinney never gambled without an ace in the hole. When Señor Villareal and his armed *vaqueros* came to claim the Villareal land, the wily Kinney was waiting with his own private army of forty free-lance gunmen. A battle was narrowly missed, and when the Mexicans rode away, Kinney looked about him and knew he was the sole owner of this vast land grant by right of force. The year was 1841. Kinney had been in Texas for only a year, but he had already made a name for himself.

As the inevitability of the war with Mexico became more and more apparent, Kinney promoted Corpus Christi as a good harbor for the landing of American troops. But within his promotional scheme there was one slight omission about Corpus Christi Bay. Kinney had not told the Army the bay was too shallow for anything much larger than a fishing boat and that larger vessels had to anchor 25 miles offshore at St. Joseph's Island and ferry themselves and their supplies in smaller boats in order to get to Corpus Christi. Nevertheless, on July 25, 1845, troop transports anchored off St. Joseph's Island and began landing operations. During these operations, a young lieutenant, who thought the coming war with Mexico was immoral, fell off the ship and had to be pulled out of Corpus Christi Bay in a bucket. This wasn't the only thing that went wrong for Lieutenant Ulysses S. Grant at Corpus Christi. While waiting for action, Sam Grant—as his friends called him—had two other embarrassing moments. He was taken by a Texas horsetrader who sold him an unbroken, rangy, mustang stallion for $12—an enormous amount of money for such rank horseflesh. And he appeared in an

THE EL DORADO TRAIL

Army production of Shakespeare's *Othello*. The latter might not
have been too bad except that smooth-shaven, good-looking Sam
Grant was a poor actor and didn't have the talent to handle the
role of Desdemona. Among the future figures of fame who derived
fun at Grant's expense were Jefferson Davis, a former son-in-law of
General Zachary Taylor and a veteran of the Black Hawk Indian
War; and Robert E. Lee; also present were two future Presidents of
the United States: Zachary Taylor and Franklin T. Pierce.

The boom days for Kinney's outpost at Corpus Christi lasted less
than a year. In February of 1846, "Old Rough and Ready" Taylor
received orders to move his troops closer to the Mexican forces at
Matamoros. During the first weeks of March, the Army's enforced
holiday at Corpus Christi came to an end. Camp followers who had
set up grog shops and brought in gambling and whoring were without customers overnight. The only men who remained behind as
potential spenders were ". . . too sick to leave the hospital at once
or were detailed to serve as a garrison for the suddenly forlorn-
looking camp at Corpus Christi." [18]

Empire building simply had to wait while Henry Lawrence Kinney marched off with the American Army to do battle at Buena Vista
with General Santa Anna, the man many believed should have been
hanged after the Battle of San Jacinto.

After the Mexican War, Kinney returned to Corpus Christi and
set to work building his empire once more. He knew he needed
customers and help. To get both, he advertised the great opportuni-
ties available for settlers, in Eastern and in European newspapers.
He purchased a steam dredging machine and set out to make a deep
water channel that would allow larger ships to sail in and dock at
Corpus Christi rather than at St. Joseph's Island. Then only two
weeks after Lieutenant Beale had delivered the news of California
gold to Washington, D.C., Corpus Christi opened its first hotel.
Board and lodging were available for $30 per month. By the end of
October, a new wagon road was completed between Corpus Christi
and the Río Grande. In short, it appeared as though Kinney and his
followers might have heard about the gold discovery, and were getting ready for the first wave of emigrants.

By December, 1848, there wasn't any doubt that Kinney and his
friends knew about the new El Dorado. By that time ". . . steamboat
*Fanny* was making fortnightly runs to Port Lavaca and New Or-

leans." [19] Now things happened very quickly. Kinney made arrangements with some traders who were making a round trip to Mier, Mexico, to mark a trail between Mier and Corpus Christi. They did this on their return trip by tying a plow to the back of one of their wagons. In this manner they turned a line of fresh earth to serve as a marker for travelers until something in the way of a more permanent road could be constructed.

On January 20, 1849, the Corpus Christi *Star* reported a shipload of emigrants was bound for Kinney's new port. Furthermore, the article pointed out that these men were going to travel overland from Corpus Christi to California. The boom Kinney had hoped for was beginning, and it was time to get ready for the trade. Fresh emigrants, their pockets jingling with cash, would need many things: a place to stay, a place to eat, a place to buy supplies, horses, and a last bottle of whiskey or brandy before taking off. They would also need guides, or at least they would be interested in buying maps; and they would need all kinds of services.

To help the gold seekers as they passed through town, a new wharf was built, and behind that a two-story brick building was constructed. Ranchers drove herds of wild mustangs into town and corraled them, waiting for the prospective buyers—most of whom had never had to put up with the habits of a wild, rank range pony. Then tradesmen began to arrive in Corpus Christi to cash in on the emigrant trade. From out of nowhere came carpenters, blacksmiths, cobblers, barbers, gunsmiths, coopers, and men who could repair or build spare parts for wagons. As in every frontier town, gamblers, bartenders, and ladies of pleasure also appeared. Even a doctor who claimed he knew what to do about cholera arrived.

The Corpus Christi *Star* printed a route for the Argonauts to follow on their way to California. All the Forty-Niners had to do was take this easy route. Why, it went through settled country all the way. They would never have to worry about being lost in the wilderness. It would be a jolly trip to Upper California and the land of gold. The first leg of this so-called easy trip followed what was left of the plow mark between Corpus Christi and Mier, Mexico. After that, it did pass through two Mexican cities of some size; and if the miners were lucky enough to have a Mexican War veteran in their midst, he might just remember how to get to Monterrey and Saltillo. Then from Saltillo the *Star* jauntily stated that all the emigrants would have to do was travel to "... Parras, and through the states of Chihuahua and Sonora to the junction of the Gila and Colorado rivers, emptying into the Gulf of California...."[20]

The major difficulty was that the country simply did not have the number of settlers in it who could offer supplies and protection to gold seekers. After Monterrey and Saltillo the only towns in all the vast area of northern Mexico's high plateau with fairly large populations were Parras, Durango, and Chihuahua City. In between these places there was a lot of vacant or almost vacant country. To cross this country was not the easy trip a newspaper explorer might outline in a column. Getting a Mexican guide was no great guarantee of help either, for the man might not know a thing about the area outside the perimeter of his own stomping grounds. Then there were the great stretches to cross where there was not much water and very little grass for the horses and mules. There were two rugged mountain ranges to get over—the Sierra Madre Oriental on the east, and the Sierra Madre Occidental on the west; and there were bone-dry deserts to wander through. Finally, the *Star* simply forgot to mention the Apaches and Comanches. Both tribes had been terrorizing northern Mexico for many years. They had been doing such an effective job that few Mexicans dared to live outside their cities. Those who did, lived in constant fear of a warrior's war cry.

But Coloney Kinney had John H. Peoples, editor of the Corpus Christi *Star*, start a promotional scheme to encourage gold seekers to come by way of Corpus Christi. Copies of the *Star* plus additional advertising copy were sent to other newspapers throughout the United States. Another phase of Kinney's campaign for the emigrant trade was the formation of a company of Forty-Niners he christened "Kinney's Rangers." These men were picked up from all over the country, and their central gathering point was New Orleans. From there 100 men sailed on a chartered steamboat to Corpus Christi, where they came under the command of Captain Walter Harvey. The actual size of the company may have been smaller. For one California emigrant, Harvey Wood, was a member of the "Kit Carson Association"—another group put together by a promoter under Carson's name but without Carson's permission or aid, and as Wood remembered it in later years, "Kinney's Rangers" had about forty men when he saw them buying horses in Corpus Christi in February, 1849.

To men with gold fever, just passing through Corpus Christi on their way to El Dorado, Colonel Kinney was the true American hero. He was that combination of gentility and violence, of manners and frontier spirit, and of courage and action. He was that great composite of landowner and thief, of horse trader and protector of the people. He was everything any man could aspire to be, and he had the empire to prove it.

One emigrant who passed through Corpus Christi and had the good fortune to dine at the Kinney home said the following about him:

> He is not yet sixty years of age and his life has been one of heroic adventure and daring enterprise and affords a rare example of what indomitable energy and well directed enterprise can accomplish. It is impossible to conjecture what improvements he will make on his possessions if he should live even ten years. He is now boring two artesian wells, one a little back of the town of Corpus Christi, and another about five miles distant, to irrigate his lands. He is a true son of old Pennsylvania and well may she be proud of him.[21]

There was the heart of the matter, the pulse-beat of a frontier-minded people on the move. There was the admiration of the strong, the doers, the takers, and the makers. But not all the promoters who called like sirens stranded on the dry and sandy beaches of the ancient inland seas possessed the Benjamin Franklin virtues of Henry Lawrence Kinney, who did help others while he helped himself. Other promoters, the true flim-flam men, were takers who gave nothing but trouble to those who listened to their come-on talks and laid cash and lives on the drumhead for something they might never get. These sellers of the dream were actually merchants of nightmares.

## MERCHANT OF NIGHTMARES

In 1849 it was hard for a man to keep his mind on his work. It was especially hard if the man was young, healthy, and read everything about the *real* El Dorado and all the men bound for California and a quick and easy fortune waiting in the earth. Young Michael Baldridge had endured it fairly well, all things considered. He was, so tradition would have him believe, doing just the right thing to get ahead in the world. All during the winter of 1849 and into 1850, Baldridge pursued his studies with a famous New York accountant, C. C. Marsh. As Baldridge later entered in his journal, Marsh had told him that he was only reviewing, and that he would have his diploma whenever he wanted it.

One morning as young Baldridge entered C. C. Marsh's office, one of those little things happened that can change a man's life. Mr. Marsh had just finished reading the daily paper and had placed it on a table. Baldridge picked it up, and as he later wrote: "The first thing that met my eye was Parker H. French's advertisement, setting forth in glowing colors the beauties of a sixty-day 'pleasure trip' to California by land and sea, and promising in happy combination novelty, romance and adventure, with bushels of gold lying about loose in the distance." [22]

Baldridge dropped the paper, put on his hat and coat, and one can only assume did not even say good-by to his mentor of accounts receivable and otherwise. He walked quickly to Parker H. French's office at 41 Wall Street, opened the door and stepped into a journey that he would never forget as long as he lived.

The man who greeted young Baldridge was Parker H. French himself, and at first Baldridge may have been tempted to go back to his accounting master. The man in front of him was not the prototype of an American Wilderness hero. He was not a Daniel Boone or a Colonel Kinney. He was closer to Kit Carson in size, and put together like a lightweight boxer who had managed to win all his bouts without ever suffering any serious damage. Baldridge described him as ". . . below medium height and weight with a build that . . . suggested more than average physical power. . . ." [23]

The things which first struck those who met Parker H. French were his commanding presence and his ability to assume leadership without being asked to do so. As another California emigrant later wrote, ". . . he appeared to be born to command, and in business— sharp practice—he had managed all his undertakings and schemes as smoothly and with as much success as if he had been a noted cavalier with a yearly rent roll of hundreds of thousands of dollars." [24]

In no time at all French convinced young Baldridge that he

should join his expedition as his personal and private secretary. If Baldridge was stunned that a leader of an emigrant party needed the services of a personal secretary, he never indicated it in his journal. However, he did write that French was planning a book about his trip to California and needed somebody to take notes for him. He also told Baldridge that the position he was offering him would include taking care of the accounts. The fee offered for this position of importance was $25 per month and free passage.

The final and convincing words, though it is doubtful they were needed, came when French told Baldridge about the existence of gold on the Gila River. This wondrous information, French told Baldridge, this guide to the fabulous gold deposits of the Gila, had come to him "... from ancient traditions, and mysterious sources, not to be mentioned at present. ..."[25]

It was the oldest confidence game in the world, but it worked. Factual information about California gold had been given the official seal by the President of the United States and everybody else in a position of knowledge and power. All Parker H. French and other flim-flam men had to do was to make a natural extension from these facts. The flim-flam men could and did say that there was gold in California; there had been gold in Mexico and Peru; there was a great unexplored section of the American West; there was, then, the possibility of finding a fortune while traveling to California. Parker H. French even went so far as to put this last lure into a broadside he circulated in New York to advertise his expedition.

And the trip would be easy—oh, so very easy. They would sail from New York to Port Lavaca, Texas—just north of Corpus Christi —in the chartered steamship *Georgia*. From Port Lavaca it would be a simple journey by stagecoach on good roads to El Paso del Norte. Of course French neglected to mention that neither the stagecoaches nor the good roads existed. Then, at El Paso del Norte the gold seekers would have an easy, really a pleasure trip, on horseback to the Gila and Colorado Rivers. From there it would be an *exceedingly short ride* to California. Again, through ignorance or a total lack of responsibility, French did not tell his customers the ride was through the Guadalupe Pass in the Sierra Madre Occidental on a trail that had been roughed in by Lieutenant Colonel Cooke and the Mormon Battalion during the Mexican War—a trail that was hard to find and hard to travel if a man did find it. There was no

43

mention in French's broadside of the dreaded Apaches who ruled
this wilderness; no mention of the dry stretches between El Paso
del Norte and the Colorado River crossing; and no mention of the
high sand dunes of the Colorado Desert between the river crossing
and California. The way French put it the whole trip was a vacation.
To make it even easier for those who signed up, he promised an
armed escort of U. S. troopers and Texas Rangers, the services of a
physician, the knowledge of experienced guides; and all the livestock, food, supplies, and equipment necessary for the journey to
California. But the greatest promise he made was of finding gold
even before the miners arrived in California. As he put it in his
broadside, ". . . gold does exist in great abundance along the course
of the Gila . . . we have the old Spanish authorities for the fact." [26]

Unlike Kinney, men like Parker H. French possessed a very small
knowledge of the country they proposed to lead men through. They
built their "factual" stories out of what they had read, heard, and
imagined. Then if, like French, they intended to go along on the
trip, they gathered as much information as they could simply for
their own protection. Their primary interest was in the fees they collected from innocent Argonauts about to sign on for a journey as
wild as that of Jason and the seekers of the golden fleece. In the
case of French's party there were two prices. If a man traveled as a
regular passenger, he was charged $250 for a trip that was supposed
to take only sixty days. If the trip went over the time schedule, the
passenger was to be reimbursed at the rate of $5 per day for each
day beyond the sixty-day mark. The other category for passengers
was what French called the enlisted man's group. Men in this category paid $100, worked their way, and apparently were not qualified
for any return on their money if the expedition exceeded sixty days.

The worst part of expeditions organized by flim-flam men was that
such men generally did not know how they were going to get their
customers to California once they had stepped ashore at a Texas or
Mexico seaport. Added to this central flaw was their ignorance
about living conditions in the port towns and along the trail; their
poor suggestions for equipment and supplies; and their tendency to
desert at the first moment of possible disaster. Because of such flaws
men like Parker H. French were sellers of an imperfect dream. The
dream they sold might give a man the hot, slamming impact of a
bandit's bullet; one last scream as an Apache arrow pinned his stom-

ach to his spine; a final tumble into space as his horse fell from a hanging-wall trail in the Sierra Madre; a choking, swollen tongue and delirious death miles from any waterhole in the Colorado Desert; or a wandering into madness in a box canyon in the middle of nowhere to die knowing that the golden dream had become a nightmare of deadly fool's gold.

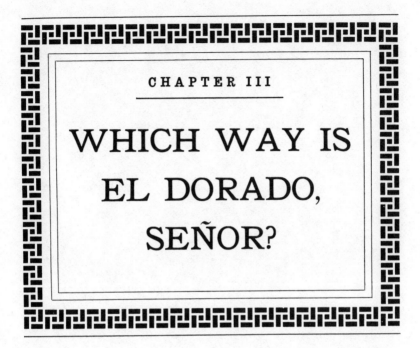

CHAPTER III

# WHICH WAY IS EL DORADO, SEÑOR?

# TO GO ADVENTURING

All during the last of December, 1848, the talk was about gold. The major problem was to get to California before it was all gone. Men with solid professions, established businesses, or steady jobs talked about the fortune to be made.

Gold fever was highly contagious that winter, and the disease continued throughout most of 1849. There was a national excitement in the air, and gold was the catalyst. Behind all the excitement, behind all the talk in taverns, or away from the dinner table while the women were in the kitchen out of hearing range, gold was the topic of the time. It had become ". . . a mass hysteria . . . ," and ". . . men decided to go to California as they might get religion at a revival, or volunteer at the outbreak of a war."[1] For along with gold fever, men found that they were stricken with the urge to go adventuring.

The Mexican War was just over, and many men had not yet settled down to a civilian routine. Other younger men who had not been part of the United States Army that marched into Mexico felt they had been bypassed. The national economy was in a slack period; and while there wasn't a depression, jobs were scarce and business was slow. But over and above these factors was the existence of the West. The West and adventure were synonymous. Everybody knew something about the West, even if what was known was as vague as a desert waterhole.

People had read about the Lewis and Clark expedition. Others had read the fiction of James Fenimore Cooper. Many men had read government reports published in the newspapers, and a large number had read John C. Fremont's account of his expedition. One

Forty-Niner wrote that it was Fremont's account of California's climate and resources that attracted his attention to the Pacific Coast, and that the gold discovery had offered him ". . . an unexpected opportunity of going." [2]

Yet gold alone was not the great drawing card, the big attraction for men to pull up stakes and go West. The idea of moving west toward the setting sun ran deep in the mainstream of American thought. Out beyond the last settlement, the last smoke from a cabin; out there in back of beyond was the American adventure. There in that great West was the unknown promise, and it was in a land where buffalo herds shook the earth as they passed, or so it was told. Out there were Indians and fur trappers. Out there was the Oregon country with its deep dark soil. Out there was California: the land of hide traders, the land South Pacific whalers sometimes visited on their way back to New England, the land coveted by Spaniards, English, and Russians; and now, by God, it was the land of El Dorado!

Still, El Dorado was a long way off, and there was much to be taken into consideration before a man headed west. The major question revolved around which was the best way to get to California. Which route took the least amount of time, offered the smallest number of hardships, presented the best odds against the loss of life, and cost the smallest amount of money? The answers to this many-faceted question depended in large measure upon where the emigrant was starting from in the States and what kind of man he happened to be.

To men from the Eastern seaboard towns and cities the logical route to consider was down the east coast of South America, around Cape Horn, and up the Pacific Coast to San Francisco. The popularity of this ocean voyage to California can best be judged by the number of vessels and passengers that sailed this route. In the morning edition of the New York *Herald* on March 23, 1849, the newspaper reported that up to that date a total of 198 vessels carrying 12,323 passengers had sailed around Cape Horn to California. But there were drawbacks to sailing around the Horn. If an Argonaut did not have much money, a sea voyage was not easy to finance. Cabin fare usually ran $300 and steerage $150. If a man did have the fare, there were other disadvantages: he might be seasick for the first few days or weeks or even for the whole voyage; the quality and quantity of the food would diminish in direct proportion to the length of the voyage; the chances that he might come to hate the captain were exceedingly good; and the 17,000- to 18,000-mile voyage might take anywhere from four to eight months.

Easterners with less money, less love for the sea, and less patience or stomach for a prolonged voyage had the opportunity of booking passage to San Juan del Norte in Nicaragua, where they could travel across country and catch another ship at San Juan del Sur. Or they could book passage on a vessel bound for Chagres, Panama, where they could travel across the Isthmus and catch a northbound ship at Panama. Either of these voyages was shorter, and appeared to offer a quick, economical, and safe trip to California. As it turned out for many emigrants, the choice of either route resulted in just the opposite of what they had expected. True enough, it was cheaper and shorter to sail directly to Nicaragua or Panama, but there the trouble began.

The journey across these countries subjected men to harder traveling than they had anticipated. Tropical disease, bandit raids, and accidents took their toll. Then when the gold seekers reached the Pacific ports of San Juan del Sur and Panama, they discovered prices for accommodations had been boosted, and they had to wait and wait and wait for a ship to appear. When a vessel did put into port, the impatient Argonauts soon discovered there was very little space for more passengers. And the space that was available cost emigrants as much, or even more, than the price for passage from the pier in New York. One pioneer recalled that he paid $1,000 for steerage passage aboard the steamship *California* when the San Francisco-bound vessel put into Panama in January, 1849.

Yet while Cape Horn and Central America routes were popular with men from the East Coast of the United States, this was not the case with men who came from America's great heartland. Whether they were town men or farmers, all the way along the Appalachians to that old jumping-off point at St. Louis, Missouri, the favorite route was the Overland Trail. Like any trail, this one had many branches. Some men headed south to Santa Fé following the traders' route. Some wandered off course on a deadly short cut through Death Valley. But the bulk of the wagon train men followed the Central Overland Crossing, the one George R. Stewart calls *The California Trail*.

The Overland Trail to California had starting points at Council Bluffs, old Fort Kearny, St. Joseph, Independence, and many other towns and outposts that served as jumping-off points for the Western frontier. These were places where the outfit was put into shape. The final supplies were purchased. The maps and guidebooks checked and rechecked. Endless conversations with men who had been there and back took place, and a guide or "pilot" was employed if the party wanted one. These were exciting places where men gathered for a migration that was unlike anything that had ever happened before or is ever apt to happen again unless man moves to other planets.

The white-topped wagons—lighter than Conestogas—the oxen and mules, the barking dogs, the campfires and the smell of woodsmoke, the talk of the adventure about to begin, the strumming of a guitar or the bowing of a fiddle—all this and much more were part of the scene at the beginning of the trail. Then the wet spring of '49 came. In April and May the wagon trains began to roll westward. They were on their way to the land of gold.

On maps or through what their guides told them men learned that they crossed the sea of grass and headed northwest toward Fort Laramie. They followed the North Fork of the Platte River for most of the way, and before they reached Fort Laramie passed Chimney Rock and Scotts Bluff. Beyond Fort Laramie was Independence Rock, and then that low defile in the Rocky Mountains called South Pass. From there they had two major choices: Go southwest to the Mormon stronghold at Salt Lake City and strike out across the Great Basin and hope to cross it without running short of water before they reached the eastern flank of the Sierra Nevada. Or head northwest to Fort Hall, then southwest to the Great Basin and bypass the alkali wasteland surrounding the western shores of the Great Salt Lake. But no matter which direction they took from South Pass, all the trails to California ultimately reached that final sawtooth obstacle, the glistening, granite-topped Sierra Nevada. The trick was to get to these mountains early enough to avoid the snow and the fate of the Donner Party. Then the hardest of all jobs was to get wagons across a path that really did not exist.

Despite the final obstacle of the Sierra Nevada, emigrants of '49 came across the plains in greater numbers than on any of the other routes. "... an acceptable figure for the whole migration would be 22,500—certainly large enough!" [3]

Large enough? Next to the Central Overland Crossing all the other routes to California saw a small amount of traffic. Yet the experience of one man is the material for an epic. Man's history is not only a matter of numbers. In the long haul it is a matter of individuals—what they saw, what they felt, and what they thought. And in that golden year of 1849 individuality was a key factor in the quest of El Dorado.

---

## THE MEXICO CROSSING

---

Around Cape Horn in a ship, across the narrow waist of Central America and up the Pacific Coast in a ship, or across the plains and mountains in a prairie schooner were three major ways to get to California. But for many other men—Mexican War veterans, Southerners, Southwesterners, and even some Easterners and Midwesterners—the trail to El Dorado was through Mexico.

They sailed across the Gulf of Mexico from Mobile, from New Orleans, and from Havana, Cuba. Their ports of call were the windswept barren Texas harbors at Galveston, Port Lavaca, Corpus Christi, and Brazos Santiago on the northern curve of the gulf shore. South from these ports, the principal starting points for the Mexico crossing were Tampico and Vera Cruz.

In the Mexican ports the *norteamericanos* were face to face with the Mexicans the moment they landed. In Texas ports they still had a long or short journey before they crossed the Río Grande into Mexico. But whether they entered Mexico directly or indirectly, the emigrants were all up against the same question. And for most Americans who spoke but one language the matter of asking the initial question was their first problem. Yet fumbling and grumbling, finding a fellow American who spoke some Spanish or a Mexican who spoke some English—no matter how poorly—they managed to ask about the routes across Mexico. What were the roads and trails leading to Pacific Coast ports? What were the roads and trails leading overland to California?

"Which way is El Dorado, *señor?*"

"*¿Cómo dice?*"

53

# THE EL DORADO TRAIL

A puzzled look on the American's face, then slowly, very slowly, another try: *"Cal-if-or-nia, por favor. ¿Donde está el camino a California?"*

*"No entiendo, señor. ¿Cómo dice?"*

Completely blank at the Mexican's reply and thoroughly convinced that all Mexicans tried to speak as rapidly as possible, a last desperate try came out from a member of the party, a sentence pulled out by somebody who either had read it or had it told to him: *"¿Se habla inglés aquí?"*

*"Sí, señor."*

Such meetings were very hard at first. But the man with some English and the man with some Spanish got together. Out of their common struggle came instructions about passports, hotels, where to eat, what to see, and with luck which route to follow.

At Vera Cruz, emigrants were to follow in the footsteps of Cortés. From the tropical heat of Vera Cruz they walked, rode horseback and muleback, or traveled in stagecoaches to Mexico City. And everything was like an outing if a man did not get yellow fever or stop a *ladrón's* bullet. But in the old Aztec capital the gold seekers were faced again with the problem of which way to go. Southwest of Mexico City was Acapulco, the old port for the Manila galleons. Northwest of Mexico City were San Blas and Mazatlán. All these places were a long way off, and in between these ports and Mexico City was a strange land, an unknown country. All of it had seemed so very easy back home in the States. Newspapers and guidebooks had made the trip into an outing with simplified instructions and maps that leveled mountain ranges. Still, Mexican guides could be hired. Though the word about them was that they were not too trustworthy. Some were in league with the *ladrones*. Others didn't know their way once they were outside their home territory. Yet a man with some cash could ride a stagecoach as far north as Guadalajara, and it took only six days and cost $60. From there to San Blas was some 300 miles. But 300 miles of what?

To men who came ashore at semitropical Tampico confusion was every bit as great as for those who landed at Vera Cruz. From this seaport emigrants had to hire a guide or use a map. They purchased horses and mules, and rode across the Sierra Madre Oriental to Mexico's great Central Plateau to San Luis Potosí. For the Tampico travelers, San Luis Potosí was the point of decision. Traveling due west, they went to Guadalajara and on to San Blas or Mazatlán. The other choice was to head northwest to Durango and cross the deep *barrancas* of the Sierra Madre Occidental on the hanging-wall mule trail to Mazatlán. But like gold seekers leaving Mexico City, men who rode out of San Luis Potosí knew they had a long journey to reach a seaport, and that the seaport was still a long way from California.

Some Argonauts who departed from Texas seaports also headed for Mazatlán, but most of these men who crossed the Río Grande were overland men. They struck out into the vast semi-arid plateau, and headed for that pinpoint on the map of Santa Fé traders. These men were on their way to Chihuahua City and the northern overland route across the dry land. They followed the desert trail toward the non-existent Seven Cities, and then headed west to the now-existent El Dorado. These questers of the golden dream crossed the Río Grande anywhere between Matamoros and El Paso del Norte. They crossed the great river of the north, traveled in the territory of the Comanche and Apache, crossed the Sierra Madre Occidental just south of Arizona, and dragged themselves across the Great American Desert. Somewhere to the northwest was California. Somewhere beyond the range of suffering and death was El Dorado.

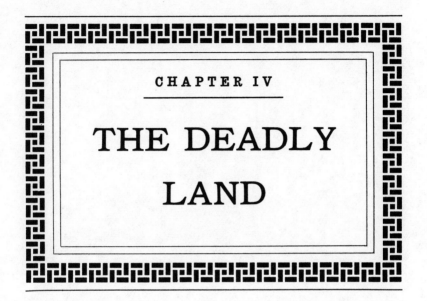

CHAPTER IV

# THE DEADLY
# LAND

## PUSH ON TO ADVENTURE

After it was all over, after the suffering and the cries of the dying, he was able to write about it with some objectivity. He even knew that his real reason for going, for enduring the long march through the deadly land was not so much for gold as it was for ". . . the same wild feeling that sent thousands . . . straggling across the lone prairies, or beating windward against the eternal westerly seas around Cape Horn. . . ." [1] Unlike most seekers of El Dorado, John Woodhouse Audubon was a trained observer, a man quite capable of analyzing his own motivations. His long apprenticeship under his father's guidance had provided him with such tools. That same apprenticeship had also provided him with a lasting curiosity. And when the chance to go to California presented itself, Audubon's long association with his father was the telling factor.

At the beginning of 1849, Audubon had more reasons to remain home than to join the gold rush. He was thirty-six years old, slender and tall; a handsome man whose face was striking with its deep-set eyes, high cheek bones, broad forehead, straight nose, sensuous lips, square jaw, and full head of long, curly hair. He was extremely alert and active, sensitive to everything about him, and moved with ease and grace in all classes of society. He might well have passed for a social dandy. But above all this, he possessed a fine talent that was coming into its own. In every sense of the word, he was "established." Even more than Victor, his older brother, John was the obvious choice to assume the role as successor to their famous father.

To make it even more implausible that John should go trooping off on a wild expedition to California, his father was very ill and no longer able to work. The elder Audubon's health had steadily deteriorated since he had lost most of his eyesight in 1846. At that time he had asked John to finish the paintings for the book about North America's quadrupeds. And now as he got ready for a trip his father would have jumped at not many years before, the old man was hardly aware of what was taking place. Ironically, as he made his final plans, his senile father's greatest joy was to have John's sister-in-law "... sing a Spanish song, *Buenas Noches*, every night before he went to bed." [2]

Despite his father's failing health John Woodhouse Audubon could not resist the expedition formed by friends of the family and placed under the command of Colonel Henry L. Webb, who had commanded a regiment during the Mexican War. But friends of the family did not turn the trick that sent Audubon off as a member of Colonel Webb's California Company. The real reason was his recollection of what his father had said to him only three years before the California gold discovery. "Push on," he had told him, "to the West, even to California: you will find new animals at every change in the formation of the country, and new birds from Central America will delight you." [3] And there was the real reason right out in the open as exposed as a blackbird bouncing stiff-legged across a patch of snow. It wasn't gold at all. It was the adventure and the chance to observe more wildlife. Knowing this and using the gold as an excuse, Audubon accepted the position as second in command under Colonel Webb. On February 8, 1849, the company of eighty men, with a capital of $27,000, boarded the steamship *Transport* and set sail from New York to Philadelphia. They were headed for Brazos Santiago and Brownsville, Texas. From there they planned to take what they thought would be an early and easy route across northern Mexico to the Gila Trail and on to California.

## THE MEN FROM WESTFIELD

Ten days before Colonel Webb's California Company said farewell to the States, The Hampden Mining Company of Westfield, Massachusetts, had boarded a schooner and set sail for Brazos Santiago.

In the fashion of the times, this company also traveled in a quasi-military fashion. No doubt the tendency to follow the movements of a military unit was due in part to veterans of the Mexican War. But it was also due to the fact that some of the organizers of these groups realized it would be necessary if not vital to have a disciplined body of men in order to cut down the risks of the tough journey ahead. Another similarity between the Hampden Mining Company and the men Audubon traveled with was the presence of at least one man who kept a diary of the trip. For during the gold rush the fad of keeping a diary or personal journal reached a peak in the United States.

The forty-six members of the Hampden Mining Company arrived at Brazos Santiago on February 20, 1849. The following morning they stepped ashore. Clarke presented a letter of introduction to Major Chapman, United States Army Quartermaster at the post and, noting that the Hampden men were from the same town as his wife, the major invited them to come to his house. As it turned out, not only was the major's wife from Westfield, Massachusetts, but she was also a woman with whom Clarke ". . . had some acquaintance." [4] So, for the men from Westfield, their introduction to Texas was more personal than it was for other gold seekers who passed through this lonely American outpost. Though Clarke does not mention in detail the nature of the reception he and his companions received from Major Chapman and his wife, it can be assumed it was at least cordial, and more than likely even gracious and warm. Clarke's description of this bleak country only makes his readers believe that the major's wife must have been overjoyed to see someone from a world quite different from this stark, windy, sandy, frontier outpost.

To Clarke, Brazos Santiago was a military station on a sand bank. It consisted of the military building, a collection of run-down shanties, and an ". . . old steamboat . . . hauled up on the sand . . . and used for a hotel, post-office, &c." [5] The rest of the company must have shared his feeling about the place, for by three that afternoon they had secured passage on a military vessel bound for Brownsville.

The Hampden Mining Company's attitude toward Brazos Santiago seemed to be universal. Other emigrants who passed this way either expressed similar feelings or expressed no feeling at all. When Audubon first saw the town from aboard ship, he wrote that ". . . not a landmark more than ten feet was in sight, and miles and miles of breakers, coming and dashing on the glaring beach, broken here and there by the dark, weather-stained wrecks of unfortunate vessels ... ended our view whichever way we looked. ..." [6] When he landed and looked around he was even more dismayed. He bluntly stated that Brazos Santiago was absolutely nothing if one removed the government buildings. He described the town's location as being one long flat about a mile wide, a flat that extended in the direction of the Río Grande, and was "... kept from the sea's overflow by a range of low sand-hills, if drifts from 10 to 15 feet high deserve the name." [7] Nor did the scenery look much better to Clarke as the Hampden Mining Company moved up the Río Grande to Brownsville. Here they stopped long enough to cross over to Matamoros, where they called on the American consul and got passports for their company. They paid $2 each to the consul for certificates and $1 each to the Mexican *alcalde* for their passports. While they were in Matamoros, Clarke looked over the town. He noted it contained about 10,000 people, and had "... more the appearance of a large brick-kiln, ready for burning, than any thing else. ..." [8]

## CALIFORNIA VIA TEXAS

The lonely beach at Brazos Santiago and the brick-kiln façade of Matamoros were not the only jumping-off places for gold miners taking the northern route across Mexico. Other parties started from interior Texas towns and crossed the Río Grande to the northwest; and some miners began their trek from Texas ports on the eastern curve of the Gulf of Mexico. Young Harvey Wood was a member of such a party.

Harvey Wood was twenty-one years old and working as a clerk in a New Jersey store when he got gold fever. He had been reading ads in the New York *Tribune* placed by a dream seller who had chosen a most adventurous name for his overland company. He called it the Kit Carson Association, though the great mountain man and scout had no connection with it. And on February 6, 1849, the

# The Deadly Land

ad for this company had a ring of great urgency, a sort of last call for California gold about it:

FOR CALIFORNIA VIA TEXAS,—Starting positively for Galveston on the 12th inst. in the fine packet ship William B. Travis. We get ourselves (all expenses paid) two mules (valuable in mining as men) and three months provision each to California early in May for $110 per man. Full particulars by D. Hough, Jr., 1 Front st. President of the Carson Association.[9]

Hough knew how to merchandise a dream. As Harvey Wood wrote many years later, Hough told them he was going to be their guide, and that he would get them through in tiptop shape. In his New York office he had "... maps of the various routes posted ... and to hear him explain how simple it was to make the journey from Texas overland to California, most any one would look upon it as a pleasure trip...."[10] However, before the party's ship had reached the open sea the members of the Kit Carson Association discovered that their mentor was no longer with them. All fifty-three of these gold-hungry greenhorns were strictly on their own.

Fifteen days later, on the last day of February, 1849, the brave and adventurous Kit Carson Association landed at Galveston, Texas. While Wood does not describe Galveston, George Evans of the Defiance Gold Hunter's Expedition passed through town just ten days later. And though he had just come from New Orleans, Evans considered Galveston to be the best-looking place he had seen since leaving Defiance, Ohio. He was greatly taken with the city's "... large squares and wide streets ... and palmetto trees...."[11] Evans was one of the few men who saw much in the way of beauty in Galveston during 1849. Another who said that he was pleased with Galveston was Thomas B. Eastland, who landed there in April of 1849, but Eastland also noted that it was "... not in a flourishing state...,"[12] and that many of the houses were closed and without tenants.

Whether gold miners liked Galveston, Port Lavaca, Corpus Christi, Brazos Santiago, or Brownsville really did not matter. All these Texas port towns were merely places to land and to leave. They were places to get all the gear together, buy horses and mules, check with local men who might know something about the trails ahead, pick up more provisions, and get rid of worthless items before beginning the long trek. And items without value were quite common among these Argonauts who had never mined for gold. Promoters of the trip were not the only men who were taking advantage of the emigrant trade.

Wood's journal makes it quite clear that the greenhorns of the Kit Carson Association bought their share of gimmicks and inventions for the quick and easy removal of gold dust. Among the worthless items they purchased was a monumental five-story gold washer consisting of five sets of sieves. These were located one above the other, and were graded to catch pieces of gold ranging from very fine to coarse. Not only was this magnificent machine without value, it was almost impossible to carry overland. Yet the ever brave Kit Carson Association did not have the common sense to leave the contraption at Galveston. These truest of believers had to admit failure by the time they had hauled the monster from Galveston to Corpus Christi and on to Laredo. For somewhere on the dusty streets of Laredo the great gold washer was given away to some Mexican women. No member of the party was superstitious enough to consider the machine a jinx. If anyone had been, it would have come out into the open here. Next to the silt-heavy Río Grande some of the men came down with Asiatic cholera, and a young man called Clark died far from his Pennsylvania home or his golden dream.

---

## THE CURSE OF CHOLERA

While the Kit Carson Association buried their comrade at Laredo and then hurried across the muddy Río Grande, John Woodhouse Audubon and Colonel Webb's California Company were not nearly as lucky. They passed through Brownsville without stopping overnight at the *Frankland,* a beached steamboat that served as the town's hotel, and Audubon's only comment about this port of entry was that it was located on a high bank across the Río Grande from Matamoros. He never mentioned Brownsville's reputation as a smuggler's paradise, as a place that had more than its quota of frontier cutthroats, thieves, and gamblers. The California Company was in too much of a hurry to observe Brownsville's cultural activities. Instead, they boarded the steamer *Corvette* bound upriver for Río Grande City.

As the *Corvette* cruised upstream the captain had a great deal of trouble finding enough deep water to keep her afloat. Often the boat hung up on sand bars. When this happened it took a considerable effort to maneuver the vessel off and get her back into something that resembled a channel. Such delays gave Audubon time to observe the various shrubs and trees growing alongside the river: mesquite, thickets of reeds, willows of all sizes, and hackberry trees. He also observed the many kinds of birds and collected some specimens. When the *Corvette* reached Río Grande City the company filed ashore and set up their camp according to the military rules set forth by Colonel Webb. This done, Audubon took a good look at the specimens he had collected on the trip. He placed the dead birds side by side, and wondered when he would be free enough of his other duties to enjoy the role of naturalist. As night came on, he was "... lulled by the mellow notes of the chick-wills-widow, and the drone of myriads of insects. ..."[13] He lay down on his blankets in the warm evening, said a short prayer for continued health for himself and his family, and drifted off to sleep in the quiet night. It was to be the last peaceful evening he would know for many weeks. Twenty-four hours later all hell broke loose, as the first member of their party was stricken with cholera.

John Booth Lambert, a young lawyer from Connecticut, became violently ill. He groaned and pulled his knees toward his chin as severe stomach cramps hit. He began to vomit in uncontrollable spasms, and felt the warm, stinking, watery excrement run out his anal opening and down his legs. At one moment he felt as though he were on fire with fever; then he vacillated to chills that made him feel as though he had been placed in an ice-water bath. All that night he drifted in and out of fire and ice, in and out of reality and illusion. By morning he appeared to be improving, and Audubon thought he might make it. Then without a scream, a groan, or a last word, Lambert was dead.

The company of men were panic-stricken. They knew very little about this dreaded disease. It was not known that it was caused by bacteria; that it was usually contracted from bad water; and that it was necessary to isolate men who had cholera in order to avoid contracting it. But all the men knew the horror of this killer fever, for between its first appearance in the United States in 1832, and 1840, cholera had killed 4,500 persons in New York City alone. As a result of the fever's history, Audubon had difficulty in getting any member of the company to help him put Lambert's body into a coffin and bury it. Finally Audubon's brother-in-law, Jacob Henry Bachman, volunteered for the grim duty.

Camping in true military style, as though expecting an invasion, their tents in a straight line allowing neither mud nor dry sand to change the camping order, Colonel Webb's California Company was wide open for the spread of this highly contagious disease. The very next night another member of the company came down with cholera. This time it was Hamilton Boden, an extremely strong young man; and Audubon hoped he might be able to withstand the onslaught. But by morning the combination of fever and chills, of spasmodic retching and defecation, had taken its toll. Constant retching had ruptured the veins in Boden's face, and his ". . . broad forehead was marked with blue and purple streaks of blood that stood under the skin and down both sides of the nose, stagnating in the delicate veins round the mouth and the large arteries of the neck. . . ." [14] Then, as Boden lay dying, the fever began to run wild throughout the company. Three men grabbed at their guts and fell to the ground, twisted and contorted with pain as the first wave of cramps hit.

Audubon and Webb made frantic preparations to get their party out of Río Grande City. They hoped that by moving upstream to Roma, Texas, they might outrun the disease, not knowing they would simply carry the highly infectious killer with them. Then, to compound their trouble, another disaster hit them. Audubon had left the bulk of the party's money with the bartender at the Armstrong Hotel, as this appeared to be the safest thing he could do. When he returned for the money he was told that two other members of the party—Hughes and White—had already picked it up. Like Job, Audubon could look about him and see that disaster was becoming a way of life; also like Job, he refused to give up. Hughes, White, and the money had vanished, but that didn't mean they couldn't be tracked down.

Audubon offered a reward for the recovery of the stolen money, and two Texas Rangers—Andy Walker and Wiley Marshall—took on the assignment. They tracked Hughes and White, and near Camargo, Mexico, caught Hughes. They tied him to a tree ". . . far off in the chaparral, where no cry for help could be heard . . . ," [15] and tried to *encourage* him to tell where he and White had hidden the money. Either Hughes was much too stubborn for his own good, or the Rangers got too careless in their methods. At any rate, Hughes didn't talk, and the Rangers brought his skull back to the barroom at the Armstrong Hotel, where it became a grisly trophy. As for White, the Rangers caught up to him near San Antonio, and shot him as he tried to escape. Apparently, though, the Rangers got some information out of White, as they did locate about two-thirds of the stolen money. While this was better than nothing, the ultimate cost of staying another week in the cholera-stricken Río Grande City resulted in the burying of more gold miners next to the muddy Río Grande. Before the party got on its way to Roma, Texas, it had watched eight companions die.

## THIS GOLDEN LURE

While the shattered company of men under Colonel Webb headed upstream toward Roma, more and more gold miners were landing in Texas ports and heading up the Río Grande, or cutting directly west toward El Paso del Norte. Through rumors, newspaper stories, government reports, and guidebooks, these emigrant parties had learned something about the trails across the northern desert of Mexico. Some knew about Lieutenant Colonel Cooke's march with the Mormon Battalion in 1846–1847, and they were convinced that if Cooke had managed to cross the Sierra Madre with wagons and a battalion and go on to California, the journey would not be difficult for small emigrant parties. Other gold miners knew about Major Lawrence P. Graham's leading the Second Dragoons from Monterrey, Mexico, across northern Mexico and over Guadalupe Pass, where they met Cooke's trail leading to the Gila and on to California. And there were other crossings of this arid country they had heard about, but none of the stories gave the actual details. None outlined the very real possibility of dying of thirst, or having one's scalp lifted by the Apaches, or of getting lost in the Sierra Madre and wandering in a maze of *barrancas* until only the turkey buzzards would be left to claim the bodies. Yet even if these men had known all these problems, even if they had had a full realization of the risks, most of them would have continued on.

Their ability to believe without questioning the reliability of the information, to believe that nothing could happen to their party or to them, was remarkable. And the men who made up these parties were believers who really thought they were off on a kind of outing to a land where gold nuggets would be scattered all over the ground. The pull of this golden lure and the chance for adventure was more than most men could resist. No better proof of this could be offered than the fact that trailing the ill-fated Webb-Audubon group was a man who seemed an unlikely candidate for such an adventure. He seemed that way until one took into consideration that he had been a war correspondent attached to General John Ellis Wool's headquarters at Saltillo, Mexico.

John E. Durivage was now returning to Mexico, following the path he had taken with General Wool and his troops. Only this time the gentleman from New Orleans, the outstanding reporter for the New Orleans *Daily Picayune,* was suffering from gold mania. Like Audubon, Durivage was attached to a company of miners for more than the pursuit of gold. Adventure called him, and he was also attracted by the challenge to report this lemming-like movement of men. He kept notes, wrote dispatches, and wherever possible sent stories back to the *Daily Picayune.* He was on the lookout for items that would give the flavor of this epic in the making.

Landing at Brazos Santiago during the first week of March, 1849, Durivage and his party immediately headed up the Río Grande to Brownsville. Here he observed the devastating effect of cholera. In a letter to his newspaper, he wrote that about one hundred persons in a town of fifteen hundred had already died. Then when he reached Río Grande City, he wrote that it was ". . . nearly deserted, the cholera having appeared and frightened the inhabitants from the place."[16] It was from here that Durivage sent his first news of Colonel Webb's California Company. In a dispatch to the *Daily Picayune,* he reported the outbreak of cholera among them.

As he moved up the Río Grande, Durivage saw more and more emigrant parties. Men were on the move from Georgia, St. Louis, New Orleans, and more places than he took time to list. It was as though all the young men in the States had left the safety of their homes and were on the move to the goldfields. Durivage reported that a vast number were also taking the Chihuahua City–Gila River route. But all the joy, all the thrill of questing was fast disappearing as cholera took more and more lives. By the time Durivage reached Camargo, Mexico, on his way to Saltillo, he wrote: "We have seen scarcely anything but suffering and death." [17] At Mier, he witnessed a religious ceremony that was to appeal to God, ". . . and solicit an exemption from the cholera in favor of Mier." [18] At its culmination the procession moved outside the church to the plaza. During this part of the ceremony one person carried the host. Others carried burning censers, and all of them chanted as they walked to a corner of the plaza where there was a table holding burning candles. Here the procession came to a halt, and everyone—priests, men, women, and children—knelt and prayed. Then, as though they were following the Stations of the Cross, the procession continued around the plaza. At each outlet of the plaza they stopped, knelt, and prayed; ". . . rockets in the meanwhile being projected, and bursting in the air with an explosion like a pistol shot." [19]

## WHIRLWIND OF DISASTER

Caught up in a whirlwind of disaster and falling way behind the other parties of emigrants the Webb-Audubon men straggled into Mier on the twenty-fifth of April. It had taken them over a month to travel about 30 miles from Río Grande City to Mier. As Audubon looked at Mier, he had good reasons to be depressed and think this might well be the terminal point of their journey. By this time he had come down with cholera and was slowly recovering. Webb also was recovering from the fever, but he was not able to continue the march. Audubon figured the journey to California would take at least another 100 days, and a tally of the remaining money showed that the company had $66.04 for each man. The trio of death, desertion, and disability had cut the size of the party to forty-eight men who might or might not be able to hold up their end of the long

69

journey facing them. Mier was a crucial point for the once supremely confident Colonel Webb's California Company. To continue into the northern desert on the trail to El Dorado or to go back to the Gulf of Mexico and catch a ship home was a very real question. To add to Audubon's consideration of this question was the fact that the men would not go ahead unless he took over the leadership of the company.

Yet despite these problems, Audubon took time to comment upon the appearance of Mier. It was composed of one large plaza with an extension of suburbs fanning out from it, like every Mexican town he had seen. But he was delighted with the grand view he had of the Sierra Madre Oriental. It was as though ". . . all the blue of Italy was again before me—all but the blue of the Mediterranean; and as the sun went down behind them, even those over whom scenery had had previously no effect, seemed to feel the beauty and sublimity of this grand and isolated range." [20]

At Mier the wagons belonging to the party broke down once again, and it was decided to sell all but one wagon. The roads and trails ahead were going to be much rougher than those they had already traveled. This decision also meant they had to cut down on their supplies. It now became necessary to select carefully only those items that could be carried by pack horses and mules. To make a sensible elimination of goods and to try and salvage part of the cost of what they had to discard, the party remained in Mier for a few days to sell such items for as much as they could get.

Leaving Mier on April 28, what was now the Audubon Company moved at a better pace. This was due to Audubon's leadership, a respite from cholera, and the transformation of the party from a wagon to a pack train. By the eighth of May they were camped at Walnut Springs, 5 miles outside Ciudad Monterrey. In their ten-day trip from Mier they had averaged about ten miles per day. They were tired, but they were moving forward at long last. Resting in the shade of Spanish walnut trees, they relaxed and enjoyed this camp where a spring shot out in a fountain and provided the luxury of unlimited water.

This was Audubon's first and only time in Monterrey, and like all other Americans he had heard about this area as a result of the Mexican War. Yet he wrote very little about the city. He did mention that he was delighted with the picturesque bridges at the city's entrance, and he noticed Monterrey's beautiful location in a natural amphitheater at the base of the Sierra Madre Oriental. However, his new position of command was foremost in his thoughts. He quickly drifted from the look of the city and its surroundings to the look of his men. They were weary and worn, and not yet broken in for the long trek facing them. Their spirits were low. They could not forget the death of their companions, or the wild fear that sent others in a frantic homeward retreat. They were not totally demoralized, but they had walked the ragged edge of daily despair, and their faces showed it. And now when they needed rest, when they needed recovery time, they had to move as quickly as they could. They were already far behind the pace they needed to keep if they were going to get through the northern deserts before the deadly summer heat arrived. The pressure was on, and even the hope of a good night's sleep was gone as each man had to take his turn at guard duty. Audubon, too, felt the strain of having to stand guard, of constantly having to watch out for thieves. "At midnight," he wrote, "I take the rounds of our camp in moonlight, starlight or darkness. . . . This gives me only six hours of sleep. . . ." [21] Six hours of sleep was only part of Audubon's trouble. He was still trying to recover from his own bout with cholera, and he constantly worried about the long trip ahead.

In contrast A. B. Clarke, who had passed that way in March, gave a complete description of Monterrey's location, of the surrounding peaks of the Sierra Madre— ". . . very pointed, and worn into various fantastic shapes by the action of rains, and deeply furrowed on the sides . . ." [22]—the citrus trees throughout the city, the American merchants in business there, the thick, adobe-walled dwellings that looked like small forts, and the Bishop's Palace, El Obispado, located on Chepe Verea Hill on the west side of the city. Clarke visited this palace which had been used as a fort to hold off the invading American Army for two days during the Mexican War, and thought it was like a European castle. He also saw the signs of battle, as there were unrepaired cannonball holes.

This difference in attitude between Clarke and Audubon regarding Monterrey was not the only instance of Audubon's inability to see Mexico's cities in the manner that he saw the countryside. In Saltillo, the next city of size after Monterrey, Audubon was able to notice the adobe walls, the fortified look of the houses, the plaza, and Saltillo's cathedral, which he thought was very beautiful. Yet even here his observational powers failed him, for he certainly did not describe the splendor of the Cathedral of Santiago, which was built between 1746 and 1801. He never even mentioned its magnificent 200-foot tower. The best he could do was say that the cathedral was ". . . the most highly ornamented I ever saw in America. . . ." [23] Audubon even failed to notice the colorful *serapes* of Saltillo. Clarke, on the other hand, found out that the city was famous for its *serapes*, and wrote that ". . . they cost $25 to $500, with fine colors exquisitely woven. . . ." [24] Durivage was even more delighted to be in Saltillo than Clarke. His great disappointment was that the Mexicans had not yet erased the marks of war since he had lived there as an American war correspondent. But he quickly overlooked that, and searched for a favorite hangout. "I found the *bodega*," he wrote, "and poor old Bocanegra, the proprietor of the same, and received a Spanish hug as an affectionate remembrancer." [25]

Neither Clarke nor Durivage had experienced the trouble Audubon had in getting from Brazos Santiago to Saltillo. His trip had been a series of disasters, and most of them had occurred within towns and cities. Yet his coolness toward cities also was a result of the fact that he wasn't a city man. For him, the natural environment made life worthwhile. This aspect of his personality comes out again and again in his drawings and his writing. The contrast between Audubon as the country man, and especially Durivage as the city man, becomes quite apparent in their descriptive writing.

Durivage was at his best when he wrote about cities and city people. He captured the flavor of city life and was excited by it. The only people who stand out in Audubon's journal were either members of his company or people he met on the trail. The difference between these two chroniclers becomes obvious on the road to Parras. Six miles out of Saltillo the road passed by the battlefield of Buena Vista, where Durivage simply noted passing a destroyed *rancho* and heading across the plain toward the mountain pass leading to Parras. Audubon wrote: "Six miles over a barren and desolate rolling prairie changed our scene, and we had a grand view of all the beauties of Buena Vista; high picturesque mountains bounded the landscape on every side; and valleys, all luxuriant in vegetation of an irrigated soil aided by the climate of the tropics. . . ." [26]

In the country, outside the fever-ridden and thief-plagued cities,

Audubon felt at home, but tragedy was not left behind. In the safe camp outside the city limits of Saltillo, outside the specter of cholera, disaster hit the company once more. A man doing his turn of guard duty lost his grip on his rifle, which fell and fired as the hammer struck the ground. This single shot in the night in a strange country "... created a breathless silence, even with the bravest. ..." [27] Were they under attack by bandits, or had they run into a raiding band of Comanches? They waited for more shooting, but there was only the single shot. The camp became a scene of wild confusion. Someone had been wounded. The men could hear a man groaning. One member of the company voiced the deepest fears of the group when he said, "My God, Mr. Audubon's killed!" [28] Relief, coupled with concern for the wounded man, came with the discovery that young Graham had been shot. Lamps were quickly brought forth.

Audubon was the first to get to Graham. He saw that the rifle ball had passed through his ankle. As he assisted the company's two doctors—Trask and Perry—with the wounded man, his ears were still ringing from the sound of the whirring ball which had narrowly missed his head. A council was held, and it was decided to leave Graham and his cousin in Saltillo until the young man was well enough to travel again. Audubon gave the two men as much money as he could from the company's dwindling funds. Meanwhile another member of the company went into Saltillo and found a room for them. There they left the cousins, wished them luck, and told them to use their own judgment about coming on to California or returning home.

Hoping that the accidental shooting of Graham was the last of their troubles, the Audubon party left the plains around Saltillo and the battlefield of Buena Vista. They headed west into the dry hills of the Sierra Madre. Slowly they climbed upward, and though they gained in altitude the days were now very warm. All around them the countryside was parched and barren. The mountains appeared to have very few trees, and all the men saw was a covering of dry brush. As they reached the top of the range, where they hoped the trail would lead them on to a grassy plain, the deadly land tricked them once again. They reached a broad plain that seemed to go on into space. It was like being at the bottom of a sea without any water. The high desert mountains lined this wasteland, and Audu-

bon looked upward and imagined that a great body of water had
gone halfway up the slopes, and changed to earth all at once. As far
as he or his men were able to see, this was a dead land. Mile after
endless mile there was no sign of water, no sign of life. No matter
which direction the men looked, they saw no lean-ribbed cattle, no
burros, no used-up horses walking along in search of a clump of grass
to nibble. This was a dead land. It was a land where the soil was the
color of dried bones, where the scraggly bushes were like pieces of
dead skin or lost scalps dropped by a vanished Comanche raider.
Nowhere in this flat, dry Bolsón de Parras, this ancient lake bed left
over from another climate, was there any sign of water; nowhere was
there any sign of life. Yet not many miles from their view of the desolate *bolsón*, Audubon's party entered a *rincón* hidden in the desert
mountains. Suddenly there was water. And with water, there was
life. Ahead of the weary emigrants was the long, narrow valley of
Parras.

## A PLACE OF DECISION

Parras in the State of Coahuila was an oasis, a place of decision for
travelers on the El Dorado Trail. Located in the eastern desert foothills of the Sierra Madre Oriental, it was (and still is) almost 100
miles west of Saltillo. It was a stopping place before striking out
onto the vast Central Plateau to head southwest to Durango, or
northwest to Chihuahua City. Here next to running water, here in
the shade of tall cottonwood trees, they camped and rested. They
got out their maps and guidebooks. They talked to local citizens and
to foreigners who had settled in this place. They talked of Mexico,
of the country they had wandered through, of the wines and brandy
that Parras was famous for, and of the *one* central issue that drove
them onward. Where, they asked, is the road to California?

In English, in Spanish, or a little of both, the answer was: "Which
one, *señor*?"

A key question at Parras got a key answer. *Which one? Which road? Which trail?* To the west across Mexico's Central Plateau was Durango and the silver mines. Beyond Durango was the winding mule trail across the Sierra Madre Occidental to the port of Mazatlán. Here a man might catch a ship to San Francisco. That, *señor*, was one way to California. Another way was to cross the Bolsón de Parras, the Bolsón de Mapimí and head northwest to Chihuahua City. From Chihuahua City there was the road to Janos in the northern foothills of the Sierra Madre. Beyond that was a trail through the Guadalupe Pass to the State of Sonora. Then to the north was Tucson, and west of there was the junction of the Gila and Colorado rivers, the Colorado Desert, and then California. That, all that, *señor*, was another way to California. Many men have traveled it, and many men have died on their journey. Watch out for three things, *señor*: *Indios*, waterholes, and the *Gran Desierto*. Two will kill you, and one will keep you alive. *Vaya con dios, señor.*

But what of Parras, some asked. Why is it here? They were told that Spaniards who had once marched north in search of gold had settled there as early as 1598. Then it was the home of the Yritilas and other Indians, but the weary Spaniards saw the water, the shade of the cottonwoods, the wild grapes, and they made Parras part of Nueva Vizcaya. At this time the pueblo of Santa María de las Parras (Santa María of the vines) first appeared on Spanish maps when Jesuits from Durango founded a mission there.

Raids by both Apaches and Comanches did not drive the Spaniards out, and gradually they took over the land that had been a desert sanctuary for the Indians. By the time Audubon and other parties of California emigrants passed through Parras, it was no longer a frontier outpost. It still suffered from occasional Indian raids, and *hacienda* owners built their thick-walled adobe homes to serve both as living quarters and as forts. After all, a man never knew when the Indians would strike again. There had been other invaders, too. The *gringo* army had occupied Parras during the Mexican War, and since the end of that war there were many bands of *ladrones* who showed no mercy if they caught a *gringo* or a Mexican of means off his guard.

When the Hampden Mining Company passed through Parras in the latter part of March—two months ahead of Audubon's Company —A. B. Clarke was greatly intrigued with the town's beauty. He

commented at length upon its plaza, its shady walks, its fine avenues, and its magnificent rosebushes. Most of all, though, he was
impressed with the wines and brandies of Parras. "In the neighbor-
hood," he wrote, "there are made annually 225,000 gallons of wine,
which is of a superior quality." [29] Clarke's only criticism of Parras
was that there were too many thieves. This, however, was a typical
complaint that each group of miners made about every part of Mexico that they passed through. Yet none of these critics speculated
about the cause of such thievery. None related it to the terrible pov-
erty they saw, to the civil unrest left in the wake of the lost war, or
to the fact that many Mexicans saw no reason to treat another wave
of invading *gringos* with kindness.

Many of the California emigrant companies that passed through
Parras failed to describe it in detail, but all of them stayed for a few
days before striking out into the great Central Plateau. And most of
the companies came away with some bottles of Parras brandy and
wine. John E. Durivage even left Parras with a Negro boy he hired
as a servant—a boy ". . . whose wardrobe consisted of a very melan-
choly-looking pair of leather breeches, a forlorn hat, a sickly shirt,
and distressing shoes. . . ." [30]

To Audubon, Parras was a town of one-story adobe houses, the
color of campfire ashes, but it was also a place where he saw fruit
trees, fields of corn and wheat, vineyards, and hedges of cabbage
roses along avenues shaded by tall cottonwood trees. In his journal
he wrote that here ". . . one might almost fancy himself again in a
country where it rains sometimes, and be almost tempted to believe
that after all, there is something worth living for in this burnt up
region." [31]

But Audubon's luck had not changed. Once again his company
was hit by cholera. This time Audubon suffered another attack of
fever serious enough for the company to have to carry him in their
remaining wagon as they left Parras on the morning of June 2 and
headed into the dry heat of the Bolsón de Parras. Unlike most gold
seekers they were not bound for either Durango or Chihuahua City.
They were on their way to Parral (now Hidalgo de Parral)—a silver-
mining town in the foothills of the Sierra Madre north of Durango
and south of Chihuahua City. Here they planned to take a trail
across the mountains into the State of Sonora, and then north to the
confluence of the Gila and Colorado rivers.

## A COUNTRY OF FEAR

Audubon remained in the wagon on the first day's march toward Parral. That night they camped at El Poso where there was water, but the gravelly hills and dry ravines offered no food for their animals. The country was so dry that even the bunch grass was brittle from the loss of moisture. To get through the Bolsón de Mapimí— that pouch of desolation—they started each day even before daylight. They moved northwest toward the blue haze on the horizon. Somewhere out there, somewhere between two and three hundred miles, were Parral and the Sierra Madre. And the men knew their only hope to escape the heat was to get into the mountains as fast as they could. They traveled onward through the mesquite and the bunch grass, but they moved with caution. They watched for the waterholes, and for stunted willows that gave them away. And they watched for a distant dust cloud that might mean the movement of horsemen. They were in the great trough or tableland that extended from the American Southwest, and they knew it served as a chute or runway for Apache and Comanche raiding parties.

The days and nights ran together in a dull, hot sameness. Audubon felt as though he were being slowly roasted. More than that, he felt he was in a country of the damned. No man should have to endure such daily torment. Yet people lived here, actually lived out their destinies in this harsh land. And what were their destinies? Roast in the summer, freeze in the icy blast of a winter norther. Try to make it on a *rancho* where it was necessary to sleep with a gun close to you for fear of Indians, or call home a dirty *poblado* where wind-blown sand made everything gritty. These were people who lived out their lives in a land that was always short of food and water. They lived out their lives with the daily taste of fear in their mouths. These people of the plateau knew the horror of an Indian raid, knew the chill of an Apache war cry. They had seen loved ones butchered, and would see such violence again. They had heard the screams of children and women as they were carried off by the raiders, and would hear such screams again.

This was a country of fear, a country where any stranger might be in league with death. The extent that fear played in the lives of these people came rushing home to Audubon when they rode into the *poblado* of Cerro Gordo. To Audubon this place was ". . . a miserable den of vagabonds, with nothing to support it but its petty garrison of a hundred and fifty cavalry mounted on mules." [32] The people on the streets hooted at them and called them *gringos*. But here they also met a small traveling circus company that pleaded with them for protection.

Audubon looked at the tall thin leader. He studied his gaunt face, and saw the high cheekbones, the high thin nose, and the deep-set brown eyes. "What do you want?" he asked.

"Only to ride with you, *señor, por favor*."

"Why?"

"*Los Indios, señor*. The Apaches."

Five of them waited for his answer: one woman and four men. Audubon thought of the possibility of their being thieves. Certainly none of them looked like bandits. They looked like what they were— a raggedy little act that might have once been part of a very poor circus. Five people waiting for a decision, five people with a terrible fear of the Apaches, but five people who were brave enough to try to make their living by entertaining other frightened people in this hostile land. There was nothing else he could do, and Audubon knew it. So they rode out of Cerro Gordo together—a company of *gringo* gold miners and a very small and poor Mexican circus—companions of the trail.

The woman, Audubon called her the Queen, rode side-saddle on a small pacing pony. One man walked behind the two pack mules that carried all their plunder, and he continually adjusted the packs. There were two horses that carried only saddles, and they were used for performances. There were four other horses that the men of the circus rode, including the mule driver. But of the men Audubon was most interested in the clown and the leader. The clown rode a jaded-looking horse, and he carried three little Chihuahua dogs with him— two inside his shirt and the other on the pommel of his saddle. The leader rode the best of their horses, a gray Arabian. But as good as his horse was, that was the end of the man's ability to defend his circus. His weapons belonged to another traveler in another land who rode out to joust with windmills. Dangling from the man's left side was a long dragoon sword; ". . . and under his right leg, at the bend of his knee, with the but of it in a sling from the *'cabeza'* of the saddle, hung a Mexican musket, made about the year 1700. . . ."[33]

During the three days the circus rode with them, Audubon learned that these people took their show through northern Mexico.

"Where do you perform?" he asked.

*"Los poblados, ciudades, las haciendas, señor,"* the leader replied, "wherever there are people who wish to see us."

As they got to know each other better, the leader told Audubon that he and his companions carried everything they owned when they made these trips. For that reason they always tried to ride with an armed party of men from place to place in order to avoid the Apaches.

"Do you earn a good living?" Audubon asked.

*"Sí, señor, muy bueno,* if no *ladrones* and no *Indios."*

On the third day's ride from Cerro Gordo, the Audubon Company and the Mexican circus arrived in El Valle. This was the next stop for the circus, and here the Queen of their show thanked them for their protection. Then she gave them ". . . a most courteous invitation to her show and fandango, the termination to every Mexican entertainment, either battle, wedding, or christening. . . ."[34] Audubon thanked her, but said he would not be able to go. Some of his men, however, accepted the invitation and when they came back to the camp talked mostly about the *señoritas* who were damned good-looking and friendly.

Leaving their circus friends at El Valle, the Audubon Company rode into the foothill country of the *sierra.* The scenery got more rugged, and to the west they saw the tall backbone of the Sierra Madre. Four days after Cerro Gordo, they arrived in the silver-mining town of Parral. To Audubon Parral was a wild and picturesque town. It was surrounded by high mountains, and the mines were on the slopes. The streets were narrow. Most of the buildings were one story high; a few were taller. At Parral they found some Americans who were in charge of some silver mines. But once again disease struck their party, and they remained for eight days. While they waited for three men to recover, they learned that the pass across the mountains was a good trail, an area where there was water and food. They decided to cross at this point and not go on to Chihuahua City and northwest from there.

In preparing for their trip across the Continental Divide, Audubon sold the company's one wagon—the Jersey wagon that had been his ambulance—for $275, but he turned down a local offer of $250 for the two mules that had pulled it. He thought it safer to have more animals than they needed. On June 28 they were ready to leave Parral, but they did not get away without tragedy striking again. Teller and Fuller died of cholera and were buried here. Once again Audubon felt he was leading a cursed party. But this feeling of depression vanished as they moved into the mountains. Even their mules sensed the difference in climate. As they escaped from the parched earth behind them, they moved as though they were racing each other, and before the day ended the company had traveled 20 miles. Part of this journey was covered in a mountain storm that hit just at dusk. They rode on for a little over a mile in the heavy rain until they came to a grassy flat. This was their first Sierra Madre camp, and they pitched tents in a thicket of mesquite and scrub oaks; dug ditches around each tent to take care of the run-off water; gathered grass to put under their blankets; and had some Parral cheese and hard bread which they washed down "... with a tin cup full of good strong Parras brandy...."[35] For the first time in the whole trip, Audubon felt he had escaped from a country of harsh extremes, a land of daily violence.

The next day the men rode through some of the most beautiful country they had seen. All about were patches of bright scarlet lilies. Overhead was mistletoe infesting the limbs of large live oaks. Then they slowly began to work their way up the narrow mule trail leading to the pass. At the top of the ridge they rested at a point that jutted out and made a natural overlook. As far as they could see the country was turned upside down in hogback ridges and deep *barrancas*. It was like looking at a stormy sea that had suddenly turned into mountains, ridges, and canyons. Audubon wrote that he "... gazed in admiration at the picturesque cliffs, ... all discolored with the iron that was here prominent on the surface, and the broad valley, widening in the distance...."[36] From this place they began their descent of the steep mule trail. At one stretch it was so sharp the men got off their mounts and led them for about 2 miles. When they reached the bottom of the *barranca*, another member became terribly sick with an attack of cholera. Four men, including Dr. Trask, remained with him, while the rest rode another 10 miles to a rolling prairie where they camped for the night. By evening, the men who had remained behind with the sick man appeared in the light of the campfire like stragglers of a defeated army.

During the next few days the company rode in and out of one *barranca* after another, crossed mountain streams, and passed through mountain valleys. The narrow passes were worn by years and years of travel, and the pack mules had to place their hooves in the same holes other mules had made. Two of their pack train missed these holes, fell over the side and rolled four or five times before recovering their footing. They got up, shook themselves, grunted, and worked their way back to the trail. Meanwhile, some of the men were suffering from attacks of dysentery. Young Liscomb got the "runs" so badly that for several days Franklin Carrol and John Tone had to ride alongside him and hold him in his saddle. Whenever the trail was too narrow to permit this, the men dismounted, walked alongside his horse, and held him. The days were hard and long as the men worked their way in and out of deep *barrancas* where the bluffs and breaks were covered with a thick forest of pine and spruce. They passed through many back-country *poblados,* but they kept moving ahead. They knew they were in country the Apaches raided, and they didn't want to stop their march until they reached a larger settlement. The hardship of the trail began to tell on them more and more, and on the evening before the Fourth of July Audubon called a halt for a day of rest.

The morning of Independence Day the men were awake at their usual time, but they knew a long day's ride did not face them. Most of the men stood next to the campfire, drank coffee and a little Parras brandy, and looked to the east at the high ridges behind them for the first light of sun. As it rose above the ridge and its rays filtered through the pines and began to clear the blue haze of the *barranca*, Audubon searched the bottom of his saddlebags. Rolled up in a handkerchief was a small American flag given to him by Hamilton Boden as he lay dying of cholera at their Río Grande City camp. Before their camp was completely in daylight, Audubon climbed a tall pine nearby, attached the American flag, said a prayer for Boden, and climbed down. The other men watched in silence. Then they gave three cheers for the Union and prepared to spend their day of rest. "Some slept," Audubon wrote, "some basked in indolence, some started off to look for game, some looked to their saddlebags and blankets; all was rest, at least from travel, and I unpacked my paper and pencils and made a sketch of the 'Fourth of July Camp.' " [37]

As the men toasted Independence Day, they faced another month of rough mountain trails. They passed through one small mining village after another—camps of isolated hope. Finally, they dropped over the last western ridge and descended into the State of Sonora. Behind them were cool mountain canyons and rushing streams. From the front, they were hit smack in the face by the hot, searing winds of the Sonoran summer. Accustomed to the cool weather of the Sierra Madre's high country, the men were not prepared for such intense heat. Audubon wrote that ". . . the dry parched bottom sent up a heat such as I do not recollect having ever felt before. I saw the men fag, get down and tumble on the grass at the sides, whenever a shady spot could be found, and the poor mules seemed completely exhausted." [38] The men vomited and felt faint from the heat, and this was only the beginning of their march across the burning land.

Ahead were all the tortures of a desert summer. For hundreds of miles the surface of the ground became as hot as a pancake griddle by midday. They reached Ures, the capital of Sonora, on August 22, and found an adobe village of about 4,000 persons—most of them Indians. The *alcalde* told them that ". . . gold abounds in the surrounding mountains, but the Apaches are so bad that it cannot be secured. . . ." [39] Weary and tired, they remained in Ures for eight days, then headed northwest to Altar.

The eight-day trek was over desolate, sandy hills. When they reached this small *poblado,* they were in a bad way. Many of them were on foot. Their clothes were ragged and torn. They had been living on half rations, going without water for as long as twenty-four hours at a stretch, finding no feed for their horses and mules, and becoming wearier mile by mile. "Yet," Audubon entered in his journal, "we are well and not as much depressed as might be supposed, and while we are short of everything, money included, our courage is in no degree lessened." [40]

Altar, though, was not the end of the desert. It was the beginning of the worst country they had to cross. From this point on there was no relief. Plants offered no shade. Cacti, mesquite, chaparral, and other thorny plants tore into the flesh. The wind was never cool, not even at night. When it blew, it burned a man's face and chapped his lips. For added torment it raised clouds of sand and dirt that hit against the skin like thousands of tiny whips. Everything that was part of this country seemed to pose a threat: the thorny plants, the rattlesnakes, the scorpions, the constant menace of an Apache raid, the shortage of water, and the heat of the sun that made a man's head feel as though it were slowly being baked over a bed of hot coals. Yet they were barely started toward the Colorado; and when they reached the river crossing, there was the final test awaiting them. Beyond the Colorado River was the last leg of their California journey, but to complete it they had almost a hundred miles of one of America's worst deserts to stagger across.

CHAPTER V

# ¡AY, CHIHUAHUA!

# TO COURT DISASTER

Before the Audubon Company managed to leave their death camp at Río Grande City in that spring of 1849, other companies of California emigrants were well on their way to Chihuahua City and El Paso del Norte. These two jumping-off points were the last safe stops for parties bound for Guadalupe Pass—the northern crossing of the Sierra Madre Occidental. Beyond either settlement only the thin line of Mexico's frontier outposts offered anything in the way of supplies or protection. To rely upon such places as Corralitos and Janos was to court disaster. These villages were in the heart of Apachería, and their existence depended upon the day-to-day whim of some of the fiercest warriors the world has ever known.

To make matters even more precarious, it was no secret on either side of the border that the Apaches hated Mexicans with a burning passion only matched by the deep fear Mexicans had of them. Unknown to gold seekers on their way to El Dorado, this fear of Apaches was founded in reality. Since the seventeenth century these Indians had been terrorizing northern Mexico. The extent of this reign of fear would have been quite apparent to emigrants if they had known that in a fifteen-year period between 1820 and 1835, the Apaches had killed about 5,000 people in northern Mexico, destroyed *ranchos, haciendas, poblados,* and driven most settlers out of the territory.

Added to the Apache threat was that of the only Indians capable of defeating them. These were the Comanches, and during the latter part of the nineteenth century they, too, made annual raids in northern Mexico. Riding in parties that numbered as many as 500 braves, they were completely organized as a military force. Each year they crossed the border and followed ". . . the Great Comanche War Trail

—which led from the high plains of Texas across the Big Bend of the Río Grande to strike at the mining communities from Durango southward, and according to some reports, as far west as the Gulf of California."[1] The southern extension of their yearly raids took them to within 300 miles of Mexico City, and within the scope of that large territory the Comanches struck at many of the communities California emigrants passed through. Between the Comanches and the Apaches the northern Mexico route to El Dorado presented an Indian danger far greater than on any other overland route to California.

But to Yankees stricken with gold fever, and dead certain of their superiority over both Indians and Mexicans, it was almost impossible to accept any concept of possible failure or defeat. Even if these men had known *all* the facts about the Apaches and Comanches, and about the nature of the country they would have to cross on their northern *jornada,* most of them would have avoided facing the possibility that they might not make it. These gold-hungry Yankees rated themselves among the very best of men.

To add to their cockiness, the emigrants also knew that Santa Fé traders had been making freight-wagon runs to Chihuahua City for many years without much trouble. Furthermore, they knew that Kearny's Army of the West had marched from El Paso del Norte across the Sierra Madre and on to California; that Lieutenant Colonel Philip St. George Cooke and the Mormon Battalion had even taken wagons over Guadalupe Pass; and that Major Lawrence P. Graham had led the Second Dragoons through the same country, all the way from Monterrey, Mexico to California, at the end of the Mexican War. And while the Argonauts might not have considered themselves as able as the Santa Fé traders, they certainly rated themselves as capable as any soldier.

No doubt if anybody had asked these men about their qualifications to make this overland trek, their answer might well have been: "By God, what makes you think we're any different than Cooke's damned-fool Mormon boys, or the pups from the Second Dragoons? If those b'hoys made it, the trail must be a goddamned post road."

The northern Mexico overland crossing was anything but a post road. It was a tough land in every respect. It could kill a man for lack of water, lack of food, lack of fodder, and lack of shade. It could kill him with the swift strike of a rattlesnake, the slow dehydration from daily dysentery, or the arrows and lances of an Apache or Comanche ambush. The major problem on the northern branch of the El Dorado Trail was very basic: to keep alive in a land that specialized in death.

---

## THE ONLY GOOD INDIAN

---

Yet the Argonauts never considered themselves as prospects for bleached bones or shallow graves to be unearthed by coyotes. As for Indians, that was not a danger to stop Americans. These were men whose history was filled with stories of Indian raids and counterraids by white settlers that drove the Indian farther and farther west. Even a man born and reared in New York City believed he was superior to any Indian if it came to a fight, while men from the states and territories bordering on Indian country were old hands at giving the "redskins" hell. They all knew how to handle Indians even if the Mexicans didn't. It was quite simple. "The only good Injun is a dead one."

This attitude showed complete ignorance of the fighting prowess of the Apaches and Comanches. The Kit Carson Association believed in this American myth all the way, and proved it at San Catarina, Mexico. Here, over 150 miles southwest of Laredo, in the eastern mountains bordering the Bolsón de Mapimí, Harvey Wood and fifteen other men from this company joined with sixteen men from the Mazatlán Rangers of Massachusetts to help the owner of a *hacienda* chase a raiding band of Comanches who had stolen forty head of horses.

The complete folly of such an act can best be understood by considering these items: the men were in a country they didn't know; pursuing Indians who knew the land intimately; and risking their lives for forty horses from a large *hacienda*. At least one of the Mazatlán Rangers should have known better. This was Captain John H. Peoples—former editor of the Corpus Christi *Star*. Peoples even told Wood and the others that they had better not rely upon the Mexicans, who would desert if they caught up to the Indians and got into a fight.

Fortunately, these *gringos* and Mexicans never found the Comanches. As it turned out, they took a long, rough ride from five o'clock in the morning until eleven o'clock at night, and succeeded in returning to the *hacienda* with saddle-weary bodies and no stolen horses.

What these self-appointed Indian fighters did not know was that while they were chasing a band of Comanches in the Bolsón de Mapimí, larger bands were striking swiftly and with deadly results around Corpus Christi. In June of 1849, the Corpus Christi *Star* reported: "One hundred persons of all ages and both sexes have been killed or carried into miserable captivity during the past month or so, and the border mails and trade are almost broken up by the swarms of Indians who are ranging with impunity." [2] By September, the same newspaper estimated that more than 200 persons had been killed by Indians within five months. During that same September a ranger post of 225 men was established to patrol the country between Corpus Christi and the Río Grande. The Comanches were hitting fast and hard, and frontier communities on both sides of the Río Grande lived with the daily threat of an Indian raid.

The Kit Carson Association's attitude toward the Apaches was much the same. With supreme confidence these young gold miners passed through Chihuahua City and rode into the heart of Apachería without even considering the danger. Harvey Wood's first mention of the Apaches simply stated that these warriors seemed to be pretty much in control of the frontier outpost of Janos, and that the Mexicans were terrified of them. At the same time, though, Wood wrote that the Apaches were friends of the Americans, and he certainly did not see them as any potential threat. To some extent, Wood's belief was true. But he failed to realize that he and his companions were trespassing through country which the Apaches claimed as their domain. Under such circumstances there was no clear-cut guarantee that *all* Apaches would look upon Americans as friends. Harvey Wood didn't know that any small party of Americans ran a terrible risk and stood a very good chance of having their livestock and possessions stolen at the very least, and of losing their lives if the raiders felt so inclined.

In contrast to the Kit Carson Association, other California emigrants became quite aware of the terror and terrible deeds carried out by the Indians. John E. Durivage, whose party arrived in Chihuahua City the same day as the Kit Carson Association, wrote that the Apaches had been active just outside Saucillo. Here, about 70 miles south of Chihuahua City, he learned that a terrible raid had taken place against a man with several women and children. They were on their way to Guajuquilla (now Jiménez) when they were attacked by about fifty Apaches who swooped down out of the mountains, instantly killed the man, ran lances through some of the women, and kidnapped one child. Durivage also reported that such brutal attacks were not limited to Mexicans, and that Americans had felt their wrath. But he was frightfully aware that it was the Mexicans who lived in a constant state of fear that the next unusual sound, the next dust cloud in the distance might mean another raid.

Another gold seeker, a member of a company from New Orleans, captured something of the terror the Apaches were causing. Somewhere between Saltillo and Chihuahua City, O. M. Wozencraft wrote that he and his companions had passed over a long and desolate stretch of country. Then quite casually, as though he were mentioning a change in the weather, Wozencraft stated he had seen a group of traders turn back because they feared the Apaches. More than that, he wrote that this region had been ". . . abandoned to the Apache for many years."[3]

Abandoned to Apaches was the curse, the dark cloud over northern Mexico. This was the key to understanding the face of fear that travelers saw in small *poblados*, which they heard about in the cities. As the gold seekers crossed the lonely stretches of country in between settlements, they began to feel uneasy, to watch the dust clouds, and to post a tight guard around the camp each night. Dreadful encouragement for security measures presented itself in tales about Americans meeting the same fate as Mexicans. George W. B. Evans of the Ohio Company entered an atrocity story in his journal: 20 miles before his party arrived in Chihuahua City an American, a man called Vaughn, ". . . was found horribly mutilated and scalped a short distance from the city. . . ."[4]

What Evans didn't make clear in his journal was that the man called Vaughn was not an ordinary victim the Apaches had hit by random chance. Henry Vaughn was a natural target, as he was a professional scalp hunter—a member of John Glanton's bounty hunters. Glanton and his followers were mostly Americans—some even runaway slaves—who had drifted south of the border to make their fortunes as legal killers. They were welcomed by the northern Mexico states of Sonora, Chihuahua, Durango, and Coahuila; for by 1849 all these governments were offering payment for Apache and Comanche scalps, the capture of Indian children who could be bartered for kidnapped Mexican children, the rustling of Indian livestock, and the destruction of Indian villages.

In Chihuahua City, Evans found that the government had posted a reward of $1,000 for an Apache chief named Gómez. At the same time, Evans also heard of the 1849 price for scalps in Chihuahua City just two months after the adoption of the *Ley Quinto* or Fifth Law. Under the terms of this infamous law, the following bounties were offered: "... $150 for each live squaw and for each child of either sex under fourteen, $200 for the scalp of a warrior fourteen or above, and $250 for each live warrior." [5] Not wishing to lose their own "hair," very few scalp hunters ever brought in a live Apache.

The only time Evans ever saw a scalp hunter in action was at El Carmen, a small village northwest of Chihuahua City. While he and his companions were unloading their horses, John Glanton and his band rode into the *poblado*. Their belts were loaded with Apache scalps, and tied on one horse was a live Apache. The captive was a weatherbeaten old woman, whose wrinkled face mirrored her mountain home. Resigned to her fate, she stared blankly at the strangers surrounding her. She had come a long way from the Sierra Madre, and she knew she was going to die. Her captor was a demon in dirty buckskin, a man without pity and without honor. After the old woman had been inspected by the authorities and verified as a true Apache, Glanton turned to a Mexican who rode with his killers. Without hesitation Glanton gave the order for the old woman to be shot and scalped.

What followed horrified and sickened Evans. In a matter-of-fact way, the act was simple, efficient, and thoroughly rotten. The only dignity was the silent death of the woman. The killer didn't even bother to find out if his shot had ended the woman's life. Pulling a butcher knife from its leather scabbard, and grinning at the crowd, he quickly sliced into the woman's skull just below the hairline. His movements were fast as he circled her skull with the sharp blade, leaving a thin red line. Next he knelt against the woman's shoulders for leverage, grasped her gray hair with both hands, and jerked upward until there was a liquid, plopping sound. With that he grinned again and held the bloody scalp aloft for all to see.

# ¡Ay, Chihuahua!

This vile business was not limited to frontiersmen who had become almost savage, nor was it limited to insane killers. Some Forty-Niners who did not fall into either classification did a short stint of scalp hunting when they passed through Mexico. One of the members from the Ohio Company—a young man from Perrysburg—wrote that some of the party took a one-shot chance at the grisly business. The writer stated that his friends received $300 per scalp plus all the livestock they stole. Then he wrote, "I was not in the Indian fighting business."[6] To many Americans it was all a matter of business. Most of these men did not see the Indians as human beings in the same sense that they saw each other, but as wild savages who posed a constant threat to the white man. The only way to protect "civilized" men was to kill these "savages."

These amateur scalp hunters didn't always find Indian fighting an easy way to pick up *pesos*. William Dunphy of Texas—later a successful California and Nevada cattleman—admitted that when he crossed from Brownsville to Mazatlán, he did some Indian fighting for pay near Durango. During a fifteen-day campaign in the mountains, he and twenty-three other men fought a number of battles with the Apaches. Dunphy and his companions quickly discovered, though, that collecting Apache scalps was not an easy way to earn money. In one major engagement Dunphy saw the Apaches kill one of his comrades and wound nine others. What he didn't know was that he and his friends had been lucky. Scalp hunters were prized trophies for many tribes. Even as mean a professional as John Glanton finally became a victim of his own trade when the Yuman Indians killed and scalped him. As one bounty hunter put it, Glanton "... lost his locks at the level of his Adam's apple...."[7]

---

## THE CITY OF THE NORTH

---

Chihuahua City during the California gold rush was an island of civilization in northern Mexico's sea of wilderness. Miners remembered it with affection, and those who kept journals wrote at length about it. To have been to Chihuahua City was to have visited one of those mysterious places on the map of the world. Santa Fé traders had been there. During the Mexican War Colonel Alexander W. Doniphan and the First Missouri Volunteers had occupied the city after their quick victory over the Mexican Army in the Battle of Sacramento, and at the end of the war the Second Dragoons had marched through the streets on their hike to California. Even so, Chihuahua City was a place of romance in the same manner as Timbuktu.

Chihuahua was a name to toss out for effect, a name that was as much a Mexican yell, a curse, or a sigh as it was anything else. ¡Ay, Chihuahua! And what did it really mean? That, too, was a mystery, something lost in time, a leftover from other men who first ventured on to the great plateau and discovered that in this violent land mistakes were final and complete. A man could die of thirst in a dry arroyo. While turkey buzzards and ants picked his bones under the scorching sun, another man could be killed in the same arroyo by a roaring flash flood that started with a cloudburst in the Sierra Madre many hours before. ¡Ay, Chihuahua!

Gold-hungry gringos, just passing through, heard all the ancient warnings. They were told of sudden sandstorms, flash floods, the strike of a rattlesnake, the whir of an arrow, and the dry canteen among scattered bones beside a dry waterhole. They were told these things, and they knew Chihuahua City was an island of hope on the long northern jornada. ¡Ay, Chihuahua!

All roads, all trails, all paths leading to Chihuahua City made men more than happy to arrive in this "City of the North." Men trekking from Parras came through the lunar landscape of the Bolsón de Parras either directly west to the foothills of the Sierra Madre to work their way north; or they left the dry, dusty, ancient lake bed and headed northwest across the semi-arid land of the Bolsón de Mapimí. Emigrant companies traveling from San Antonio and Laredo had to climb the dry, rugged ridges of the Sierra Madre Occidental without benefit of a true path, only to wander on to the Bolsón de Mapimí. Men crossing the Río Grande farther north at Presidio del Norte had to make a semicircle around the Big Bend country, and then headed into the Bolsón de Mapimí. And the emigrants who forded the river at El Paso del Norte had the choice of making a wide detour through rugged, dry foothills where Indians waited or of trudging through Los Médanos—incredible, rolling sandhills that stretched for miles like a series of lost beaches in need of an ocean.

# ¡Ay, Chihuahua!

These were the ways to Chihuahua City, and they offered no easy going. These were routes of biting northers and freezing sleet in the winter; of hot, searing winds that scorched and chapped the skin in the summer; and of eternal wind at any season that peppered a man's face with sand, grit, and fragmented pieces of eroded stones. These routes offered no rich cities, no decent little villages once a man said *adiós* to the key jumping-off points. Between these ports of the frontier and that island called Chihuahua City, there were only poor *poblados,* crumbling *haciendas,* and undermanned military posts waiting for the final Indian raid. It made no difference whether a man lived in a *jacal* with a thatched roof and walls made of thin sticks chinked with clay; a thick-walled adobe *rancho;* or a walled and guarded fort—the problem for all was the same. They were people living in a land where living was not encouraged. Nowhere in this vast country could a traveling emigrant expect to buy much food, for people living with the specter of starvation were not merchants by nature. Nowhere in this country of seasonal grass awaited by all animals could a man always expect to find good grazing for his livestock unless he arrived just as the season started. Nowhere in this high plateau of little rain and fast run-offs could a man always expect to find water in a riverbed or waterhole. The ways to the "City of the North" were not designed for the weak, the sick, or the coward. The ways to Chihuahua City truly tested a man's desire to get there, and challenged his willingness to make the long *jornada.*

The Hampden Mining Company arrived in Chihuahua City on April 15, 1849. They had made remarkable time—about 500 miles in eighteen days. They were lucky, and they knew it. There had been plenty of water; plenty of grass; plenty of food in the *poblados*; and they had no trouble with Indians. Their timing had been just right, and their selection of a trail like drawing to an inside straight.

Two days out of Parras they had stopped at the village of San Lorenzo and purchased loaves of fresh, hot bread the women were taking out of small adobe ovens. When they rode away from San Lorenzo their guide got lost. But just at dusk they met a party of mounted and well-armed Mexicans who directed them to the public road. They were very fortunate, indeed, and A. B. Clarke knew it. All along their route he saw many crosses in memory of persons killed by Indians, and the whole country was terrified of another raid. As confirmation of their good luck they met another party of Americans who had not been so fortunate.

Four days away from Chihuahua City they came upon this party of twenty-eight men who had come by way of Corpus Christi and Monclova. They told Clarke they had made the mistake of taking the desert route from Monclova through the driest part of the Bolsón de Mapimí. "They went without water three days at one time, lost one man who went to look for a mule . . . ,"[8] and felt their tongues swell, their lips puff out, blister, and crack as their skin shriveled with the daily loss of moisture. Unlike these wanderers of the desert, the Hampden Mining Company reached the "City of the North" without enduring such torment, without thinking that each day might be the last.

At one in the afternoon the Hampden Mining Company rode into Chihuahua City; found a corral for their animals; rooms for themselves; and at four o'clock Clarke attended his first bullfight. He went to the *corrida,* he said, ". . . not only to gratify my curiosity, but to judge for myself the effect of such a spectacle, on a people who make it their chief amusement."[9]

The bull ring was built in the shape of an amphitheater, and enclosed about an acre of ground. The building was octangular, constructed of bricks ". . . with an arched covered gallery, at the circumference, with settees for the spectators."[10] These were the best seats available. Below these were rows of stone seats that extended to the heavy wooden plank fence seven or eight feet above the arena. Clarke estimated that there were about 3,000 people in the stands.

His attitude toward the afternoon's *corrida de toros* was typical of American miners who saw a bullfight in their journey across Mexico. He failed to see the ritual beauty. To him the whole spectacle was a symbol of degradation. His vision of the "moment of truth" was focused on the bloody and dying bulls and the gored horses with their intestines dragging on the sand. The performance filled him with utter disgust for people who watched it with such fascination, and led him to the conclusion that people who delighted ". . . in such cruel performances, must naturally be fit candidates for robbers and assassins."[11]

But the bullfight was the only disappointment for Clarke in the "City of the North." On the next morning he started his day with

"... a bowl of chocolate, very rich, for one quartillo, about three cents, and a dish of tripe and parched corn, for the same."[12] He called upon the prefect, showed his passport, and notified the rest of the company that they were required to do the same. Then he asked some American merchants which route to California was the shortest. They told him that the Guadalupe Pass was the quickest, but they also said it was rough and dangerous. With all necessary business out of the way, Clarke proceeded during the next two days to explore Chihuahua City, which he liked so much that he said, "I am of opinion, it would make a pleasant place of residence."[13]

Clarke and the other men of the Hampden Mining Company found Chihuahua City the island of civilization they had heard about. The main part of the city was beautifully laid out in a Roman grid pattern. The central plaza faced the imposing cathedral and the *casa de ayuntamiento* (town hall). The principal streets were wide and paved with river cobblestones, and were washed down each morning with precious water. Unpaved streets were swept clean and sprinkled with water to keep the dust from flying as horses and carriages passed by.

In the plaza more water from the Río Chuviscar filled a beautiful fountain. This lavish use of water in such an arid land was a grand thing for the dry and thirsty traveler to see. To accomplish this vision of a land with water to spare, the city had constructed a stone aqueduct that brought river water into the heart of the city. With water came the other touches of beauty: grass in the plaza, roses and other flowers, and tall cottonwood trees.

Near the plaza was the central marketplace. Here Clarke saw Mexicans and American merchants from Santa Fé carrying on a brisk trade. He found that a man could buy a fine meal for as little as six cents. But most of all, he was fascinated with the people. The "City of the North" was a crossroads of the frontier, and the people matched its location. Clarke saw dark, Indian *peones* whose lot was not better than a slave's; proud *rancheros* with broad-brimmed sombreros, silver hatbands, tight-fitting jackets with silver buttons, tight breeches that flared out at the bottom and were trimmed up the side with silver buttons, a broad red sash around the waist, and high-heeled boots that were beautifully tooled and accentuated by silver spurs with sharp-toothed rowels. He saw the padres with their stark black habits; military men with their colorful uniforms; weatherbeaten emigrants in heavy and rough clothing showing the wear and tear of the trail; long-haired, lean men who were deeply sun-tanned, who wore buckskin clothing and Indian moccasins, and were pointed out as professional scalp hunters. There were merchants in the clothing of their trade, and beautiful, wealthier women who stepped out of carriages and went into the cathedral or visited the market. Clarke noticed their expensive clothing, and was intrigued by their beauty; he wrote of their ". . . deep black eyes, shaded with long lashes, glossy raven hair, which they arrange with good taste; complexions coming nearer to the brunette than any other which we have among us, and almost universally contrast well with a fine set of teeth." [14] Clarke had been a long time on the trail. He had seen more than enough of parched country, and was delighted to walk about the "City of the North," admire its beauty, and be amazed at the conglomerate of people.

In Chihuahua City a man had a sense of security in the middle of nowhere. Here he could forget where he had been and where he had to go. Here he could rest, sleep in a hotel, eat a decent meal, buy a drink, look at women, buy supplies, ask about the trail, forget about Indians, visit a church (even though it was Catholic), and get ready for the long drag ahead.

The Kit Carson Association arrived in the city on May 1, and Harvey Wood wrote that they attended church one Sunday morning and a bullfight in the afternoon during their week's layover. Then they ". . . bid goodbye to Chihuahua, starting out with our animals feeling much better and with more experience in packing a mule. . . ." [15] John Durivage also arrived in Chihuahua City on May 1, and he stayed at a hotel owned by an American named Riddle. Durivage thought the accommodations excellent for a man and his horse. "The price of board," he wrote, "is $1.50 per day and 37½¢ for each animal." [16] O. M. Wozencraft noted that he and his companions had stayed in the city, and that they had ". . . spent some time here in resting and refitting, and attended the bullfights in the large amphitheater. . . ." [17] George W. B. Evans of the Ohio Company wrote at length of the city, and no small wonder. Evans had come the long way—over 1,000 miles—from Port Lavaca to Presidio del Norte and through desert mountains and the Bolsón de Mapimí.

After the long, dry ride from Port Lavaca, Evans felt that Chihuahua City was an oasis. In his descriptions of the city's beauty the abundance of water and food was stressed time and again. He gave a vivid picture of the market with its vendors and their fruit, vegetables, and meat. The meat he saw was ". . . neatly skinned, excepting the head, which was always laid on the wooden bowl containing the meat as an index to the kind."[18] He indicated the costs of various items in the market, and was astounded by the very high price of tobacco and the fact that women smoked *cigarillos*.

During their stay in the "City of the North" from June 23 to July 16, the members of the Ohio Company contracted with local merchants for ". . . leather canteens, pinole and beef. . . ."[19] Evans explained how *higote* or dried beef was prepared by mixing beef, lard and pepper ". . . by the process of cutting and pounding, so . . . that no fear need be apprehended of its preservation in all kinds of weather. . . ."[20] Then, Evans pointed out, all that was necessary was to toss a small piece of this meat ". . . into a pan or kettle of boiling water with a little flour or corn-meal. . . ,"[21] and a very good dish would be cooked in a short time.

The beauty of the city, the abundance of food and water, the different types of people, the local customs were memories that California emigrants had of the "City of the North." One image took hold most of all, one memory left the deepest impression—the Cathedral of Chihuahua. In spite of the anti-Catholic bias of most miners, a bias that came out in their journal entries about the "priest-ridden" country, the miners were overwhelmed by the church's grandeur. Even the magnificent cathedral at Saltillo had not impressed them as Chihuahua's did. Perhaps the very fact that such a building existed in this remote city was the key factor in their astonishment, or maybe the hardships of the trail made them more receptive to a monument of civilization.

Evans even took the time to measure the Cathedral of Chihuahua and claimed it was 180 feet long and 180 feet wide. Like many other miners he was intrigued with the building. He described the two high steeples and the large clock between them which kept good time and tolled the hours so loudly that the sound could be heard throughout the city. At the back of the cathedral, he saw the large dome surmounted by a steeple of smaller size. In true Yankee fashion, Evans inquired about the cost of the cathedral. He was told that the bulk of the money had been raised by taxing the local silver mines at the rate of "... six cents on each mark of silver. ..." [22] What he did not know was that the cost was even higher. The actual tax was one *real* or twelve and one-half cents for each mark or about one-half pound of silver taken from the mines. Nor did he know that the ultimate cost for the construction of the Cathedral of Chihuahua came close to a million dollars, and that from the laying of the cornerstone on April 22, 1726, almost one hundred years passed before the building was completed.

Men approaching the "City of the North" claimed they could hear the great bells in the cathedral towers from as far away as 25 miles. The sound came to the travelers as a symbol of civilization, a song of welcome letting weary men know that the end of one stage of a wilderness journey was near. Thomas B. Eastland, who passed through Chihuahua City in September, 1849, also commented upon the cathedral's bells. His party was coming toward the "City of the North" by way of El Paso del Norte. They had taken the southern route out of San Antonio and had been on the trail for more than one hundred days when they "... heard its large and sonorous Bells afar off—many days had passed since our ears were greeted with the sound of 'Church going Bells,' and our thoughts joyfully turned towards home. ..." [23]

The baroque style of the cathedral's front was an incredible sight to the emigrants, and they stood in the plaza and looked upward at the whole façade that had been carved from buff-colored rock. They looked at the six sections of the façade divided by vertical columns. Between the columns they saw the shell-shaped niches containing stone figures of the twelve apostles. Below the figures was the top of the arch for the main entrance, and the emigrants never forgot the two massive, hand-carved, wooden doors that stood more than twice the height of a tall man. Then reaching skyward on both corners of the front wall were the tall, column-fluted bell towers. Each tower contained three sections, and each section was smaller than the one beneath. The whole effect was one of looking into space and seeing a man-made monument diminish in size as it moved farther away from its earthly base.

If the gold-fevered Americans remembered nothing else about the "City of the North," they remembered the Cathedral of Chihuahua. In the morning it seemed to capture the golden hue of the rising sun, by high noon the color was the glare of the desert, and by evening the soft colors of twilight gave the building a shade of peace to complete its changing day of color. It didn't take a religious man to realize that this monument to Catholicism was also a monument to man's ability to endure and to create beauty in a land that offered in exchange only a daily challenge of hostility and brutality, a daily threat of death. *¡Ay, Chihuahua!*

## NORTH OF CHIHUAHUA, SOUTH OF THE RÍO GRANDE

Outside the limits of Chihuahua City the California emigrants wasted no time as they headed north. The way to Janos, the last frontier outpost before the Guadalupe Pass, was across a tawny land overlooked by barren desert mountains, where dry arroyos might be occupied by waiting Apaches. Most companies of miners rode at least 15 or 20 miles on their first day's march from the "City of the North," and frequently their first camping ground was the Hacienda Sacramento. As at Buena Vista, the proud Yankees entered in their journals that they had seen the battlefield of Sacramento where Colonel Alexander W. Doniphan and his First Missouri Volunteers had routed the much larger army defending Chihuahua City in this crucial battle of the Mexican War.

When Thomas Eastland camped here in 1849, he wrote that ". . . the Mexicans say if the Americans had fought like *Men* instead of *Devils* the result would have been different." [24] True enough, the American victory over a larger and well-fortified force might have seemed as though the *gringos* were in league with the Devil, but the Mexican Army was defeated by its inability to believe that *gringos* could fight, and its belief that the rules of classical warfare would carry the day.

General Alejo García Conde prepared his forces in proper textbook fashion for a classical defense of Chihuahua City. He had selected the narrowest part of the Hacienda Sacramento, and had his men placed in twenty-eight trenches in the desert hills. In an arroyo General Conde had a troop of mounted lancers waiting to

charge into the enemy after the terrible rifle and artillery fire of his
main force had struck the key blow. It was all neat and beautifully
arranged, and the general could look at his deployed army of 1,200
horse soldiers, 300 artillerymen, 1,200 infantrymen, and 1,400 civilians, and see that he had set a perfect trap for the 1,200 *gringos*. It was
all beautiful, and it was all wrong. What General Conde didn't know
was that before February 28, 1846, ended, he would realize the folly
of sticking to formal military tactics against men who presented a
battlefield formation that was never included in any military history.

Dressed in buckskin, in incomplete uniforms, in civilian clothes;
wearing sombreros, military hats, and no hats at all; their hair strag-
gly and shoulder-length; their beards unkempt; these crazy *gringos*
came at the Mexican Army like something out of a nightmare. This
wasn't an American Army. It was an organized gang of border bandits, frontiersmen, scalp hunters, farmers, and Santa Fé traders. All
the Mexicans could truly focus on were four parallel columns of white-
topped covered wagons moving onto the battlefield. Three hundred
and fifteen of these wagons belonged to Santa Fé traders; eighty-
five belonged to the First Missouri Volunteers. And the wagons
came at the general's carefully placed army at an angle, not straight-
away as any proper army should have done. This unorthodox movement did away with General Conde's fixed line of fire.

To add to the confusion for the Mexican forces, the Americans
were interspersed between the wagons in compact units of marching
infantry, hard-riding cavalrymen, and dead-shot artillerymen. The
whole scene was like watching a series of moving forts—forts that
outflanked the main Mexican line of defense, caught General Conde's
mounted lancers in their arroyo and cut them to pieces with artillery
fire; took a deadly toll of the troopers on the hillsides as these border
and frontier Americans calmly used their expert marksmanship to
zero in on the bright Mexican uniforms as though they were enjoy-
ing a Sunday turkey-shoot. All the while, the American band played
"Yankee Doodle." Then Colonel Doniphan—the red-haired, handsome Irishman, the astute frontier lawyer with a talent for leadership—gave the order to charge.

Wild, yelling farm boys, cool frontiersmen, and even the notorious
ex-Chihuahua scalp hunter—James Kirker—advanced on the Mexican position. The whole battle lasted no more than three hours.
Then the Mexican forces broke and ran in panic toward Chihuahua
City. As they fled, the excited Americans chased them, shot, clubbed,

# ¡Ay, Chihuahua!

or cut them down with sabers, and ran some into the hills where they were killed by Apaches who were sitting and watching the battle as though it were a sport.

As the shouting and shooting ceased, the white-topped wagons came to a halt. It was time to straighten out the supplies and trade goods, as some of the traders planned to set up shop in Chihuahua City the day after the battle. It was time to rest, to count the dead and wounded—300 Mexicans and 2 Americans had been killed— and time to celebrate and tell the first versions of stories that would someday bore the family back home.

This, then, was what had happened in this lonely stretch of land. This was the place of victory and of death that passing miners saw when they pitched camp at Hacienda Sacramento. But all the action was gone, and only men who had been there on that bloody February day saw anything other than the tawny plain and the barren desert hills. To these men who rode or walked with the First Missouri Volunteers, this battlefield of Sacramento was a place of ghosts. To these men there were the remembered sounds of rolling and creaking wagons, horses' hooves striking the earth, teamsters swearing and whipping the frightened animals, rifle and cannon shot, men yelling, cursing, and screaming, and then the cries and moaning of the wounded and dying. To these veterans of that time of glory and hell there were remembered sights of the crazy covered wagons rocking and swaying over the uneven ground, the sweating and plunging horses and mules, the clouds of dust and gunsmoke, the sight of Mexican cannonballs moving so slowly through the air that soldiers watched them and ducked out of their path, the remembered faces of men who fought alongside one another and then camped in Chihuahua City's main plaza the next day and watched for a glimpse of a dark-eyed *señorita,* the look of the wounded men with blood staining their bandages and with pale white faces grimacing in pain or relaxed in shock, and the faces of the dead Mexican soldiers who were already beginning to look not quite real. All that one day—that day that was so short and so terribly long—was there for men who had followed red-haired Colonel Doniphan; but for other gold seekers the battlefield of Sacramento was only a stretch of ground where some other Americans had won a battle. To them, it was a place to stop for the night, to brag about how damned good Americans were, and then to break up camp in the early hours of dawn and hit the trail for California.

# THE EL DORADO TRAIL

## JANOS: THE LAST OUTPOST

Most gold seekers took between ten days and two weeks to make the trip from Chihuahua City to Janos. On the journey they traveled through the natural chute of this vast tableland, passed through Governor Don Angel Trias's Hacienda Encinillas, the *poblados* of El Saucillo, Galeana, the ruins of Casas Grandes, town of Corralitos and the last outpost—Janos.

All during 1849 and 1850 companies of California emigrants passed through this isolated northwestern corner of Chihuahua. Despite the fact that such journalists as John E. Durivage of the New Orleans *Daily Picayune,* John S. Robb of the St. Louis *Weekly Reveille,* and John H. Peoples of the Corpus Christi *Star* were among the men who traveled this route, none took time to describe the ruins of the ancient Indian city of Casas Grandes. One of the few gold seekers who did so was George Evans of the Ohio Company, and he was truly impressed. To him, it was like ". . . a large deserted castle, now in complete ruins . . . undoubtedly erected by the Aztecs.. . . ." [25] What Evans saw was not a castle, it was a decaying and deserted city where the Mogollón-Anasazi Indians once had had a thriving agricultural civilization—a city of adobe houses, cobblestone-faced pyramids, cobblestone platforms for astronomical observations, and an aqueduct system of stone-lined canals and reservoirs. As the gold seekers saw it, Casas Grandes was a city of a vanished people, a city returning to the earth that had been used to build it.

Though the builders of Casas Grandes were gone, none of the California emigrants was unaware of the Indians who now ruled this land. When Harvey Wood of the Kit Carson Association passed Casas Grandes and rode into Janos in May of 1849, he saw that the town was ". . . in the possession of six Apache Indians, who were amusing themselves by riding from store to store and making the proprietors furnish liquor or anything else they demanded." [26] That same month John Durivage looked at Janos and thought it ". . . a

104

town of very little importance and *muy pobre* in all the necessaries of life." [27] He noticed that it was a garrison town where constant warfare with the Apaches was causing a steady drop in population and where those who managed to hang on had no inclination to fight off the natural decay of their houses when a more dangerous foe was so near at hand.

The Hampden Mining Company took eight days to travel the 269 miles from Chihuahua City to Janos. They had combined forces with the Mississippi Company for added protection, and except for A. B. Clarke they arrived in good shape for the mountain trip over the Guadalupe Pass.

During the ride from Chihuahua City, Clarke's knees had become so badly swollen he had to be lifted on and off his mount. To add to his suffering, his eyes were terribly inflamed from the constant glare of the sun. There was nothing to do but leave him in Janos until he was able to travel. Before his companions moved on, they found a room for him in the *alcalde's* home. It wasn't fancy, and Clarke complained about his bed—his blankets placed on cow hides on a hard-packed dirt floor. But in the midst of his own self-pity, he was carefully nursed and fed by the *alcalde's* mother, who was concerned about his *reumatismo doloroso*.

The *señora* was well versed in native medicines, and though Clarke protested at first, he soon gave in. By the end of a week he wrote, "I am using *aguardiente* and red pepper, hot, upon my knee." [28] In addition, he was using mesquite gum to relieve the inflammation of his eyes. As primitive as the *señora's* remedies seemed to Clarke, they didn't do him any harm. And either the treatment or the rest or both worked well enough so that he was ready to travel again within two weeks.

He joined a Missouri Company of seventy emigrants, and prepared to leave Janos. The *alcalde* refused any payment for taking care of him, and said he had been a victim of *mala fortuna*. "I however," Clarke wrote, "made him the small present of a fine shirt, a box of caps, and a purse. For the old lady, I could think of nothing in my possession but a tea-spoon." [29]

Janos was a frontier outpost, and it had been one since the Spanish had established it in 1690. At Ramos Pass to the south of the town, a cluster of crosses signified the long state of war between the presidio and the Apaches. Janos was not a place to tarry. The California emigrants moved in and out of it with a haste born of fear and fever. The fear was of the violent land in this heart of Apachería, and the fever was to get to El Dorado before all the gold nuggets had been picked up and pocketed. It took the same number of letters to spell *adiós* and Janos, and gold seekers were inclined to equate one word with the other.

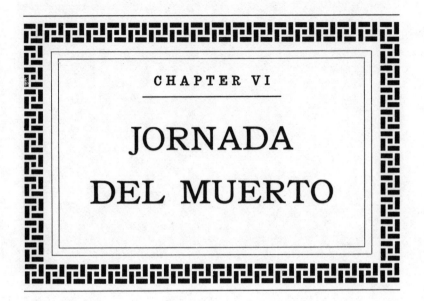

CHAPTER VI

# JORNADA
# DEL MUERTO

# THE LOWER ROAD

Northwest of Chihuahua City was the hardest journey of any branch of the El Dorado Trail. Or to put it another way, southwest of El Paso del Norte a man did well to stay alive even if the Apaches didn't collect his scalp. Starting from either of these frontier cities, these wilderness ports, the California emigrant had no trouble in finding traps to test his courage and stamina; and the worst trap of all was the trail leading northwest out of Janos.

In that corner of upside-down country, that heartland of Apachería, was the Guadalupe Pass. Some called it Cooke's Wagon Road, but they hadn't been there; nor did they know what Lieutenant Colonel Cooke and his Mormon Battalion had gone through while crossing the mountains with wagons. To make matters even more difficult for the naive and innocent gold seekers who took this route, most of them were almost worn out by the time they reached Janos. Yet ahead of them were bluffs and *barrancas*, Apaches and Yumas, and the wasteland of the Colorado Desert.

Emigrants coming southwest from El Paso del Norte to Janos usually had made the long haul from Texas over what was called the Lower Road. Like everything else in this arid and barren land, the name was a mirage and not a reality. Guides could lead a caravan through this country, and some companies even made it on their own. Yet the Lower Road was not much more than a hopeful line on a not too accurate map.

The first attempt to establish a wagon road from San Antonio to El Paso del Norte and on to Chihuahua City took place on August 27, 1848. On that day, Colonel John Coffee Hays—frontiersman, Texas Ranger, and soldier—headed a band made up of fifty Texans and fifteen Delaware Indian guides. Among the Texans was Samuel A. Maverick, a close friend of "Jack" Hays. Maverick was making the trip because he was despondent over the death of his eldest daughter, Agatha. Hays knew this, and he persuaded Mrs. Maverick that the trip would save her husband's life. "Don't you see Mr. Maverick is dying by inches?" Hays said. "Everyone remarks how gray he has grown, how bent and feeble he looks, and this will be the very thing for him—he always thrives on hardships...." [1]

Whether Samuel Maverick thrived on hardship or whether he was simply a tough man to kill was never really decided. But the trip with "Jack" Hays didn't lack for hardships. Their survey party got lost, had difficulty in finding enough water and grass to keep their horses alive, and the men ended up eating "... mule-meat and polecats..." [2] in order to avoid starvation. At that, they only got as far west as Presidio del Norte, just north of the Big Bend country. Then they gave up and returned to San Antonio.

The Hays-Maverick expedition arrived home in December 1848, just in time to see the movement of the United States Army into the same country with surveying parties in search of a route to El Paso del Norte that could be used as a wagon road. Lieutenants William H. C. Whiting and William F. Smith headed one of these parties, and on a return trip from El Paso del Norte to San Antonio in the spring of 1849 they established what came to be known as the Lower Road—the route Argonauts followed and the route partly followed today by the Southern Pacific's tracks. Yet to call it a road in 1849 was to stretch and strain the imagination. Furthermore, to call it a road was to give greenhorn gold seekers a false impression of what to expect.

## THE DETERMINED TEXANS

The "Strentzel" party gathered near the present location of Dallas, Texas, on March 29, 1849. There were about 135 people outfitted and ready to take the new Lower Road to El Paso del Norte. From the Pass of the North, they planned to move their wagons over the mountains on Cooke's Wagon Road, head northwest to the Gila Trail, cross the Colorado River, and make the trek over the Colorado Desert. It was brave and bold, and among the 135 people were 9 wives and 25 children. Their friends had tried to talk them out of it, but these Texans were determined to get to California before all the gold was gone.

No logic appeared to dictate their actions, for all logic made the journey absolute folly. Women, children, and wagons? My God! What made these people think they could do what was hard and sometimes fatal for frontiersmen and soldiers? What made them think they could just up and cross the arid Texas plains, the mountain stronghold of Apachería, and the Great American Desert?

Were these people utterly mad, or were they so naïve that they truly didn't realize what they were doing? The only answer that made sense was that they were both mad and naïve. They were possessed with a dream—a dream made out of myth and reality, out of pieces of truth, scraps of lies, and great chunks of ignorance. But the essence of this dream was that the *real El Dorado* had been found, and it was in California! And men possessed of the El Dorado dream thought it worth the risk of a *jornada del muerto:* a journey of death.

Years after it was all over, Dr. John Theophil Strentzel wrote: "We had not even a guide to direct us the way. Nothing except a map and compass to go by, the country was entirely unknown to us, not one of the party even having been through it."[3] Even Strentzel's son-in-law, John Muir, must have been impressed by the journey these innocent Forty-Niners had been willing to try, and had accomplished.

The first part of their trip was not bad at all. For 300 miles as the Argonauts headed southwest toward El Paso del Norte, they traveled through a fertile country that offered plenty of grass and water, enough trees for wood and for shady places to noon, and they were not bothered by the Comanches who lived in this area. They traveled slowly because the heavy spring rains had made the soil soft, and wagons sometimes bogged down and had to be pulled out. And they were bothered by frequent, heavy rainstorms. But the honeymoon aspect of their journey lasted for only 300 miles. The final 500 miles to El Paso del Norte tested their willingness to endure; and their ability to survive as they crossed a vast dry plain that was practically without timber and grassland. It was very short of drinkable water, since it was full of alkali and salt.

"About the last of May," Strentzel wrote, "we all came near being lost for want of water." [4] They traveled for two days and one night without finding a waterhole. The last one they had found had been so brackish they couldn't drink from it. The only thing that saved them was that they had been wise enough to leave each good water-hole with an extra supply for the next day's journey. So they moved ahead with what little water they had left in their canteens. Strentzel's wife was ill. The children were crying for water. The teams were staggering. The wet spring had turned into a hot summer that threatened to bake the land and boil the blood of any animal crossing it, and Strentzel's water supply had dwindled to one quart. The only hope was with the water hunters of the party—men who had volunteered to ride ahead and search for springs. Strentzel used the last of his water to the best advantage. Taking a spoonful at a time, he moistened the throats of the children and his wife. All the while, he watched his team stagger and almost fall; and he looked at the never-ending dry land; and wondered how he—a learned physician from Poland, a man also trained in the art of viniculture—had come to emigrate to Texas and to strike out for California. All his attention focused through his blue eyes at the horizon as he watched for the water seekers. He stared and wiped the sweat from his brown curly hair. Then almost at the last moment, almost when he was ready to accept his fate, the water hunters appeared.

They took shape in the distance, and shouted, "Water! water!" In a ridge of sandhills some ten miles away, they had found pools of fresh water. Moving as quickly as they could in the stifling heat, Strentzel and the other men unhitched their teams to drive them ahead. Meanwhile other men took kegs and canteens and made the round trip to water. Some teams were so spent from this long drive that it took them all that night to reach the waterholes. Then with a stroke of desert irony, the very next day the company was deluged with a rain-and-hail storm.

The company camped next to the pools for one whole week. They had come a long way and had suffered much. At one point prior to running out of water, they had lost thirty-five head of horses and mules to a raiding band of Comanches. As in the case of finding the waterholes, they had been lucky about the stolen stock. Sixty men tracked the unsuspecting Comanches, caught them off guard, and got the animals back from the surprised warriors without firing a shot. But such luck couldn't hold out, and it didn't. By the time they reached the Pecos River they had buried their first friend. Mr. E. J. Syms had been in bad health even before they had started their pilgrimage, but he had insisted on going. The trip, he had said, would be good for his health. Just after the affair with the Comanches and before they found the pools of water, three ministers in the party read religious services over Syms. After that his "... body was lain coffin-up in a deep dug grave, carefully covered and then all the wagons in the train driven over it, so as to obliterate the site as much as possible to prevent desecration by Indians."[5] Mr. Syms was only the first of the party to perish. By the time the company had reached the Pecos River, only 30 miles beyond the sand hill waterholes, five more persons were buried as the trail took its toll.

The Pecos River presented an unusual barrier in this dry land. While it was a narrow stream, it was running fast and deep. And a man could look in any direction until his eyes ached and not see anything he could call timber, anything that could be used to construct a raft. Still these emigrants weren't about to be stopped. Two wagon bodies were covered tightly with canvas and made as waterproof as possible. Along the sides of the wagons the men tied empty kegs for buoys. Next, they fastened ropes to the ends of the wagons. Then two men swam across the river with the loose ropes. In this fashion a makeshift ferry was formed. The wagons and all the goods and people were pulled over; the animals swam across, "... and by evening the whole train was safely over and ready for marching."[6] It was time to camp and go fishing. This the men did, and that night they had pan-fried fish while they calculated that they had about 200 more miles of dry country between the Pecos and El Paso del Norte.

Beyond the Pecos the dim markings of a trail gave way to a road of sorts made by "... a large train of emigrants from Western Texas...."[7] This party was just three days ahead of Strentzel and his companions of the trail, and it made them happy to know that friends were so close. But friends nearby could not make up for a scarcity of water, and during the last 80 miles to El Paso del Norte it became necessary to divide into smaller groups so that enough water would be available at the few shallow waterholes along the route.

On July 2, 1849, Strentzel and the whole company arrived in El

Paso del Norte, and it was like coming to an unexpected oasis. The company found that the Mexicans were very friendly, that fresh fruits and vegetables and other supplies were for sale. They rested here for twelve days and prepared for the trip over the Guadalupe Pass and the Great Desert. While they recovered from their three months on the trail the make-up of the company changed. Some gave up and headed back home over the same country they had just crossed. Many sold most of their belongings and their wagons, and purchased pack animals for the rest of the trip. Some elected to remain in El Paso del Norte; ". . . while the men with families, and a few others, patient and level headed men who were willing to travel slowly, organized and resumed their wearisome journey, through the horrible Apaches, to the gold-fields of the Pacific coast." [8]

## EL PASO DEL NORTE: FRONTIER CROSSROADS

When California emigrants came out of the wasteland of south-western Texas and crossed the Río Grande, El Paso del Norte seemed like another mirage. There were cottonwood trees, gardens, vine-yards. There were adobe houses with reed-covered overhangs that shaded entryways, a town plaza, and a block-shaped church that looked more like a fort except for its almost isolated bell tower. But this wasn't a mirage, an Indian village, or a small *poblado*. This was the Pass of the North, and it already had a long history as a cross-roads of the frontier.

By the time of the gold rush, El Paso del Norte had been in existence for almost three hundred years. Three years after the New Mexico Pueblo Revolt in 1680, the Spaniards had built a presidio next to the Río Grande, and began using this place as a supply depot and rest stop in their military campaigns against the Pueblo Indians. Even after they had defeated the Pueblos, they were faced with more Indian trouble as the Apaches and Comanches waged a hit-and-run war against them during the rest of Spain's time in the New World. As this brutal war raged, El Paso del Norte served as a vital link in the Spanish chain of presidios and outposts established to defend the northern Mexico frontier.

The life-saving water of the Río Grande and the fertility of the river bottomland helped to make the Pass of the North a true oasis in the long *jornada* between Chihuahua City and Santa Fé. When the official Spanish government inspection team, headed by the Marqués de Rubí, visited here in July of 1766, his Captain of Engineers, Nicolas de Lafora, wrote an enthusiastic account of the region's agricultural production. He commented on the various fruits and was especially interested in the vineyards that were carefully tended by the inhabitants. And like all people who passed this way, Lafora noted that a "... passable wine and better brandy ..." [9] were produced at this outpost.

To Santa Fé trader Josiah Gregg, El Paso del Norte was a pleasant stop between Santa Fé and Chihuahua City—a place to rest and enjoy himself before he had to face Los Médanos, that waterless region of windblown, shifting sand dunes some 30 miles south of the Río Grande on the road to Chihuahua City. In his classic *Commerce of the Prairies,* Gregg described the Pass of the North as having a population of almost 4,000 people "... scattered over the western bottom of the Rio del Norte to the length of ten or twelve miles." [10] He also observed that these settlements were more like plantations than a town, and that there were many vineyards, cornfields, and orchards. Gregg was pleased with the wine and brandy, and wrote that Americans called these products "Pass wine" and "Pass whiskey," and that they were a most profitable trade article for the markets of Chihuahua and New Mexico.

The McCoy brothers from Independence, Missouri also penned their impression of El Paso del Norte as it was in 1848 when they stopped there on a trade run to Chihuahua City. John McCoy summed up their feelings by concentrating on those things which had annoyed Alexander, Samuel, and himself. One bother was the constant wind that picked up sand and grit and deposited it as a daily coat of dust on everything left outside, and that filtered through the cracks and crevices of all dwellings. Another nuisance was the governmental red tape involved in securing a *guía* or trade passport. Like most Americans they hated this type of governmental interference with free enterprise. "Declare what you are carrying. Declare where you are headed. Don't make a mistake. If you make a mistake, if an inspector finds an error in your declarations, your goods will be subject to confiscation." To traders who had made the long wagon trip from Missouri, all this paperwork was a damned pain-in-the-ass.

After 1848 El Paso del Norte became more than a frontier port, a checkpoint for travelers and traders crossing the border into Mexico. Overnight the gold rush changed this quiet town into a bustling, brawling frontier crossroads.

Weary men—and sometimes even women and children—trekked in from Texas or the harsh lands of northeastern Mexico. Some of these companies had taken as long as four months to come from Gulf Coast ports or inland departure points such as Austin and San Antonio. To these dead-tired people El Paso del Norte was a welcome sight, even if their own built-in prejudices told them to distrust the dark-skinned Mexicans. At last they would not have to worry about finding the next waterhole before nightfall. They could replace the liquids in their dehydrated bodies. And all types had come in from the desert. There were discharged Mexican and American soldiers, Santa Fé traders, buckskin-clad frontiersmen and scalp hunters, Indians who had drifted into town to trade for a bottle of "Pass whiskey," outlaws on the dodge, and gold seekers bound for California.

To Argonauts this was the last place to rest, purchase supplies, ask directions, secure passports, and enjoy themselves before striking out for Janos and the trail to the Guadalupe Pass. Most gold seekers had Joseph Pownall's attitude toward the Pass of the North. This New Jersey Argonaut walked the streets of the town in June of 1849 and was impressed with the shrubbery and trees that nearly hid the flat-roofed adobe buildings. And small wonder, for Pownall and his party had been on the trail, on that Lower Road through southwestern Texas, since late March. To him this wasn't any ordinary town. This was the only piece of earth that hadn't been a threat to his life in months.

Some emigrants, though, simply couldn't overcome their backgrounds, couldn't accept the notion that they were entering a new world and beginning a new life. Such a man was Thomas B. Eastland from Nashville, Tennessee. In a letter to his wife from El Paso del Norte, Eastland expressed his horror at the daily sight of mixed-bloods. And his own prejudice colored everything he saw so that the *plaza pública,* the church, and even the wine became something to disparage. All he could believe was that this was the end product of darker people and the Church of Rome.

The one thing Eastland admired was on the American side of the Río Grande. This was Coons' Ranch, and here Eastland claimed one could see the difference between Mexicans and Americans. At Coons' Ranch there were well-built houses, an orchard, two large vineyards, and about 4,500 acres of irrigated land. Yet what Eastland either didn't know or ignored was that Benjamin Franklin Coons of St. Louis, Missouri, had just recently purchased this ranch. Prior to that it had belonged to Señor Juan María Ponce de León, who had been granted this tract of land in 1824. So what Eastland credited to Coons was the hard and creative work of Ponce.

But Eastland was a bitter man by the time he had reached El Paso del Norte. He had allowed Colonel John "Jack" Hays to talk him into taking the Lower Road. Hays had made extravagant promises about this route to the gold fields, and to top off everything he let it be known that they might get rich even before they arrived in California.

If Eastland ever asked him about this, the newly appointed Indian Agent for the Gila River territory probably told him, "Not many know it, but the Gila is as rich with gold as any lode in California."

Then to cap his persuasive argument for going along with him, Hays made it clear that to travel with him was to travel with the U. S. Army exploration party under the command of General William Worth. What more could any emigrant wish for? Here was military protection from Comanches and Apaches. Here were guides who knew the lay of the land and where to find waterholes, and here was the promise of striking it rich even before reaching California.

Nothing turned out as the glib Hays had promised. Because the military had orders to build a road as it proceeded, the expedition moved with incredible slowness. General Worth died of cholera, and everything was delayed while the military readjusted itself to the command of General Joseph E. Johnston. By the time Eastland reached El Paso del Norte he was far too angry and discouraged to see anything worthwhile about this crossroads of the frontier.

During the peak of the Argonaut rush through Mexico in 1849–50, company after company straggled into the Pass of the North. Some men, like Thomas Eastland and his son Joseph, came with

THE EL DORADO TRAIL

built-in prejudices. Added to the attitudes of such men was their own weariness and their bitter memories of the Southwestern desert. Other men came to El Paso del Norte in better spirits and with a much different frame of mind. These men came with the flush of adventure and the anticipation of discovery.

Such a man was Benjamin Butler Harris. A tall, blond Tennessean, an ex-lawyer and ex-schoolteacher, Harris had come to Texas before the California gold strike in search of better health for his ailing liver and had promptly come down with what he called "Brazos fever." This rawboned Tennessean with high cheekbones and a nose that would have been at home in Dante's Tuscany joined Captain Isaac H. Duval's party when it headed out of what is now Johnson City, Texas, on March 22, 1849. He was on his way in search of better health and the land of gold.

The Duval party traveled by horseback and muleback, and many of the men were former Texas Rangers. No mistake about it, young Harris was traveling with a rough breed of men. Just how rough they were became brutally apparent to Harris when he saw one man knife another in the stomach over such a minor question as the cooking of beans. And though there were two physicians in the party, the wounded man died two days later. Yet this violent streak, this hardness about life and death carried these men across the Southwestern desert in good shape and fast time; and when they reached El Paso del Norte they were ready for a *fandango* and the products of the vineyards.

Harris liked the Pass of the North. After his Texas home and his time in the desert, this was a lively place. He and his companions enjoyed themselves while they purchased supplies for the next leg of their journey, and they were too satisfied with the fine wine made from Mission grapes to complain about having to pay twenty-five cents each for passports to cross into Mexico.

Many of the *gringos* who walked the streets of El Paso del Norte and who drank "Pass whiskey" in the *cantinas* during these gold-rush years were typical of the stereotype of the Forty-Niner. They wore rough, heavy clothing that was much too warm for this hot climate. They had beards and long hair that made them look much older than they really were. They were boisterous, proud Yankees; winners of the Mexican War; distrustful of people a shade darker in color, and apt to equate crude behavior with manliness. This was

118

what one might expect to find among ex-soldiers. Other emigrants were quite different, and they broke the single-dimension picture of the Forty-Niner. Some were family men whose behavior was tempered by wives, daughters, and other females. And some were peace-loving men who had been against the Mexican War, against slavery, and who truly believed in equality for all men. Then, as in all mass movements, there were some individuals who had a flair that set them off from the usual run of Argonaut, the usual run of citizen anywhere in the world. One such character was yet another Harris, but he was not related to Tennessee Harris of Duval's party.

Lewis Birdsall Harris was a most unusual emigrant. A native New Englander who had migrated to Texas prior to the discovery of gold at Sutter's Mill, Harris was thirty-three years old when he hit the trail from San Antonio in the spring of 1849. Traveling with him were his wife, Jenny; two Negro slaves, Bob and Jane; the Cal Thorn family; a close friend called Cornelius; and Captain Herman Thorn who was doomed to drown at the Colorado River crossing. None of this was typical, as most emigrant parties did not take along their wives and children; and most of them moved in larger groups. Yet the most unusual aspect of the Harris party was their major mode of transportation.

Unlike other gold seekers, Harris had considered the possibility of not being able to find enough timber to construct rafts for river crossings. To take care of this problem, he designed a boat-wagon in which the body was patterned after the typical river flatboat. His creation was put together with well-seasoned lumber, calked tightly, and ready for water. Its first test was the Pecos River, and the men pulled and paddled it across without any difficulty or any leakage in the strange amphibious wagon. After this trial run, Harris and company were ready for any river they might encounter on the trail to El Dorado. And the first public view of this craft took place when they arrived at the Río Grande. Once again they used lines and paddles to maneuver their craft to the Mexican shore. While they made their way across, astonished residents of the Pass of the North stood on the riverbank and stared with wonder at this peculiar wagon.

Being a very practical Yankee, Lewis Birdsall Harris took full advantage of El Paso del Norte's markets. He loaded his wagon and pack animals with fresh apples, green corn, grapes, and flour. Then between this stop and Santa Cruz in the State of Sonora, Harris and his party added even more to their supplies. On the other side of the Guadalupe Pass, they killed wild cattle at the deserted Rancho San Bernardino, and jerked as much beef as they could carry. From Santa Cruz to Tucson, they stopped at other *ranchos* that had been left to the Apache raiders. At these places, Harris wrote that he "...found the peach orchards hanging full of ripe fruit and lived on peach cobbler for a long time." [11]

In contrast to Boat-wagon Harris the adventures of some emigrants bordered on outright farce except that what happened to them was real, was hell on men and animals, was often dangerous and sometimes fatal. The misadventures of Colonel Sam Whiting's expedition along the Lower Road was a surrealistic nightmare for this party as they crossed the vast reaches of southwestern Texas. Many years later, Augustus W. Knapp wrote of his experience with this party; and even though he was many miles away in distance and many years in time, the memory of how the party suffered remained vivid.

They started out with 200 mules for riding and packing, and that seemed a good idea. But nobody had bothered to consider the problem of feeding these animals in country that would hardly support a swarm of grasshoppers. Somebody came up with the notion that the party would have more than enough food if they just carried enough *panoche*—a mixture of ground parched corn and sugar. So they purchased five tons of *panoche*, to be carried in one wagon pulled by twelve yoke of oxen across hundreds of miles of rough plains covered with mesquite and prickly pear cactus, waterless stretches of wind-blown sand, and across rivers with quicksand bottoms and rushing high water from the spring run-off. It was a brave trip for the one hundred who started it, brave and foolish to the point of almost being suicidal for everybody.

Sam Whiting was anything but a natural leader, and if he knew his way across this wilderness, he managed to keep it a secret from everybody including himself. As the days became weeks and the weeks eased into months, the Whiting expedition disintegrated into a fight for survival. They were lost, and everyone knew it. Their animals were dying, and they saw them die. And as their oxen dropped in their yokes, the emigrants slaughtered and ate them, and kept their hides in case they should need them. Mile after weary mile they plodded on. They watched the horizon until their eyes burned from the glare. Then as they became more tired than they had ever dreamed, companions began dropping behind. They dropped out of sight, out of the dulled consciousness of men afraid of collapsing, and nobody bothered to go back and look for them. Nobody bothered, and yesterday's messmate never appeared again unless he flew overhead as part of a turkey buzzard's last meal. Yet despite their bad planning; despite such insanities as losing three men when they pursued "... a mirage for nearly half a day. . . ;" [12] despite their lack of leadership, and their callous disregard for companions in trouble, they finally wandered into El Paso del Norte in the late spring of 1849.

They must have seemed like a legion of walking dead as they crossed the Río Grande and approached the *plaza pública*. Many had worn out their shoes and had walked the last 200 miles across the blistering hot earth and the prickly pear cactus in improvised buckskin moccasins fashioned from the green and uncured hides of their slain oxen. They had endured mile after endless mile of prairie-dog towns that twisted ankles, and ". . . abounded with rattlesnakes and tarantulas of the largest size. . . ." [13] They had watched companions drop dead alongside them, and they had even fought a wind-driven, roaring grass fire that passed by and left miles of blackened stubble to cross. It was as though the very earth were scorching itself to deny even the poorest of feed to their starving mounts.

To Augustus Knapp and the other survivors of this ordeal in the desert, El Paso del Norte was much more than a frontier crossroads, a wilderness port for men on the move. This adobe town near the banks of the Río Grande was a paradise. But here in the safety of this Mexican town, Knapp's strength gave out. He came down with a fever, and in a few days he was so sick he could not go on with his companions of the trail when they were rested and ready to move. With bloodshot eyes and a temperature that made him feel as though he were still walking the desert with shaky strides, Knapp waved farewell and good luck to the men who had endured the long march with him. Then as they moved out of sight of his brush hut alongside the river, Knapp truly believed he would never see them again. He was convinced his luck had run out, and that it was his fate to die in this alien land.

But fate plays many strange tricks. Just as Knapp was resigning himself to the inevitable, a most unusual vision appeared at the opening of his hut—a vision that filled the doorway of his grass and reed shelter. What his fevered eyes focused on stood well over six feet tall, had strong, muscular arms that carried no flabby fat and were tremendously powerful. Yet what he saw was not a vision or a mirage or a fever-inspired illusion. What he looked at with utter astonishment was a rawboned woman with bright red hair and blue eyes. She was of heroic proportions, and could have been a model for the mythical pioneer woman. This guardian angel at Knapp's doorway was not a Calamity Jane wearing man's clothing and looking more masculine than feminine. On the contrary, she wore a dress that she filled out with ample endowments in all the right spots. She was all woman, much woman, and there was no mistake about it.

To Augustus Knapp or anybody else on either side of the Río Grande, there was no need for introduction. Only one female in the whole Southwest looked like the Amazon standing before him, and that was "The Great Western." Her real name and origin were not even important, and Knapp made no mention of them in his memoirs. To him in that hot summer day of 1849, "The Great Western" was going to take care of him in his time of need. Where she was from and who she was didn't matter.

He did know she had been a camp follower during the Mexican War and had won the lasting respect of the soldiers by giving aid to the wounded during and after the battles, and he had heard that after the war she had settled near Coons' Ranch on the American side of the Río Grande and opened a saloon. He also knew she was feared by Mexicans and given a wide berth by Apaches who eased in and out of both settlements. The Mexicans didn't wish to offend her because of her temper and ability to use a pistol, and the Indians ". . . seemed to hold her in perfect awe, and had a superstition that she was a supernatural being." [14]

Augustus Knapp remembered "The Great Western" with as much respect and awe as the Mexicans or the Indians. She fed him and nursed him in his makeshift hut. One day a party of Apaches stopped at his shelter, looked him over, and asked if he were an American. Knapp indicated a "yes" to the question, and the Indians informed him he wouldn't be harmed. At the same time he was told that if he had been Mexican that would have meant his death. When "The Great Western" heard about this, she quickly moved Knapp to her saloon, where he met a daily stream of unusual characters.

During his stay with this oversized female savior, Knapp never bothered to ask how she came to be where she was, or figured it was better not to ask questions. If he had, he might have been able to clear away her misty past. As it is, she is as much legend as truth, as much fabrication as fact. She might have come from Missouri or Tennessee. Her maiden name possibly was Bourjette, Bouget, Bourdette, or Borginnis. She may have once been Mrs. Davis or Mrs. Foyle. And there are even stories that indicate she was a camp follower during the Seminole War. Yet some things about this remarkable woman are fairly definite.

"The Great Western" did serve as a cook for the 7th Infantry officers' mess at Fort Texas (later Fort Brown). She did assist wounded men during and including the battles up to Buena Vista. And she did go along with Major Lawrence P. Graham's battalion of Second Dragoons as they headed out of Monterrey, Mexico, in 1848, and began their long march to California. However, she became sick at Chihuahua City and remained there when the troops moved on. After that she endured a period of bad health and hard times. Or so Lieutenant William H. C. Whiting entered in his journal when he met her near Coon's Ranch in April of 1849.

The fame of "The Great Western" was no ephemeral thing. She was not one of many frontier characters who moved across the colorful panorama of Southwestern history, only to be forgotten and to die lonely and unknown after she had lived beyond the first excitement of the frontier years. Both Argonaut Knapp and road surveyor Lieutenant Whiting as well as all the other soldiers, miners, frontiersmen, and Indians she knew would have been amazed to know that when "The Great Western" died she received a military funeral and burial. Yet this is exactly what happened when she "cashed in her chips" while running a saloon in Yuma, Arizona, in 1866. By then she had married a man named Bowman, and she was buried in the Fort Yuma cemetery alongside her favorite frontier soldiers.[15]

El Paso del Norte was a rendezvous for adventurers, for characters who were larger than life, who were cast in a different mold, for types like "The Great Western," Boat-wagon Harris, Texas Ranger John "Jack" Coffee Hays, scalp hunters like James Kirker and John Glanton, and the steady line of gold-fevered Forty-Niners who crawled in from the vast reaches of the plains. To all of them, this was the place to call a halt. This was where gold seekers such as H. O. Harper of St. Louis, Missouri, could buy a bottle of "Pass whiskey" or "Pass wine," go to a *fandango* with a dark-eyed *señorita*, and try to forget that between the Pecos and the Río Grande two of his friends had been killed and scalped by Comanches. This was the place to revive the inner man and to tell yourself you were tough enough and had guts enough to keep moving. This was the Pass of the North, the crossroads of the Southwestern frontier.

## THE BLOODY ROAD TO JANOS

On any map, even one scratched in sand by a sunburnt man squatting on his haunches, the road from El Paso del Norte to Janos looked like a Sunday's outing in a family buggy. To men just in off the Lower Road; to men who had almost become accustomed to a flat, dry plain only broken here and there by an eroded arroyo, sand dunes, and prairie-dog towns; to men who had almost forgotten that a sip of water now and then wasn't a normal amount; to men almost out of the habit of having enough food to ease constant hunger; and to men who had seen six or seven hundred miles of a land without shade from the burning sun, a land where there were no forests but only greasewood, mesquite, and prickly pear cactus or a growth of lonesome willows and maybe a stunted cottonwood or two next to the river; to men who had become accustomed to such a landscape, the road to Janos sounded like a post road with all the fixings. And they said so with great conviction. They would bring a Mexican back to camp, misunderstand his English and murder his Spanish, but believe he had said this trip to Janos would be easy. They believed it because, why hell, because they were badly in need of an easy trip.

"Hell, pilgrim, this fella says it ain't no more than seventy or eighty leagues to Janos."

"The hell he does. You just don't understand his lingo."

"Tell him, fella. Tell him what you told me."

"*Sí, señor. Ciudad Janos es setenta, sea ochenta leguas.*"

"No, no, tell them in English. They don't know a damned word of Spanish."

"*Sí, señor. Ciudad Janos es* maybe seventy, maybe eighty leagues."

"See, see, what'd I tell you, and he even says there's Americans in the towns—silver miners and store owners."

"Did you say towns?"

"That's what I said."

"Towns? What you drinking, pilgrim? You had too much 'Pass whiskey'?"

"Goddam! I'm not pulling your leg. You know I always share. No siree, I ain't had none of that stuff these people call whiskey. There's at least one place, a town they call Corral—something or other."

"Corralitos, *señor*."

"See there. See, just like I told you."

"Oh hell, didn't you talk to anybody except this here Mex?"

"Sure, I talked to a scalp hunter. He says there's this other town out there, and he talked some about Americans, too."

"Sweet Jesus Christ! A scalp hunter! What the hell was a scalp hunter doing in that country? You mean we got to fight Indians, maybe Apaches? Is that what you call an easy trip?"

The talk would go on. One after another the men would gather around. They'd compare maps, tell what they'd heard, and they'd come up with their own notions about the lay of the land. They'd talk about the Apaches, about the waterholes between El Paso del Norte and Janos, and about names of what might or might not be towns. Then they'd always come back to the one dream they wanted to believe; they were going to have an easy road to Janos. Most of the way, at least half, they'd be on the regular road to Chihuahua City. Sure, there was some dry and barren country, and Apaches to watch out for. But what difference did any of this make to a man who damned near had his brains baked, and who almost choked for lack of water between the Pecos and the Río Grande. Nothing could be worse than what they'd already been through. And the rested *gringo* with a little "Pass whiskey" on board would say to the Mexican patiently trying to warn him, "Don't you go to worrying about us Yankees. There ain't nothing we can't handle if we set our minds to it."

So they headed for Janos. Some parties left the Pass of the North as they had found it, and both Mexicans and Americans had good

125

memories of their meeting. Other parties didn't leave anything
except bad feelings. Joseph Pownall of Hackettstown, New Jersey,
indicated in his journal that some of his party had caused a considerable amount of trouble before they left. They took the law into
their own hands, and shot and killed a Mexican who—they claimed
—had stolen three of their mules. Then, not satisfied with their vigi-
lante "justice," they ended up ". . . *stampeding* the whole place. . . ." [16]
Then to add insult to murder, they proceeded to take their time in
getting out of town until they were warned by a messenger from the
American consul that the militia was getting ready to come after
them. At this point they "took the hint and packed up immediately
if not sooner and vamosed." [17]

It was no wonder the citizens of El Paso del Norte were upset over
this brutal killing by these *gringos* at this time; for during that same
June of 1849, two more Mexicans were shot and killed by Argonauts
of the Texas party headed by Captain Isaac H. Duval. The three
killers were ex–Mexican War volunteers—John Brazelton, Calvin H.
Rolfe, and William Hammock. As with the Pownall party, the reason
given for the killings was the theft of mounts and equipment. However, a third man was badly wounded by Hammock without any
reason at all. Benjamin Butler Harris wrote that this shooting took
place when the party's gunslingers saw Mexican soldiers rushing to
the presidio and decided to make them drink some wine with them.
They stopped the colonel, who was on his way to his command post.
Then when a bugler rode at a gallop by them and blew the alarm,
the men ordered him to halt. When he faiied to comply, Hammock
shot him in the back.

Again as with Pownall and his party, Duval's men were sent a
note by the American consul. In this note the consul advised the killers to surrender, as some 700 Mexicans were ready to come after
them. They refused, eased out of town, and camped on the Chihuahua Road near a steep bluff where they figured to put up a last-
ditch fight. But the expected cloud of dust from the Mexican cavalry
never appeared on the horizon, and the Duval men moved on down
the road as they headed for Corralitos and Janos. Still, Duval kept
a rear guard; and as they rode through the tableland beyond El
Paso del Norte the next day the expected dust cloud finally appeared
in the early afternoon. By now they were more than 20 miles south
of the presidio, had met up with a party of Santa Fé traders, and

were establishing their night's camp. They quickly readied themselves for battle, but no battle took place. A dozen or so men galloped into their camp, and the *gringos* took them prisoners. The Mexicans said that they were custom-house guards who had been sent out to protect the Santa Fé traders from *ladrones* and Apaches.

Not totally content with this information, the Duval men continued to question their captives. The Mexicans insisted they were not an advance guard for the army, and they informed their captors that after they had left El Paso del Norte the soldiers had marched into town, got drunk, and there was no chance of immediate pursuit.

Though there was no danger of pursuit for either Duval or the Pownall parties, there were other dangers on the road to Janos. The trek across almost waterless sand hills, that miniature Sahara, Los Médanos, could be a danger if the wind blew too hard. There was always the possibility of an attack by *ladrones,* and there was the constant omnipresence of the Apaches. No traveler on the road to Janos dismissed that unseen threat of violence that might suddenly streak out of a deep arroyo or appear as a thin wake of dust behind galloping war ponies rushing down the foothills of the Sierra Madre with the sound of ear-piercing yells from ruthless warriors—yells blending into one shrill note of terror for the men who heard them.

Joseph Pownall sensed this threat to his life in Corralitos and Janos. These were towns where fear was a way of life. At any moment, on any day, the unthinkable could happen. Outside the reach of the towns, beyond the presidios, out of sound and sight of the Mexican soldiers was the evidence of horror, and it was there for anyone to see. The *poblado* that was now only a name on a map, the *poblado* where turkey buzzards still searched for a meal from the dead as they slowly circled over the gutted buildings, the deserted *ranchos* with tall grass, good springs, cottonwoods shimmering in the afternoon breeze—all the ghosts of those who died or vanished after enduring and living through an Apache raid—this is what Pownall and all the other California emigrants saw on the road to Janos. They shuddered, and they wondered why the townspeople of Corralitos and Janos allowed these butchers to come into town and trade stolen goods from murdered families. But the Argonauts were only passing through, only taking a first and last look at the country these Mexicans called home.

The extent of Apache domination, and the effect of their brutal

raids was also quite apparent to the Duval party as they reached
the Río Santa María and the silver mines of Corralitos. Here they
saw that there were at least fifty guards protecting between one hundred to two hundred miners, and they saw that armed escorts traveled with each ore train bound for the mills at the town of Corralitos.
Here, too, they learned that the richest of the silver mines was owned
by an American and his Mexican wife. This was Lewis Flotte from
Baltimore, whose wife was the daughter of the old Santa Fé trader
Robert McKnight. Flotte's mine was at the town of Barranca, and
had the same name. The ore was exceedingly rich; and when John E.
Durivage passed through the area in May of 1849, he noted that
when Flotte's workers weren't bothered by Apaches, the profit ran
as high as $1,000 per week. But if any Argonauts thought of follow-
ing Flotte's lead and remaining here to prospect for silver instead of
continuing the journey to California, such ideas were quickly damp-
ened by the all-too-visible signs of perpetual danger from the
Apaches.

Corralitos and Janos were not normal towns. They were communities under constant siege, communities always ready for the worst
and thankful for those days of peace they enjoyed only because
the Apaches needed some place to trade. But the possibility of attack
was always present, and the residents of these towns built their
adobe homes to serve as both dwellings and forts. These structures
were complete with parapets and portholes, and if any member of
Duval's party ever doubted the need of such precautions that doubt
was removed during their stay in Corralitos. At high noon one day
a band of Apaches suddenly appeared on the outskirts of town and
quickly rustled some of the horses feeding there.

The Apache menace became even clearer to various parties of
Argonauts as they followed the Río Casas Grandes to Janos, and
headed out for the Guadalupe Pass, riding through a country of
good grass and plenty of water. In this fertile land, more than one
company of emigrants had encounters with the warriors of Apachería. Joseph Pownall wrote that his party had camped no more than
15 miles outside Janos when they were suddenly confronted with a
band of Apaches. To Pownall these warriors seemed to outnumber
his party by at least three times. They were savage-looking men, and
all of them were armed—". . . some with bows and arrows, some with
lances and others with guns. . . ." [18] Tension was somewhat relieved

when one of the Apaches rode toward them carrying a white flag. The emigrants quickly searched for something white to wave and ended up holding a sheepskin aloft. Slowly and cautiously, the Indians rode into their camp following an Apache who was tall in the saddle and who rode bolt upright. As the Apaches dismounted for a talk, the miners were astounded at the size of their leader.

The man who was obviously the chief of these Mimbreños Apaches was no ordinary man. He stood well over six feet tall, though the bulk of his height was in his powerful torso. His legs were short and bowed, and on a lesser man would have seemed comical. Not so with this man, for his large head, his alert, deep-socketed eyes, his jutting chin, and his high-bridged nose curving downward toward a wide and sensitive mouth marked him as a man to be reckoned with. This was Mangas Coloradas, called "Red Sleeves" by the *gringos.*

In his description of their meeting with Mangas Coloradas and his braves, Joseph Pownall wrote that they wanted tobacco; but were most interested in a Negro member of their company. Apparently, this was the first Negro they had ever seen, and they were very curious about his color.

Other parties of Argonauts had meetings with Mangas Coloradas on the trail outside of Janos, but none ever reported a direct conflict with him. John E. Durivage wrote of a story he had heard at El Galeana, near Corralitos, in the spring of 1849, about a battle between a party of Texans and a large band of Indians on the western side of the Sierra Madre, a battle in which only two of twenty Americans escaped with their lives. However, Durivage only reported hearsay. Proof of this battle was not recorded by other gold seekers who kept journals, and it is highly unlikely that such a conflict would have been overlooked by the considerable number of Argonauts who took this route, if there had been any substance to the story.

The closest thing to a conflict between Argonauts and Mangas Coloradas occurred when thirteen-year-old Tom Edwards of the Duval party exchanged shots with the chief because he wanted to kill an Indian in revenge for the death and scalping of his grandfather back in Texas. Fortunately for Duval and his company the great Apache chief was not hit, nor did he lose his temper. Instead he signaled for a parley as both miners and braves began shooting

129

and getting into position for a battle. Both sides withdrew and waited until late in the afternoon for their meeting. By that time all the hotheads had cooled off, and the parley began.

After saluting Duval and exchanging greetings, Mangas and nearly a hundred of his men gathered around young Tom Edwards and stared at him. The nervousness of the moment was broken as Mangas kept muttering in Spanish that the boy was a *muy malo muchaco*.

Having finished his message to the nervous boy, Mangas Coloradas then made it clear to Duval and the others that the Mimbreños were not enemies of the Americans. The Mexicans were *their* enemies. Then he spoke of how he had offered guides to Lieutenant Colonel Cooke when he passed through the Mimbreño homeland. Finally he came to his proposition. Why couldn't the Americans and the Apaches combine their strength and wipe out the Mexicans? He offered the land to the Americans as the spoils of a certain victory, and he and his people would take all personal property and scalps. The final point in his argument was that the Mexicans all wore crosses and were nothing but a bunch of damned Christians. On the other hand, the Apaches and the Americans were heathen *gringos*.

Captain Duval and his men turned down this generous offer from "Red Sleeves." But fondness of Mexicans played no role in their decision. The Duval party disliked Indians even more than they disliked Mexicans, and they were not about to halt their rush to El Dorado, even for the promise of an empire.

Fortunately for northern Mexico Mangas Coloradas never got together with Parker H. French when he and his gunslingers were in the Corralitos-Janos area the following year. If they had, northern Mexico's history might well have been even more violent and bloody. A proposition of conquest and the chance to rule a huge stretch of territory would have appealed to French. For by the time this flimflam man from New York had arrived in the country of the Mimbreños in the fall of 1850, he was a bitter man who was out for blood, vengeance, and anything of value he could lay his hands on.

Parker H. French was one of those characters who turned up in one wild venture after another in the American West, and very few of his activities were truly within the law. Before he vanished into the nether land of history—for nobody ever reported his death—

French had been a flim-flam man, a bandit, scalp hunter, mutineer, district attorney, newspaper editor, California State Assemblyman in 1854, one of William Walker's revolutionaries, Minister of Walker's Nicaraguan government in Washington, D.C., a Confederate spy, and a Union spy. Wherever there was any action and a chance to fleece an honest man, French was certain to turn up if he had heard about it. And like all such characters, he had a knack for knowing where his facile talk, false promises, and fast gun would pay off.

The motive for French's appearance in Apachería stemmed from his feud with a group of the emigrants who had agreed to hire French as their guide to California. All these men had been drawn into his web in New York. There he had distributed printed broadsides that described the easy route he intended to follow. He had placed ads in newspapers, and had run his operation out of a Tammany Hall office. In addition to maps, stories of a fortune to be made on the Gila River even before reaching California, French gave his business an added note of respectability by flashing a letter of credit issued by Howland and Aspinwall. This was the ace in his hand. Nobody would doubt his intentions when they saw such a letter from the most respectable owners of the Pacific Mail Steamship Company. And he was right, nobody did.

French promised the anxious Argonauts that he would guide them to California in sixty days for $250 per man. Also, he vowed that if the time schedule was not met, he would refund $5 per day for each day beyond the sixty-day schedule. This was not an opportunity to be missed. He quickly gathered 120 paid customers, and 50 enlisted men who had paid part of the fare and were to work out the rest, or had been enlisted as full-time employees for the trip.

On May 13, 1850, Parker H. French's Overland Expedition to California set sail from New York aboard the steamship *Georgia* bound for Havana. French easily made himself popular with the other passengers when he bought 150 bottles of champagne for them and the ship's officers. His generosity was not without reason. Many of the passengers asked if they could join his expedition, and French agreed to take on these additional Argonauts. Five days later as the *Georgia* steamed into the harbor at Havana, the expedition was considerably larger.

In Havana the Lopez Insurrection against the Cuban government

131

was on, and for three days the *Georgia* and two other steamships—
the *Ohio* and the *Falcon*—were held in the harbor by the guns of
Moro Castle and various Cuban guard boats stationed near them.
The delay was slight compared to other delays the gold seekers
would face later, and on May 23 they sailed into the harbor at New
Orleans. They were lodged in the St. Charles Hotel and encouraged
to join the Lopez revolt in Cuba. But even the promise of free land
failed to arouse any interest. The men had already missed their connection with the Galveston steamer *Palmetto,* and were losing precious time. They had signed up for a trip to El Dorado, and they
weren't about to be sidetracked for anything else.

By June 4, three weeks out of New York City, the men stepped
ashore at Port Lavaca, Texas. Wagons, supplies, and mules were supposed to be waiting and ready to go. As usual, nothing had been
done, and more time had to be wasted while everything needed for
an overland trip was purchased and made ready. To compound the
difficulty for these city men, French purchased unbroken mules, and
turned over the taming of these wild animals to one *vaquero* and
the greenhorn gold seekers. What followed was utter chaos, and only
very good fortune kept these men from getting anything worse than
bruises. Young Baldridge, who had hired on as French's secretary,
cited an example of the artful kicking of the mules during this train-
ing period for man and beast:

> For instance: while I was trying to manage a particularly "oneasy
> critter," holding him by the head I stooped to pick up my rietta,
> when he surprised me by a stunner, which sent me to grass and
> nearly knocked me out. For the life of me I could not see how it
> was done, but the boys said he did it fairly and I was not entitled
> to claim a "foul." [19]

The problem of breaking mules for harness and riding was only
the beginning of a series of difficulties that beset this expedition on
its way to Cooke's wagon road and that "easy short cut" to the confluence of the Gila and Colorado rivers. It took them one month to
travel about 150 miles from Port Lavaca to San Antonio. As one
member of the party put it, "If this was a pleasure trip, it must be
a left-handed one, anyway." [20] The spellbinding French had promised them an outing to the gold fields, but the reality of the journey
quickly convinced them that he could not be trusted in anything he
said or promised.

## Jornada del Muerto

The men complained about the food, the camp sites, the eternal dust, and the muggy, hot summer weather in which frequent showers only added to their discomfort and made the going that much tougher for them and their mules. Men and mules were tortured with a constant swarm of large mosquitoes, and added to their misery was the growing belief that French had no more than a vague notion of which trail or road was the correct one.

At San Antonio, French produced his letter of credit from Howland and Aspinwall. Using this to procure drafts, he then purchased supplies at the U. S. Army post. Altogether, he spent close to $2,000. These drafts were never recognized by Howland and Aspinwall. Why this letter of credit had no value is also one of the many mysteries about French, for there is no definite indication that it was a forged document. Rather it is speculated that it was to be used for aiding the revolution in Cuba. As things stood, by the time the Army learned French's letter of credit was worthless he and his expedition were well on their way to El Paso del Norte. Nevertheless officers were put on their trail, and they carried a warrant for the arrest of the smooth-talking New Yorker.

Meanwhile, trouble continued to plague this party of emigrants. French had hired four Texas Rangers as guides and interpreters, but he constantly bickered with them about the direction, camp sites, and everything else that came to his mind. This interference with men who knew the country and their jobs almost ended with a gunfight between French and one of the wagon masters. The only thing that prevented it was that the Texan calmly told French if he wanted to draw against him to go right ahead. Then he added the final touch that made French back off, "But if you do, see that you make sure work, for if I live two seconds you are a dead man." [21] Along with this showdown between the Texan and French, the party had a long list of complaints ranging from the dreadful summer heat and shortage of water to delays caused by Comanches who wished to trade with them and the constant worry about rattlesnakes which were striking their livestock on a daily basis. Along with these complaints was the observable fact that their equipment was beginning to wear out, that miles of forage had been destroyed by a lightning-set grass fire, and that accidents were beginning to take their toll. One member of the party was accidentally shot to death by a companion. Another man fell from his wagon seat and was badly injured when a wagon containing a ton and a half of

133

bacon rolled over his chest. The most disturbing thing of all was that the promised sixty-day trip to California had long been exceeded.

When approached about his failure to meet his announced timetable, French calmly assured all the paying members of his party that there was nothing to worry about. After all, hadn't he promised to pay $5 per day to each man for each day beyond the sixty-day schedule? Then, too, all of them should bear in mind that they would surely find gold at the Gila River and arrive in California as rich men. Why, there was nothing, absolutely nothing at all to worry about.

The old come-on no longer worked. Too much had happened, and most of it had been bad. French's charm had been fine in a Wall Street office as he outlined their journey on his large wall map. It had been exciting to be one of his men aboard the *Georgia* while there was plenty of champagne to drink, and the riches of a King Midas to talk about. And it had been all right in New Orleans, even though they had missed their steamer for Galveston, for it was difficult to be angry when a man was staying at the St. Charles Hotel and taking his meals in the city's best restaurants. But all of that was too many months and too many miles behind them. It wasn't any better than a mirage on the 800 miles of plains between the Pecos River and the Río Grande at El Paso del Norte. As the men neared the Pass of the North, the split between these disgruntled gold seekers and French and his cronies grew wider and wider. It was no longer a matter of daily gripes that affected any party on the trail. The break between French and the men who had put their trust in him approached an outright feud as they reached the Río Grande, just opposite El Paso del Norte.

Two and a half months on the trail had removed the barriers that concealed the contempt the men now held for French. They were ready for any excuse to bring matters to a final head. At the new American town of Franklin, which had grown overnight in the vicinity of Coons' Ranch, the excuse presented itself: the officers from San Antonio caught up to the party with an order for the arrest of Parker H. French for his worthless "letter of credit."

Before he could be arrested, French crossed the Río Grande into Mexico. The officers waited in Franklin, hoping their quarry would not be able to resist the supplies he had been forced to leave. While they waited for him members of the party proclaimed that French had broken his contract. Therefore they were entitled to take the gear and do with it whatever seemed best. As Charles Cardinell recalled in a series of articles in the 1856 San Francisco *Daily Chronicle*, ". . . a meeting was held of the entire company, which decided to take possession of the property and sell it. The company divided the proceeds and split up into various parties to make their way overland to California as best as possible." [22]

At this time Cardinell claimed that the total strength of the party numbered 250 men. When the lawmen departed for San Antonio without having caught their man, the members of the party knew they outnumbered French and his men. But they had not counted on the possibility that such a man would never rest until he had taken revenge on them. Knowing French's ego and everything that had happened on the journey to El Paso del Norte, it was foolish for this group to break up into small parties. But prudence played no role with men anxious to get to California. Some of the newly formed companies headed south for Durango, where they planned to cross the Sierra Madre and drop down to the port of Mazatlán. Some went southwest to the *sierra* and the trail to the port of Guaymas on the Gulf of California. Others followed the original plan and struck out for Cooke's wagon road over the mountains to the Gila Trail.

In less than a month the folly of not remaining together as one large company for mutual protection became a matter of life and death at the silver-mining town of Corralitos. In this foothill town of northwestern Chihuahua, French and some ten or fifteen gunmen caught up to one party of his former expedition.

The emigrants had just finished a long day's ride. It was twilight as they unpacked the mules and washed their backs to keep them from developing saddle sores. In their journals both Cardinell and Baldridge recalled the events in much the same manner. Suddenly there was the sound of yelling or war whoops, as though they were being attacked by Apaches. A Canadian named Spafford Rounds shouted, "That is French and he comes for no good; we must not permit him to come into our camp!" [23]

Gunshots echoed off the dry foothills, and the first shots from French's gang took their toll. French shouted, "Shoot Cooper!" Hearing this, Cooper fired first, but he was shot through the thighs and dropped to the ground with both legs badly broken. The whole battle lasted a short time. But before the gold seekers could drive off French's gang Wright took a bullet through his head that splattered his brains on men beside him. Nelson was shot through the back while trying to assist a wounded comrade, and was dead within a few hours. Holmes, the old man of the party, had both arms shot off. It seemed to Cardinell that his friends were dropping all around him.

Yet while French had the advantage of surprise, he did not get the easy victory he had anticipated. Some of the miners retreated to cover behind their wagons. From there they opened up with a deadly round. Before they had finished five outlaws were dead; and French had been hit with a bullet that ripped through the palm of his right hand, broke his wrist, and rammed through his elbow. As he and his men rode off in retreat, Cardinell said that French's shattered hand hung to his wrist by skin alone.

The Argonauts had won the gunfight, but the price had been high. There was no surgeon in Corralitos for the wounded, and the best they could do for the dead was to roll them in their blankets and bury them where they had been killed.

After the battle, the *alcalde* of Corralitos and other citizens approached the scene. Seeing the aftermath of this affair, the *alcalde* feared the French gang would return and attack the town itself. He quickly sent a rider to the presidio at Janos for a company of Mexican Lancers. When the soldiers arrived he stationed part of the company at the entrance to Corralitos and kept the others within the town.

The gunfight at Corralitos caused another delay in the movement of these men. Before they could travel they had to secure care for their wounded. Then they had to get back the frightened horses and mules that had run off during the battle. Some were never recovered, and the survivors of the fight assumed that French's men had run off with them. The other animals were being held by local residents. With the help of the *alcalde* these mounts were rounded up and turned over to their owners.

The gold seekers were not bothered by French again, but after they had departed, one story has it that the wounded gunman was given shelter and medical aid in the home of Lewis Flotte, owner of the Barranca Mine. According to Flotte's combination mine superintendent and schoolteacher French was brought into the house in bad shape. His right arm was so badly shattered, the wound so filled with dirt, that there seemed little chance he would survive.

Still, French was not a man to give up very easily. This little man with small, deep-set gray eyes knew what had to be done if he were going to keep on breathing. He requested that someone be brought in who could amputate his arm. Such an individual was brought to the house, and in a later interview he told of how he had tried to anesthetize French but failed:

> He couldn't be stupefied. He had already drunk quarts of Mescal; and I tried him with Spirits of Nitre, after which I administered about an inch of chloroform. After all he was conscious of everything that was done, though probably less sensitive than if he had taken nothing." [24]

Under primitive conditions that would have killed most men, French's arm was cut off just above the elbow. Then it was cauterized with red-hot powdered charcoal. Ten days later the flim-flam man from Tammany Hall was on his horse again, and he rode out of Corralitos and headed south toward Durango. One-armed French, as he was now to be known, had paid his toll on the bloody road to Janos. And it hadn't taken the Apaches to collect payment. The job had been accomplished by the innocent gold seekers Parker H. French had cheated and misguided in the barren and lonely wilderness.

## THE GUADALUPE PASS

Northwest of Janos was that "easy" pass across the Sierra Madre Occidental, that pass called Guadalupe. All Argonaut companies taking this branch of the El Dorado Trail had this route marked on their maps, circled, and underlined. From the Guadalupe Pass the journey to California was going to be child's play. The Indians would be friendly, and this included the Apaches, who only hated the Mexicans. Supplies wouldn't be any problem either. Word was that it would be easy to pick up supplies before they made the last dash across the Colorado Desert. Oh, there might be a shortage of water on the desert, but it was not a great worry. After all, they had already learned how to get along with a small water supply for a few days.

Then, to make things even simpler, the route over the *sierra* was well marked. All they had to do was follow the trail Spaniards and Mexicans had been using for centuries. There'd be mule tracks, even marks from big wheels of Mexican *carretas,* and tracks from U. S. Army wagons. Didn't Lieutenant Colonel Philip St. George Cooke and the Mormon Battalion take wagons over these mountains in jig time? Didn't Major Lawrence P. Graham and the Second Dragoons get across without any trouble? This was going to be a waltz after what they'd been through on the desert. Yes, sir, there wasn't going to be anything to it.

Looking westward from the gravelly tableland of Janos, a man could see the rugged, high range of mountains that made up the Sierra Madre. Somewhere in that maze of contorted earth the Animas and Guadalupe Mountains converged on each other in Apachería. Somewhere out there, two or three days away from Janos—or so men said—was a wagon road through these mountains. Once they had reached that Continental Divide, they would be only a whoop-and-a-holler from California.

The trouble with the Guadalupe Pass was the same kind of trouble emigrants had been having all along the way: the spoken word, the guidebook maps or the maps scratched in the ground didn't really indicate what kind of country they were planning to take wagons through. True enough, Lieutenant Colonel Cooke and the Mormon boys had made it with wagons in the fall of 1846. But what emigrants didn't know or simply ignored was that the Mormon Battalion had gone through hell in following General Stephen Watts Kearny's orders to establish a wagon road through the mountains southwest of Santa Fé.

And Cooke's battalion had been fully prepared for the worst possible as they headed into the mountains. Three outstanding guides rode with him. All were noted for their ability in the wilderness. The head guide was half English and half Cherokee. His name was Pauline Weaver, and he had been a trapper and hunter for the Hudson's Bay Company. But he didn't like cold weather, and by 1830 he had established himself in the Southwest. The other guides were a mixture of French-Canadian and Indian. One was Antoine Leroux, a mountain man's mountain man. The other was a man called Charbonneau, who appears to have been none other than Baptiste Charbonneau, the son of Toussaint Charbonneau and Sacajawea of the

Lewis and Clark Expedition. In addition, Cooke was given further guidance by Apaches sent to him by Mangas Coloradas, who had promised General Kearny that he would see that Cooke was helped in his search for a wagon road. Yet despite all this well-qualified assistance, Cooke and his men had a very rough time of it.

Cooke thought the mountain scenery was grand and picturesque; but if there was a true wagon road he never found it. Reports in such newspapers as the New York *Courier and Enquirer* and the Corpus Christi *Star* gave Cooke credit for developing a wagon road. What these newspapers didn't know, or simply left out of their stories, was a true description of how Cooke and the Mormons got across the mountains.

These hardened soldiers made their way across the *sierra* by pulling wagons up with ropes, hacking a path through stones and uncut timber, and they lost wagons and mules in the process. When they finally dropped over into the State of Sonora, all they could claim was that wagons could be brought over the mountains. All it took to do it was men willing to make roads, act as draft animals, and take wagons apart in order to raise and lower them in places where sheer cliffs barred their way.

The Argonauts knew none of this, nor did they know of the troubles that the Second Dragoons under the command of the whiskey-loving Major Lawrence P. Graham ran into in 1848. Graham and many of his troopers were drunk during most of their march beyond Janos. They got lost in the mountains, and sober Lieutenant Cave Couts considered it a miracle that they got through at all.

Under the drunken prodding of Major Graham, the troopers worked their way upward by following a shallow stream in a narrow canyon. As they moved along, billowy thunderheads began to blow in on a Pacific wind. Lieutenant Couts watched the clouds get darker and darker, and began to worry about the possibility of what might happen if it began to rain.

"Look, Major," he said, "and see where the marks of a torrent stand upon every tree, bush, and precipice along the Cañada? Send a party *one day* in advance to repair and construct our way? Send two or more men to find how many days before we leave the Cañada?" [25]

Major Graham's reply was instant and final: "No! No! No! Sir, I know my duty and have men enough to do *anything* in a few minutes. No one shall go in advance of the command!" [26]

No one went in advance of the command. The senior officer was not about to listen to suggestions from a junior officer. Such arrogant stupidity rankled the tall, thin Lieutenant Couts who carried himself as straight as a ramrod. But the same West Point tradition that had designed his posture also had conditioned him to follow a superior officer's orders at all times and without exception.

On their third day in the canyon the clouds gathered in even heavier masses, turned black, and then the rain began to fall. But it didn't come down in a light shower or a momentary cloudburst. The rain came in torrents, and it fell so quickly and in such great quantities that it was as though a new deluge was about to flood the earth. Couts watched the water rush down from the mountain heights carrying soil, rocks, limbs of trees, and even dead tree trunks. He watched the shallow brook they were following become roaring, rushing river. Within minutes the water level rose from just enough to cover the pebbles and rocks to a muddy monster fifteen to twenty feet deep. Before the troopers could make a move Couts saw one, then two more wagons swept downstream. Men and mules struggled and scrambled for higher ground, desperately trying to get beyond the raging waters. Wet, weary, and stunned, they reached higher ground, and made a wet camp. Here for three days they waited for the storm to let up. The break came after the third day, but not before it had hit them once more with renewed fury.

On midnight watch during their second night at their high-ground camp, the wild torrent swept over the camp. The men fought to save wagons, mules, and themselves. At the peak of this flood a ". . . hospital wagon with a sick man was carried off in the current . . . , but the man succeeded in clinging to a tree which he caught hold of until the next morning." [27]

By the next day Major Graham's wet and tired command succeeded in climbing out of the last *barranca*. They crossed the Continental Divide somewhere in the vicinity of Guadalupe Pass and reached the mesa where the deserted Rancho San Bernardino was located. What Lieutenant Couts called "Camp Inundation" was behind them.

Into this maze of *barrancas*, hogback ridges, and cliffs that looked as though they had been sheared off with a giant butcher knife of creation came the Argonauts. They came on foot, on horseback, on muleback. They pulled wagons with oxen, mules, and their own

hands. Some of them knew where they were going, or, at the very
least, thought they knew. Others didn't know at all, but had hired
guides who might or might not be reliable. Their approach toward
Guadalupe Pass came from a number of directions.

Some companies came south from Santa Fé, but turned west before arriving at El Paso del Norte and headed into the Animas
Mountains. By this route they hoped to cut sign on Cooke's Wagon
Road near the pass, and eliminate many miles from their journey.
Others came southwest from El Paso del Norte to Corralitos and
Janos, while many parties moved northwest from Chihuahua City
to Janos. These emigrants passing through Janos truly believed they
would hit Cooke's Wagon Road without any trouble. But what they
and the gold seekers coming through the Animas Mountains didn't
know was that the approaches to the Guadalupe Pass were tricky
from any direction.

This country played no favorites. In fact, it tended to make the
points on the compass into a kind of shell game. If you were very
lucky, you hit the pass on the nose, and got across without too much
trouble. If you were running true to form, nothing about this pass
turned out to be easy. And if you hit a streak of bad luck, the Guadalupe Pass was elusive, the mountains almost impossible to climb, the
Apaches unfriendly, and the weather either blistering hot or wet and
freezing.

But rough going didn't stop gold seekers. Company after company
of them wandered into the Sierra Madre searching for Cooke's
Wagon Road and the tracks of Graham's soldiers. To Apaches watching from the peaks or trying to barter or steal something from the
steady line of cursing, sweating *gringos,* it must have seemed as if
all the *norteamericanos* were stumbling through Apachería. Warriors visited their camps, and sometimes managed to trade some
food for clothing or something else that caught their fancy. Other
times they managed to steal a mule or a horse when the *gringos*
became careless. Such was not the case with Robert Watson Noble
and his *vaqueros* who traveled this route in April and May of 1849.

Noble was an old hand in the Southwestern wilderness, and he
knew the Apaches would be tempted by the trail herd of mules that
he and his men were driving to California to sell to the goldminers.
With the financial backing of Samuel P. Parkman of Guanajuato, this
trail herd of mules and wagons had started from Chihuahua City on

April 10, 1849. Along the way they had passed many Forty-Niners; and even as they entered the mountains beyond Janos they found companies who were trying to find the wagon road to Guadalupe Pass. On April 23—thirteen days out of Chihuahua City—Noble had his first encounter with the Apaches.

He had picketed his mules near two camps of gold seekers—one from New Orleans, the other from Hartford. They had made camp early and were settling down for a rest when some Apaches came into their camp. The warriors were riding at an easy pace, and indicated they were interested in doing some trading. But Noble was not at all sure about their intentions. He and his *vaqueros* had driven the mule herd over 300 miles, and they were not in the mood to lose any of them. The meeting with the Apaches was an uneasy one. Noble was suspicious, and he figured they were tempted by the sight of the picketed mules. After a slow but meaningless talk with these Indians, Noble was convinced there might be trouble. That night he kept a double guard around the mules. Even so the Apaches did stampede them during the night, and it was only the quick work of the *vaqueros* that prevented the loss of any animals.

The next day Noble and his men drove their herd about 15 miles, and reached what must have been the pass itself. At times it was impossible to move the wagons until they doubled the teams on them. What road there was became more difficult to travel as it climbed upward. At day's end they camped in an area between two high peaks, and Noble wrote in his diary that they ". . . were surrounded by high mountains on all sides . . . ," [28] and that it was difficult to find a level place for wagons to stand.

Throughout the passage from Janos over the Sierra Madre to Santa Cruz, Noble found the going rough. What was called a wagon road was, at best, a mule trail. While he admitted his wagons were the large, ten-mule, Missouri type, he also pointed out that his men had to cut a road in places. Sometimes they used as many as sixteen mules to pull each wagon up a mountainside. Then upon reaching the top of a ridge, they frequently had to unload the wagons and take their goods downhill on pack mules. Hard as the trail was, though, Noble saw that there was plenty of grass for the livestock, no shortage of water, lots of timber for shade, wood, and wagon repairs; and plenty of game animals to keep fresh meat in camp. The only suffering Noble and his *vaqueros* had to endure in the trip from Janos to Santa Cruz was the backbreaking labor of getting the wagons in and out of *barrancas* and up and down steep mountains. Yet because of the extra animals from their mule herd and their own know-how, they covered the distance from the tableland of Chihuahua to Sonora's Santa Cruz Valley in twelve days, averaging slightly over twenty miles per day.

Following closely behind Noble and his trail herd of mules were two parties that crossed the pass during the second week of May, 1849. Among one company was John E. Durivage. A member of the other was A. B. Clarke, whose swollen knees had forced him to remain behind at Janos while his companions of the Hampden Mining Company had gone on ahead.

Durivage looked at the Sierra Madre country with amazement and was awed by its deep valleys and high mountains; like Noble he was impressed with the abundance of wild game, plenty of water, meadows of grass for the livestock, and the thick groves of oaks, cedars, and pines. But he worried about the possibility of an Apache raid, and was extremely apprehensive about the steep mountains that shut out the setting sun early in the afternoon and stood as blue-shadowed obstacles that looked like a final barrier for the movement of wagons.

Three days before reaching the pass Durivage looked upward at the sawtoothed peaks, the almost perpendicular mountainsides, and thought it would be impossible to take wagons across. Pack mules, yes. Wagons, absolutely out of the question. To make the trail appear even more impossible, he looked at the trace of what he thought was Major Graham's trail, and all along the way, he could see "... broken wagons, and harness. ..." [29]

A. B. Clarke, however, rode in a wagon all the way over the pass. He had managed to hitch a ride with the Governor McNees party of Missouri. Clarke traveled in good company, as McNees had been a Santa Fé trader and had been in California when gold was discovered. Now he was on his way back with a company that numbered over seventy men, five wagons with four pairs of mules per wagon, and a cavayard of extra mules to replace any that got injured or became too worn out to continue. The men of the company were a cross-cut of the Trans-Mississippi West. There were Mexicans, Irish, Scots, Negroes, ex-fur trappers, Mexican War veterans, and any other type that might be found close to the frontier. "We have nearly

all the lingo of Babel," Clarke wrote, "a motley crew, but good-
natured and sociable." [30]

Like Durivage and his party, Clarke was with a group of men
who were trying to follow Major Graham's nonexistent trail. As they
approached the central ridges of the *sierra*, Clarke figured that if
there had ever been wagons in this confusion of mountains there
couldn't have been very many, as there simply wasn't much indication of a wagon passage. "I do not believe," he wrote, "that Hannibal
carried his baggage into Italy by a more difficult mountain passage.
We passed over some ravines, the sides of which seemed pretty
closely approaching the perpendicular." [31]

Apparently, the perpendicular did not frighten Clarke as it did
other emigrants. For while he commented on the upside-down geography of the Sierra Madre, he observed the natural beauty of the
land as they crossed the Guadalupe Pass and the Continental Divide.
He even mentioned that while they rested on this passageway between Mexico's great Central Plateau and the Pacific watershed
leading to the Sea of Cortés, he got out of the wagon and slowly
walked around to exercise his sore legs. As a casual afterthought he
commented that during his long, rough wagon ride he had been
reading Edwin Bryant's *What I Saw in California*.

But Clarke and Durivage were only two of many emigrants who
worked their way across Guadalupe Pass during 1849 and 1850. And
while their experiences had much in common with all these Argonauts, some of the others wrote of different aspects of this mountain
trail. Benjamin Butler Harris, of the Duval party, was interested in
wild turkeys he saw near the summit. George W. B. Evans of the
Ohio Company called it "Warloop Pass," and wrote that he had
never seen ". . . a place better adapted to Indian ambuscades and
concealment than this. The hills are steep and rugged and the deep,
dark and gloomy ravines almost numberless, and the mountain sides
covered with a growth of low and heavy-topped trees—white and
jack oak, cedar, ebony, and occasionally wild cherry." [32] Lorenzo D.
Aldrich of Albany, New York, complained of having to cross a creek
fifty-two times during one day's travel as they dropped down from
the pass. Two members of the Peoria Company, who hit the pass by
coming northwest of El Paso del Norte and through the Animas
Mountains, wrote of the difficulty they had in getting their wagons
up and down the steep inclines. Casper S. Ricks never forgot how

they let the wagons down with ropes; and Quaker Charles Edward Pancoast always remembered how they drove between eight and ten oxen to the top of a hill, and had them pull the wagons up "... by ropes at least a hundred feet long. ..." [33] But of all the emigrants who crossed the Guadalupe Pass, none left a better description of it than artist H. M. T. Powell of the Illinois Company.

> ... an interminable jumble of peaks, rocks, deep, dark ravines, and gullies in endless confusion, through which no waggon could pass by any possibility. We found the road exceedingly rough; many of the declivities and acclivities being such as appeared almost impracticable. One place in particular it was not only fearfully steep, but it took a very short turn on the outside a steep descent, where to upset was to be utterly lost.[34]

And Powell's fears of the steep descent were brought home to the party before they reached what they believed to be Cooke's old trail. Two of their wagons turned over and a buggy went off the side and landed bottom up.

Wagons turning over, oxen falling in their traces, men straining like beasts of burden trying to save their outfits, and a steady cursing of Cooke's so-called wagon road didn't prevent Powell's observing the beauty of the land. Down from the summit and alongside a creek, he took time to list the kinds of trees he saw: "... walnut, sycamore, cedar, blue ash, scrubby oak, small white mulberry and willow and a scrubby tree with red, smooth bark; the South Carolinians call it Red Skunk; I suppose it is a kind of laurel." [35]

Time out for the classification of trees, time out to do a sketch of a mountain, and time out to enjoy fresh venison cooked over a bed of glowing mesquite and pine coals as the night of endless stars settled early in the deep *barranca*, a night when Powell stretched out on pine needles and heard the far-distant first bark of a coyote as it echoed from mountain wall to mountain wall.

The men of the Illinois Company, like all the other emigrants on the move, had their roots in America's wilderness experience. Even if they hadn't come of age on the frontier, they knew about it. They knew about it through family stories, folk tales, popular accounts, and government reports. The nation was still young enough to feel the pull of the wilderness. Pioneering and hitting the trail across an unknown ridge to an unmapped land for an untapped treasure was a natural American adventure. The man from New York City and the man from a small hamlet next to the Missouri River had this one thing in common. It was the steady attraction to the lonely and unsettled areas on the American map. And here next to a campfire, in the darkness of a Sierra Madre *barranca,* Powell and all the other emigrants felt the steady pull of their heritage.

## BEYOND THE PASS

Between 20 to 25 miles beyond Guadalupe Pass emigrant parties came to the abandoned Rancho San Bernardino. Situated in a basin forming the headquarters of the Yaquí River, the adobe buildings of the ranch were in the shadow of the hills bordering the western side of the valley. H. M. T. Powell wrote that it was a large establishment built within a quadrangle of about three acres. "On the West side are the main building and offices. On the North, a range of houses or rooms extended the whole length. A long bastion is placed at the North East corner, and another at the South West. Near the latter is what we supposed to be a furnace for melting ore." [36]

All the emigrants, soldiers, and other travelers who saw Rancho San Bernardino were duly impressed. Often they were upset that the owners had allowed themselves to be driven off such good land by the Apaches. This typical attitude of Argonauts about giving in to Indians was expressed by John Robert Forsyth of Peoria, Illinois. To him the answer to the Indian problem was to dig in and put up a better fight. After all, here was land worth fighting for: good soil, plenty of water, and abundance of grass for livestock, and tall cottonwoods for timber. With a feeling of superiority over the Mexicans, and absolutely no understanding of the ferocity of the Apache warriors, Forsyth saw the whole problem as one in which the Mexicans were not willing to put up a battle. All the Mexicans ever did was ". . . take to their houses, barricade the doors, and permit the Apaches to take blackmail without molestation. . . ." [37]

But gold seekers didn't face the same terror that the Mexicans did.

They didn't live out each day waiting for a deadly screech, the whirring of an arrow, or the sound of pounding hooves. The man from New York, Boston, Peoria, or New Orleans could take time to examine a deserted *hacienda*. He could hunt wild cattle that had once been domesticated and had belonged to the owners of this ranch. He could write about the fierceness of these longhorn cattle, and tell the folks back home how they ran as fast as a horse, charged through brush thickets as though their hides were like a rhino's, attacked a man at the slightest provocation, and were even hard to drop with a rifle ball.

One of the members of the N. Adams Company told A. B. Clarke of the experience he and a comrade had in killing one of these longhorns. He and a man from Mississippi spotted an old bull grazing on a knoll. Both men dismounted and tied their mules to keep them from running away. Then they stalked the bull until they were within rifle range. Slowly and carefully, both men drew a bead and fired. To their amazement, nothing happened. The animal didn't fall, nor did it run off at the sound of rifle shots. The Mississippian decided to move in closer and fire another shot. Once again the man aimed, fired, and the bull didn't drop. But this time the bull took action. It charged off the knoll and rushed straight down the hill at the astonished hunter. Before the man could move, before his friend could fire another shot, the enraged bull hit the man full force and tossed him into the air. Stunned and gasping for breath, the Mississippian had not even tried to get back on his feet as the bull wheeled in its tracks and lowered its head to gore him. The other Argonaut quickly fired another shot into the wild bull. With blood spurting from its wounds the bull wobbled, gasped, and made one last attempt to move forward, only to drop dead within a few feet of the bruised Mississippian. This story of how fierce a longhorn could be thoroughly convinced A. B. Clarke that these wild cattle were wilder and more dangerous than any buffalo.

Wild and tough as they were, the abandoned cattle of Rancho San Bernardino were a welcome change in diet for the emigrants. Companies of gold seekers feasted on this beef, and many took time to jerk some meat to see them through the leaner miles ahead.

From Rancho San Bernardino the emigrants took between five to seven days to travel the remaining distance from the Sierra Madre heights to the Santa Cruz Valley in northern Sonora. This descent on the Pacific slopes usually covered about 130 miles, and took a route that closely paralleled the present boundary between the State of Sonora, Mexico, and Arizona. The first stop beyond the western hills in back of the deserted *hacienda* was about 25 miles from Rancho San Bernardino at Agua Prieta or Black Water Creek.[38] Most of the emigrants who came over Guadalupe Pass mentioned this creek, and indicated that the trail to it was a good one. After Black Water Creek the trail became more and more of a road. The gold seekers traveled through broken land and moved from the heavy timber country into the warmer regions along the eastern outskirt of the Sonoran Desert. The tributaries of the Río Sonora and the many springs provided them with a surplus of water. There was plenty of grass for their livestock, and wild cattle and game animals to add to their own larder. But all along the way they saw plenty of fresh Indian signs. And while they had not been attacked, they were concerned about the possibility of a raid. To offset this problem, most parties made certain that their guards were constantly vigilant.

Once they were out of the mountains the Argonauts made fast time into Sonora's frontier community of Santa Cruz. Again, as in Corralitos and Janos, they were aware that the daily life in Santa Cruz was dominated by fear of the Apaches. When John E. Durivage, his Negro servant, and a Mexican boy first approached the town on May 23, 1849, they were greeted as though they were an attacking band of Indians. Soldiers rode toward them at a gallop, calling them Apaches. Durivage and his companions turned and were ready to retreat when the soldiers saw who they were and stopped their charge. To Durivage and all the others who passed through the beautiful Santa Cruz Valley, the notion of any people allowing any Indian tribe to keep them in such a state of terror was almost beyond belief. Why? Why, these *gringos* wondered, do these people allow such a thing to take place?

"Did you see their soldiers?" one Argonaut would ask another.

"You mean what they call *soldados*? Ain't they a sight! No wonder the damned Injuns give 'em hell."

"And their rifles, did you see their rifles? Did you ever see rifles that old! Be damned if I'd shoot one. Be afraid it'd blow up in my face."

"That ain't all either, pilgrim. I took a gander inside their fort. What they call a cannon might just barely ease a ball over the wall. And they ain't got more than maybe some forty soldiers, and they spend more time with their uniforms than anything else. You'd think they was getting ready for one of them masked balls."

"I hear they got something like a hundred and fifty soldiers there."

"Aw, hell, maybeso, maybeso, but what's the difference? Jesus, friend, you could have a whole goddamned army of soldiers like that, and they wouldn't even earn their keep. I see this one skinny greaser all dressed up in a fancy uniform standing on top their guard tower today. Be damned. I like to laugh fit to bust a gut. There he is like a lonesome rooster trying to see if any hawks are coming in for the hens."

"Well, at least they keep a lookout."

"Hell, friend, you think that makes a difference? I'd be damned worried and so would you if I had to count on them *soldados* I seen at the fort."

Conversation after conversation would go this way. Few *gringos* considered the Mexicans their equal as human beings. Too many things were different. They were darker. They let priests push them around. They ate strange food. They talked another language, and spoke so fast it was hard to pick up much more than a word or two. But worst of all, the emigrants saw the Mexicans as people who were allowing Apaches to push them right out of their homes. To the self-righteous Yankee, to the Yankee on the move heading for the gold country, the fact that these Mexicans had been fighting a border war for a hundred years or more never struck home. These Yankees were only intruders of the moment, travelers on their way, strangers in a strange land. Few of them understood or made any effort to understand the Mexican culture. It was simpler to criticize, toss everybody into a neat pigeonhole, and get on with the business of going to California.

The gold seekers looked upon Santa Cruz with both delight and despair. After the long dry hauls across the Southwestern plains and the Mexican tableland, and after the hard work of crossing the Sierra Madre, the location of this town was a beautiful sight. The mountains to the east and west were well timbered. The Río Santa Cruz ran a steady and clear stream of water. The valley was broad and fertile, and as they descended the last ridge to the valley floor they saw tall cottonwoods, fruit trees, and cultivated fields of corn and wheat. After all they had been through this was a sudden entrance into paradise. But as they rode and walked into this frontier town their vision of a paradise underwent changes. Closely examined, Santa Cruz—town of the Holy Cross—was tarnished around its edges, a bit run-down, and in places crumbling and very near the edge of collapse.

Most Argonauts who wrote about Santa Cruz described it in much the same manner. Clarke noticed that portions of the town were in ruins. To Durivage, this place was ". . . the poorest of the poor." [39] Pancoast liked its location but thought the town was on the scrawny side. Others, like Aldridge and Harris, mentioned the fear of Apaches that pervaded the atmosphere. Ricks complained that the ". . . Governor of Sonora had ordered a duty of $40 to be levied . . ." [40] on each wagon passing through—a duty Ricks never paid. Another thing which rankled the gold seekers was that they had difficulty in purchasing supplies or felt they were taken by jacked-up prices.

To these Yankees the people of Santa Cruz were indolent and stubborn. All they wanted was to get as much money as they could from the passing emigrants. What could any white man expect from such people? They were all alike, no matter where a man went. No wonder they couldn't beat the damned Indians. On and on it would go. The *gringo* didn't understand why these people didn't do things the way they were done in the States. He never comprehended the game of bargaining for goods, and he usually paid the first price asked. He paid it, and then complained that *all* Mexicans were thieves. The damned "greasers" were just out for all they could get.

Yet even with no understanding of the culture, even though they paid the highest possible prices for anything and everything they purchased, the Argonauts were getting a bargain they would yearn for when they reached California. John Forsyth of the Peoria Company wrote that vendors charged him one cent apiece for apples and peaches, that eggs were the same price, and that he paid twenty-five cents for a whole chicken. A member of the Little Rock Company bragged that he traded about seventy-five cents' worth of cheap jewelry for ". . . two and one-half bushels of unbolted flour, several pounds of sugar, and several other little articles." [41] What everything really came down to was that the gold seekers were weary of their journey, tired of trying to speak a foreign language, disgusted with what they considered to be an inferior people who were thieves by nature, repulsed by the domination of the Catholic Church, and concerned that all the gold would be gone by the time they reached California.

Yet there were exceptions to the rule. There were Argonauts who enjoyed their stopover in Santa Cruz. Such a man was John Robert Forsyth of Peoria, Illinois. He visited the church, commented on its Gothic architecture and the lifelike statues of holy figures adorning the interior. He was intrigued with Mexican women, attended a *fandango,* and never forgot the gaudy and gay style of clothing worn by both sexes. During his visit he saw all that he could. He went into a saddle shop, a blacksmith shop, and even visited "... three or four shoemakers all making fine light shoes for ladies. ..." [42] He was interested in the native method of carrying firewood in a huge pile on a burro, examined the construction of a *carreta,* looked over the barracks, observed the grass roofs of the houses which gave them a distant "... appearance of small patches of wheat ...," [43] and watched the women washing clothing and bathing in the Río Santa Cruz.

Quite unlike most men who passed this way, Forsyth was totally aware of the Apache menace and what it had done to this community. And as he and his party left Santa Cruz and rode northwest toward Tucson, he entered in his journal that "... it looked melancholy to see fine old Houses with large fruit trees planted around & every indication of a once flourishing place to see nothing now but the hateful Buzzards & the prowling wolf." [44]

## THE ROAD TO TUCSON

From Santa Cruz to Tucson is a little more than 100 miles. Travelers usually averaged about 20 miles per day on this stretch. Some took less time, some took more. The determining factors for the time of this journey were up to the individuals. Some men were too tired to move quickly. Some suffered too much from the desert heat, as they usually reached this region in late summer or early fall. A few curious emigrants took time out to visit and examine the remains of old Spain that marked this route: Tumacacori Mission, Tubac, and San Xavier del Bac.

An easy day's journey from Santa Cruz brought the gold seekers to Tumacacori Mission. The strange name which the men couldn't pronounce was a Pima Indian word that meant "curved peak." It had been the name of the Pima village when Father Eusebio Francisco Kino first visited it in 1690–91. However, Tumacacori Mission wasn't built until the early 1800s, and the guiding hand for this work was that of Father Narcisco Gutiérrez. The *padre* and his Pimas constructed a building that would last, and would withstand Apache raids. But they never quite finished the bell tower or the cemetery's mortuary chapel. This was a puzzle—especially the unfinished bell tower—to the emigrants who passed this way. Equally puzzling to them was that there were no *padres*. What the *gringos* didn't know was that the combination of Mexico's Independence in 1821 and the constant terrorizing of the valley by Apaches had driven all missionaries away. When the Yankees first saw Tumacacori standing in its isolated glory in the Santa Cruz Valley, flanked by the western slopes of the Santa Rita Mountains, it was as though they had discovered a plague-stricken settlement. Everything gave the appearance of a sudden vanishing. To make the situation even more mysterious, Tumacacori Mission was cared for and watched over by the willing converts who awaited the return of the Black Robes.

Powell of the Illinois Company took time out to visit Tumacacori Mission. He sketched it showing its arched and graceful entrance; the unfinished bell tower that looked as though it might have fallen during a frantic battle against the Apaches; the heavy, thick walls; the high, narrow, deep-set windows; the tall white dome over the altar at the north end of the church; the walled cemetery behind the north end of the building; and all the surrounding structures that made up this mission. In addition to his sketch, Powell wrote a detailed description of Tumacacori. This included a rough measurement of the interior, a word picture of the carved, gilded, and painted altar dome; and a passing comment that one of the three bells had fallen to the floor from the square tower. Then, like many men who visited the old mission, Powell took a key which he intended to keep as a souvenir. But the taking of a key was nothing compared to what other emigrants did. Many of them camped overnight inside the church, built their fires on the floor, and corralled their livestock within the walled cemetery.

An easy day's ride beyond Tumacacori travelers came to the Presidio of San Ignacio de Tubac. Established in 1752 to guard Spain's missionary efforts in northwestern Mexico, Tubac was already in bad shape when it was visited fourteen years later by the Marqués de Rubí and his inspection team on December 20, 1766. There was a shortage of guns, lances, and swords; and the four-pounder cannons were ". . . neither good looking nor well made." [45] But what the Spanish inspection team considered poor military equipment was first-rate compared to what the Argonauts found at Tubac.

When the Illinois Company saw it in October of 1849, H. M. T. Powell didn't even consider it worth sketching. He commented that its roof was missing, that the walls were filled with holes for muskets, and summed up his feeling by calling it ". . . a mere pile of tumble-down adobe houses." [46]

Benjamin Butler Harris of the Duval Company noticed the many bullet marks on the walls of the buildings. Harris also picked up a story from somebody that only about six months prior to their arrival, hundreds of Apaches had attacked Tubac and rode away only after incredible butchery turned the outpost into a bloody slaughterhouse. Whether such a battle had taken place or not didn't really matter, for as the California emigrants learned, Tubac had been raided time and again by the Apaches. Tubac and disaster were synonymous, and the emigrants quickly passed through this place that reeked of death.

The landscape of the Sonoran Desert made its first impact upon the emigrants outside Tubac. Here, as they continued on to Tucson, they left the cottonwoods, willows, fruit trees, and the fertile land of the Santa Cruz Valley. All around them the country was dry, sandy, and barren. Cacti of many types replaced trees. Mesquite and the grease-wood hugged close to the earth, and the heat of summer or early fall made each mile into a series of painful and almost sickening forward steps. To add to the traveler's misery, there was very little drinking water once the road veered away from the Río Santa Cruz, and a man had to be extremely careful if he wished to get away from the burning sun in the limited shade of a mesquite. This was rattlesnake country, and every spot that offered any shade at all was bound to have rattlers.

Without question, one of the most intriguing sights for the California emigrants on this stretch of trail was the giant saguaro. John Forsyth even took time to measure one. He found the saguaro he picked for this honor was thirty-five feet, five inches tall, and that it had a circumference of twelve feet, four inches. Forsyth was astounded by this cactus. He counted the fluted indentations that were so much like a Corinthian column, and found there were twenty-nine. Then he made the following notation in his journal: "I could liken it to nothing but some stupendous deity of the Hindoos." [47]

The very nature of the Sonoran Desert seemed to cause men to reach for similes and metaphors that possessed some religious connotation. And no wonder, for the world they trekked through might well have come out of the Old Testament. All about them were strange plants. Mirages played tricks with distance, size, and reality itself. Added to this was what the *padres* had left behind—the truly incredible Catholic churches built by missionaries and now occupied by faithful Indians awaiting the return of these Spanish shamans. All these things contributed to a sense of mysticism that touched even the most cynical and destructive. And the pinnacle of this experience for these men was just 9 miles south of Tucson. It was the mission San Xavier del Bac; the mission that was called by some La Paloma Blanca del Desierto or the White Dove of the Desert.

Founded by Father Kino in 1700, San Xavier del Bac took its name from Saint Francis Xavier, Apostle of the Indies, and from the Pima word "bac," which meant a well or spring of water. Long before the gold rush the mission had changed from Jesuit to Franciscan control, when the Jesuit order was expelled from Mexico in the summer of 1767. In the years between then and the final collapse of Spain in the New World, the Franciscans built and decorated what turned out to be the most magnificent mission in the Southwest. It was this monument to a Christian God, guarded by pagan Papagos, that startled and amazed the weary Argonauts.

When Durivage passed by this mission in the latter part of May, 1849, he thought it a grand building that, no doubt, had been constructed at a high cost. He looked at its interior walls covered with paintings. Then in a mood of sadness, he wrote, "... solemn mass is no longer heard within its walls, and smell of mold has displaced the fragrant fumes from the burning censer." [48] Powell of the Illinois Company also noticed these paintings, but his feeling about them differed from those of Durivage. To Powell not one had any real worth. Nor was he impressed with the images of saints. But he thought it was a fine building even if the roof leaked and allowed water to run down the walls and over the paintings.

Of all the emigrants who stopped to look at San Xavier del Bac, Forsyth was truly impressed by what he saw. To him the Moorish quality of the mission with its spires, domes, and minarets was highly unusual. Added to this, he was entranced with the paintings, statues, carvings, Gothic entrances, marble floors, and the fine garden surrounded by a stone-capped brick wall. He thought the church was an incredible mixture of influences that only could be matched in the Holy Land itself. Finally, in an almost typical American concern for facts, he took time to count 300 statues that were nearly life-size. As for the paintings, he wrote, ". . . they were almost countless . . . Domes, Ceilings & all were covered with them." [49]

Yet no matter how much Forsyth, Powell, Durivage, and other emigrants admired what they saw at this mission, the mark of the vandal marred the passing of the Argonauts. The stolen painting—later dropped in the Colorado Desert—the smashed statue, the missing part of a carving, and the inevitable names, dates, and trail news items cut in the adobe walls or wooden pillars with a bowie knife—all signified that the ignorant and the defilers also made the great trek to California.

La Paloma Blanca del Desierto was the final place of beauty on the northern branch of the El Dorado Trail. Less than a day's ride from there the Argonauts came to Tucson—the last Mexican town they would see on their trip. Unfortunately, Tucson offered very little in the way of man-made beauty, and its surrounding desert terrain was not admired by men who had a lot of desert yet to cross. At best, Tucson was a place to pick up information about the trail ahead and to barter for supplies. At worst, Tucson was under constant threat of Apache attack, for this Sonoran *pueblo* was ". . . the most northern presidio of the frontier. . . ." [50] More than once this Mexican outpost had been besieged by as many as ". . . 1,000 to 2,000 warriors." [51] It was not a place in which to linger, and the emigrants didn't see it as one.

Robert Noble and his mule herd stayed in Tucson only one day. The Little Rock Company quickly passed through, but did take time out to comment that the Apaches kept the inhabitants inside the town. Durivage thought the saguaro cacti more interesting than the town. Benjamin Hayes observed that the town had a couple of blacksmith shops and a shoe factory. John Forsyth watched a funeral and was fascinated by the ceremonies. Benjamin Harris mentioned that he saw at least four or five hundred other Argonauts in the little town during his two-day stop there. A. B. Clarke looked with wonder at Indian baskets woven tightly enough to hold milk and other liquids. And as he rode out of the *pueblo* on a hot June 1, 1849, he "... purchased a basket of milk, holding more than two quarts...," [52] and poured it into a gourd that he tied to his saddle. If any general attitude can be applied to most emigrants who passed through Tucson on their California journey, it was "stated" by the artist H. M. T. Powell—who did not think it worth sketching.

Tucson was a town of flat-roofed adobe houses smack in the middle of a nowhere that had become a somewhere to gold-fevered men. Tucson was a somewhere to get extra water, extra melons, and extra food of any kind. Tucson was somewhere to ask about the trail ahead. And while descriptions of the trail to the Gila and the Colorado did not sound pleasant nor easy, nobody said it was long. And most important of all, at Tucson men heard about Mexicans who had already returned from California with as much gold as they could carry. All that gold just waiting to be picked up, became even more important with only some 250 miles left to travel to reach the Colorado crossing and the entrance to California. The emigrants knew the trail ahead was through part of America's Great Desert and would not be easy. But they'd already been through country that might have been a model for the canyons and plains of Hell. So, with an anxious *adiós* they headed out of Tucson and hit the Gila Trail.

## THE GILA TRAIL

Trail driver Robert Noble knew all the tricks for getting through the desert, and he left the vicinity of Tucson in the second week of May, 1849, before the blistering summer heat set in. Noble was prepared for the worst between his Tucson camp and the Río Gila. He and his fourteen trail hands filled water kegs with about 150 gallons. He didn't want any of his men or mules dropping on the trail for need of water. At five o'clock in the evening he gave the order to move out.

All that first night Noble and his trail herders moved northwest toward the Río Gila. At ten o'clock the next morning he called a halt. Through the heat of the day he and his men camped and rested. In the early evening, as the sun began to set, they moved on. By the next morning they arrived at the Gila in good shape. Noble calculated they had traveled 105 miles through ". . . a perfect desert where there is nothing for man or beast to eat or drink." [53]

But like others who left Tucson and struck out on the Gila Trail, Noble and his men only had entered the desert. The fact that the Gila at least provided water was one of two positive things he could count on before he reached its confluence with the Río Colorado. The other aid for travelers in this desolate country was the existence of the Pima and Coco-Maricopa Indian villages scattered along the Gila.

Noble and the other emigrants who rushed through this area on their way to California were happy to discover that these friendly farmers of the Gila had become accustomed to the appearance of strangers of a different color long before the gold rush. The first wandering strangers they had seen had been the surviving members of Cabeza de Vaca's party—including Estevánico, the giant Negro slave. And these strangers, who would touch off the search for the Seven Cities of Cíbola, had visited these Indian villages just about 300 years prior to the discovery of gold in California.

In this country of bare and sandy earth, this country of cactus, isolated clumps of mesquite, greasewood, and sagebrush, there was little to break the vision of desolation other than the sparse and occasional growth of willows, cottonwoods, and rank grass that grew in some places next to the river. And the Río Gila wasn't anything to write home about. Rather, it was more like a meandering line of brown, liquid mud. Yet the Pimas and the Coco-Maricopas built their villages next to this river, and used its water to irrigate crops of corn, melons, beans, pumpkins, peas, and other fruits and vegetables. These crops in this wasteland were never forgotten by the men who were just passing by. Travelers remembered that these gardeners of the Gila, these farmers of the desert, were lifesavers in every sense of the word.

Most Argonauts liked these Indian farmers very much, and had the highest praise for them. However, as in all meetings between the emigrants and the Indians, there were always some whites who did not trust any Indian. Yet even these biased critics traded goods with them for food, and admitted they were peaceful.

When Durivage first saw the Pimas, he had almost perished and was totally exhausted. Some miles before reaching the Gila, he had given up and lain down to die. All that saved him was the courage and concern of his Negro servant who forged ahead to the Gila, got water, brought it back, revived Durivage, and helped him the rest of the way. As Durivage recovered, he observed the Pimas, and considered them a very handsome people. "The men," he wrote, "are well formed and athletic, the women bright eyed, talkative, and symmetrical. The prevailing costume is the breechcloth for the man, and a scant serape, or blanket, pinned around the loins of the women, reaching nearly to the knees." [54]

Yet even though these Indians were a great help to the emigrants, one dreadful fact remained. It was a long *jornada* between Tucson and the Pima Villages alongside the Gila. Many men almost died on this trip, and others did. All along the way, dead livestock, discarded wagons and supplies marked the Gila Trail. When A. B. Clarke traveled this route the weather was so hot he could hardly bear it. He and his exhausted companions walked and stumbled through the sand, following one another's dust clouds, trying to avoid thorny plants and buzzing rattlesnakes that seemed to be beneath anything that offered the least bit of shade. Then, as their mules gradually gave out, Clarke later recalled that most of the suffering animals were shot. Clarke avoided this, but when he could no longer stand his mule's soft, choking neigh for help he did what he could. He took his leather water container, found it had lost half its load because of leakage, but still went to his mule's aid and gave the animal what little water he had.

Upon reaching the Gila and the first villages of the Pimas, many gold seekers decided there had to be an easier way. Taking a heavily loaded wagon the rest of the way wasn't worth it. They were next to a river. Why not use it? Camps were pitched, and men with know-how went to work. Pimas with long thick hair twisted like horsehair ropes atop their heads, their bodies naked from the waist up, gathered around these strange men and watched. They watched with great curiosity as the men began to take their wagons apart to build

rafts and flat-bottom boats. The Indians gathered up the extra supplies the emigrants had dumped to make the wagons lighter, and
they watched with great interest as the gold seekers launched their
strange boats to become sailors of the Gila.

Of all such voyages, one of the most unusual took place in the fall
of 1849. The Peoria Company had made its way to just beyond the
Great Bend of the Gila. But the party was beginning to break up.
Some members had better horses and mules, and they wanted to
hurry on at a faster pace. Two men—Eugene and Myron Angel [55]—
decided they could move even faster by walking, and they made up
eighty-pound packs for themselves, and took off across the desert
on a hike that very nearly proved their undoing. Another faction of
the Peoria Company set up a tent under the broiling sun, posted a
sentinel, and held a secret Masonic meeting in which they determined to leave their slower companions to fend for themselves.
When all the splitting-up was over, Quaker Charles Edward Pancoast said that he and the others were left with ". . . all the 'Crippled
Ducks' to take care of." [56] Well, maybe their animals *were* giving
out; and maybe they couldn't shoulder a pack and walk off, but
there was nothing that prevented a bunch of "Crippled Ducks"
from taking to water in good fashion.

They built two rafts from the sideboards of their wagons, fashioned oars, attached ropes for lines, made do with two stone an-
chors, and erected a shed on one raft to shelter a Missourian's
pregnant wife. All this took five days. Then, on November 5, 1849,
they were ready to go. A few men were sent on ahead with the
lighter wagons and the livestock to wait at the Río Colorado. The
rafts were launched, and the voyage began. Pancoast went with the
wagon men, and by the time they reached the Colorado the four
men and one woman who had taken the rafts had been waiting for
them for six days. The voyage, they said, had been easy and there
really wasn't much worth mentioning.

Nothing worth mentioning, ". . . except that on the third day out
the Woman was taken with Labor Pains." [57] They quickly landed
their makeshift boats on a sandbar next to a thicket of willows. Here
the husband took some blankets and pillows, carried his wife to
what seclusion there was, and delivered her of a baby girl while the
others waited on the boats. That evening the other men came ashore
and helped the new father carry his wife and child back on board.

The next morning they continued on their voyage with the little baby girl that all the men wanted to name Gila. The second day after giving birth the baby's mother was once again preparing the meals for the men, and continued to do so during the rest of the voyage.

For companies who did not build boats or rafts, the trip alongside the Gila to its junction with the Colorado proved to be a route marked with the stench of dead oxen, mules, and horses that were being eaten by turkey buzzards. All along the trail were the droppings of parties in distress: yokes, chains, wagons, spare axles, cooking utensils, mining equipment, gunpowder, firearms, fishhooks, and even buttons. The soil the men and their animals moved through was sandy dust with the consistency of ashes. "All our camps are 'dust holes.' We eat dust, drink dust, breathe dust, and sleep in dust!" [58]

To the overland companies the march along the Gila was a march through a kind of desert they had only imagined. Yet even in their imaginations they had never conjured a true picture of what it was like to cross such a land. Dust, sand, a botanical world of thorny plants and trees, distant mountains that looked like the work of evil stonemasons and gave no indication of water or life—this was the Gila Trail. And in 1849 and 1850 the Argonauts traveled it in great numbers. During the clear desert nights the route was outlined up and down the Río Gila by campfires. The flickering golden markers were like a crooked chain of nuggets—a chain of men with a golden dream, a chain of men bound for the Colorado crossing and the riches of California.

## ACROSS THE RÍO COLORADO IS CALIFORNIA

Throughout mankind's history the crossing of rivers has marked a shedding of boundaries, an advance into a new or strange land, and the change of individual and national destinies. Thus for the Argonauts the Río Colorado was the final step on their quest. On one side of the river was Mexico, and behind these men was the long journey they had traveled. On the opposite shore was California and what these emigrants thought would be a short trip to the fulfillment of a golden dream.

They gathered on the banks of the river. Here at the confluence of two desert rivers—the Gila and the Colorado—the men following the northern branch of the El Dorado Trail through Mexico came together. They met and exchanged news, laughed and joked about their experiences with the Spanish language and the Mexican customs, made light of adventures that had almost proved fatal. But they were almost silent about the dead, and tried to remember only the good things, those things that still gave life to companions lost in the desert or buried in a foreign town or alongside the trail. They talked about the trail ahead, the trail in California; and compared information as they tried to sort out the truth. They exchanged news about parties of Mexicans who were already returning from California with saddlebags and pack saddles filled with gold. They joked about using pods from mesquite trees to feed their horses, mules, and oxen; discussed methods of crossing the river; wondered whether or not they could trust the Yuma Indians who had offered their services to swim their animals across; agreed it was a good thing that the United States Boundary Commission had stationed soldiers on the California side of the river at Camp Calhoun. They knew the soldiers would protect them, give food to people running short, suggest the shortest and easiest route to the gold country, and help them cross the river into California.

All this was true for gold seekers who reached the Colorado crossing no earlier than the last week in September of 1849. For others, they simply had to make it on their own as they had all along the trail. Camp Calhoun (named for Senator John C. Calhoun) was not established until October 2, 1849. At that time Lieutenant Cave Johnson Couts and a company of the First Dragoons, who were guarding Lieutenant Amiel W. Whipple's survey party, opened this forerunner of Fort Yuma at the site of the old Spanish mission, Puerto de la Purísima Concepción. The purpose of Camp Calhoun and its soldiers was threefold. They were to offer protection and aid to the soldiers and scientists of the boundary commission, watch over the various Indian tribes, and help the weary and worn gold seekers on their way to California.

Camp Calhoun proved to be a constant headache as far as Lieutenant Couts was concerned, but for Argonauts it was both a morale booster and a lifesaver. However, Lieutenant Couts never met the early emigrants of 1849; and in general he had a very poor opinion of gold seekers. His opinion might have been somewhat different if he had talked to the very self-sufficient Robert Noble, to tough Harvey Wood of the Kit Carson Association, to Dr. Oliver Meredith Wozencraft, who ferried the river in an oxhide bull-boat, or to journalists like John E. Durivage of the New Orleans *Daily Picayune,* and John S. Robb of the St. Louis *Weekly Reveille.* Still, Lieutenant Couts had always tended to be a kind of ramrod personality. Any looseness or laxness in behavior was more than he could stand. His report of his unfortunate march through Mexico with the Second Dragoons and the drunken Major Lawrence P. Graham indicated only too well that Couts was a man who could not tolerate what he considered to be any sign of weakness.

The first view Lieutenant Couts had of the Colorado was when the Second Dragoons reached it on November 22, 1848. At that time Couts was seething at having to take orders from Major Graham, but he did notice a small party of Mexican miners returning from California with gold. Then as the Second Dragoons slowly moved across the Colorado Desert, Couts said, ". . . Mexicans, from Sonora, are passing us daily on their way to the *abundancia,* the gold mines! This is all we can hear, The Mines!" [59] What Couts didn't know, at that time, was that the Mexican miners from the State of Sonora had already taken a considerable amount of gold from the Mother Lode, and were only returning to Mexico to get their families. But while Couts thought this early rush of miners was large, the next year, as he recrossed the Colorado Desert and built Camp Calhoun, it seemed to him that the trail had become a crowded road with thousands of Forty-Niners on the move. Worst of all, most of them were on the edge of starvation, and near the end of their endurance.

Lieutenant Couts wrote at great length in his journal of the troubles he had with the Argonauts. To him they were a constant bother. They wanted him to make maps for them, give them directions, listen to their tales of how the Yumas had stolen their livestock; and then they would beg him for extra food, and even had the gall to steal U. S. Army mules and blame the Yumas for it. Yet Couts was under orders to help these people, and help them he did, even though he thought that most of them weren't worth the trouble.

Mostly, Lieutenant Couts had far greater respect for the tall, muscular Yumas who swam livestock across the Colorado River for a fee, and frequently were cheated out of that by the gold seekers, whose attitude toward the Indians was one of disdain, distrust, and dislike. As Couts saw it, the emigrants constantly provoked the Indians.

But as in most of his generalizations, Lieutenant Couts had a tendency to lump the weak and strong, the good and bad, into one category. He was too much of a perfect West Point product to realize that his concept of human behavior didn't always apply to civilians, or even to fellow Army officers. Yet even with this attitude, and to a great extent because of it, Couts proved to be a great aid to the emigrants at the Colorado crossing.

The river crossing was no easy matter, and many men and animals were drowned in the attempt. George Evans of the Ohio Company described the river as he saw it on the first of September in 1849, and he thought it was "... about two hundred yards wide, with a five-mile current. ..." [60] Melting snow in the faraway mountains had kept the river level high and swift during the late spring and early summer, and Evans observed the damp beach marks of higher water that had receded not too long before their arrival at the crossing. Then, in a matter-of-fact fashion, he stated that the place they selected for their crossing was not nearly as wide as others which sometimes reached a maximum width of 2 miles during the heavy run-off season.

But more than Evans or the others who were strictly overland men without the ability to cope with river crossings, it was men like Boat-wagon Harris who set the pattern for dealing with the Río Colorado. Harris sailed all the way down the Gila, and arrived at its junction with the Colorado after Lieutenant Couts had established Camp Calhoun. When Couts saw Harris's boat-wagon, he offered him $75 for it. Harris turned him down, but while he was at the Colorado he did earn sixty silver dollars for ferrying a company of Mexicans across. The temptation to stay at the crossing and pile up money as a ferryman entered Harris's mind, but he felt he could make even more money by getting on to the gold mines.

During Boat-wagon Harris's short stay at the Colorado crossing the river claimed the lives of four men. The tragedy struck when Captain Herman Thorn and three of his men tried to cross the river on two log canoes lashed together. The swift current upset their craft, and before anyone could act the four men were swept downstream and drowned. Captain Thorn's body was recovered and given a temporary burial. But about three weeks later, in the second week of November, the body was uncovered and Couts sent it on to San Diego. As in all his other reactions, Lieutenant Couts followed the rule book to the letter. Along with the body he sent the following letter to Major William H. Emory:

Major:
I have succeeded in making a box that will probably carry the remains of the lament Captain Thorn to San Diego. In the absence of all material and conveniences for effecting this desired object properly, my carpenters have done better than I expected of them. I send the whole under the charge of Mr. Wiatt, a citizen, with one of my teamsters and a dragoon. They will procure a fresh team at Salvation Camp, and should reach San Diego by the 23rd instant. It will not, of course, be necessary for the teamster and dragoon to return.

I have the honor to be, your obedient servant,[61]

After the tragic death of Captain Thorn and his men it became obvious that the powerful Yuman swimmers were the only men who could safely fight the rapid waters of the Colorado. The only solution to the dangers of this crossing was to find a safer method of navigating the river. So, taking his cue from Boat-wagon Harris, Lieutenant Couts and his soldiers established a ferry service for the emigrants. This cut down on deaths from drowning, just as the presence of soldiers cut down on the occasional death of an emigrant at the hands of the Yumas.

The ferryboat was built upstream on the Gila by a man called Moore who sold it to the Army. The fare for crossing was set on a double-standard basis: one fare for Americans, another fare for Mexicans. Both Americans and Mexicans paid $4 per wagon and 50 cents per man, but Americans only paid $1 per head for livestock while Mexicans paid $4 per head. Furthermore, if the Mexicans were returning from California they were charged a tax on the gold they were carrying. The idea of taxing the Mexicans didn't come from Lieutenant Couts, nor did he like the notion nor follow it to the letter.

Couts had been issued this order by Colonel James Collier, who had been with Captain Thorn's party, and who was on his way to San Francisco to assume his post as newly appointed Collector of Customs. As Couts put it, Collier gave him the following order: "...make all the Sonoranians passing out of California with gold, pay a duty on the same, and for my trouble, to put the whole of it in my pocket. Certainly!" [62] The amount of money could have been considerable. Not only did the Mexicans have the techniques of how to get gold out of the earth, but between 1848 and 1850 Mexicans came north to California at the rate of about 10,000 persons each year.

Estimates of the number of Americans who crossed the Colorado into California during these same years vary considerably. Though any examination of journals, diaries, letters, newspaper stories, and other accounts makes it clear that during 1849–1850 the number must have been quite large. Perhaps a conservative estimate for those years is that at least 10,000 Americans used this route. Most of these emigrants traveled through some part of Mexico either by intention or by an ignorance of geography. However, they did know that one of the major points on their maps was the confluence of the Gila and Colorado rivers.

Considering the number of Americans and Mexicans who crossed the Río Colorado at this point, it is understandable that more than one man decided to cash in on the need for ferry service. Among such men was Dr. A. L. Lincoln of Illinois, a relative of Abraham Lincoln. Dr. Lincoln had come to California through Mexico in 1849, but returned to the Colorado and started his ferry service at the beginning of 1850.

In good faith, Dr. Lincoln hired nine able-bodied men who had just come out of Mexico and wanted to earn some money before they traveled on to California. What he didn't know was that he had hired the notorious scalp hunter John Glanton and his men. This turned into a fatal error, as Glanton quickly assumed the position of authority and ordered his men to destroy the ferryboat the Yumas were using in their business. The Yuma chief tried to avoid conflict, and offered to split the business with Glanton, telling him that the Yumas would swim all livestock across the river and that Lincoln's ferry could take all baggage and men across. Glanton's reaction to this proposition was typical of the man. He kicked the chief out of his hut and beat him over the head with a stick. But the Yuma chief

165

was the last Indian that Glanton ever mistreated. That night the Yumas killed the scalp hunter, Dr. Lincoln, and all but three of the ferrymen, who managed to escape and make their way to California.

The Colorado crossing was not usually that violent. Though this brief Yuman uprising caused enough fear in California, so that Governor Peter Burnett sent something over sixty men under the command of General Joseph C. Morehead of the State Militia to chastise the Yumas and guard the emigrants. On the way to the Colorado this makeshift army grew as it picked up volunteers from emigrant parties. By the time it reached the crossing what was to become known as the "Gila Expedition" had grown to an army of about 125 men. The outcome of this defense of a dead scalp hunter—a man the army wouldn't have associated with had he been alive—was a long march, not one Indian killed, and a debt for the new State of California of $120,000.

Before and after the "Gila Expedition" or the "Glanton War," crossing the Colorado was an act of arriving. The Argonauts wouldn't listen to Lieutenant Cave Couts or anyone else about the journey ahead. Across the Colorado was California. Once they had crossed the river they were within striking distance of that quick and easy fortune that awaited them in the Mother Lode. They'd been told about the Colorado Desert, but it was only 90 or 100 miles across. Sure, they'd heard all the stories about sand dunes over fifteen feet tall. But they knew about Cooke's Wells; they knew a miracle had occurred in the desert—water had cut through the banks of the Colorado far upstream and formed New River near what was now called Camp Salvation; and they knew they had come this far, so they could stand a little more hardship to reach their journey's end.

What they wouldn't believe was that it was going to be more than a *little* hardship before they crawled out of the Colorado Desert. It was going to be a season in Hell. Men and animals would drop alongside each other for lack of water. Cooke's Wells would be hard to find, and if found, would turn out to be all right for a small number of men and mules. But these wells and others never had enough water for the thousands of dry throats and swollen tongues. And some waterholes would be covered with green scum and mosquitos, or might even be polluted by bloated and half-eaten carcasses of dead mules and oxen. Then, as if to make an insane jest of their own time in the sun, some emigrants left a weird sight for others to see.

These men mocked death by standing dry, almost mummified horses, mules, and oxen in a line alongside the trail as ghostly markers on a deadly path.

The brave companies of men, women, and children had arrived in the promised land. Once across the river it was only a matter of a few weeks more of overland travel. After that, all the companies would be busy picking up golden nuggets. After all the hardships, all the weary months, the dream of El Dorado was in reach. Company after company, man after man crossed the Río Colorado. There were companies named after states: New York, Ohio, Missouri; companies named after towns: Hampden, Massachusetts; Peoria, Illinois; Victoria, Texas; and companies named after individuals: John Audubon's Company, Captain Duval's Company, and the Kit Carson Association. All these companies had names that were familiar to them, names to remind them of a place they knew, or a person they believed in even if he really wasn't along to lead them through the wilderness. And once across the Colorado, these emigrants felt the elation of having done what had been romantic at the beginning, then tiring, plodding, and finally a daily match with death in their day-by-day push onward.

But like everything else on the northern branch of the El Dorado Trail, the last barrier turned out to be almost the final and complete barrier. The golden color in their eyes turned out to be the glare of a fiery sun. The *real* El Dorado was still ahead. Worse yet, it was hiding in the earth. Crossing the Colorado only meant the Argonauts were that much closer to the elusive El Dorado. It didn't mean they had arrived—for yet ahead of them was the final *jornada del muerto*.

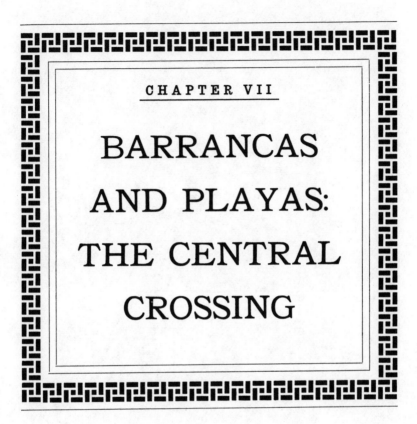

CHAPTER VII

# BARRANCAS AND PLAYAS: THE CENTRAL CROSSING

# FALSE TRAIL SIGNS

The combination of deception, misinformation, and wishful thinking formed the mental mirage for men who followed the northern branch of the El Dorado Trail, but these men had no monopoly on ignorance or self-delusion. Argonauts who elected to take the central crossing to Mexico's Pacific Coast seaports also were followers of false trail signs.

Albert Maver Winn—a natural frontiersman from Vicksburg, Mississippi—and Joseph Wyatt McGaffey, a gentleman from New Hampshire, were companions on the northern branch of the central crossing between Corpus Christi and Mazatlán. Their route took them through Parras, across the Central Plateau to Durango, and over the Sierra Madre Occidental to Mazatlán. Others who followed the same route, or a variation of it, were such different personalities as Dr. Lewis C. Gunn, a Philadelphia physician; William Perkins, a gentleman from Canada; Samuel McNeil, a rustic cobbler; George McKnight and the men from Perrysburg, Ohio; Thomas B. Eastland and son Joseph from Nashville, Tennessee; W. Augustus Knapp, who had been restored to health by "The Great Western"; and none other than the notorious Parker H. French.

The southern branch of the central crossing had its beginning either at Tampico or Guadalajara, depending upon whether the gold seeker was coming west from Tampico or northwest from Mexico City. The ultimate destination of this branch of the trail was the Pacific Coast seaport of San Blas. Among the men who took the Tampico route were ex-Reverend Daniel B. Woods and that incredible master of misspelling, Thomas Sayre. Heading northwest out on the Mexico City–Guadalajara route were elderly Daniel Wadsworth Coit, who carried his sketch pad and watched out for a load of coins he was taking to California to trade for gold; ex–Santa Fé trader Josiah Gregg; and New Englander J. A. Perry, who possessed an uncanny ability to find bad food and poor lodging.

Not all these gold seekers were optimistic questers, but most fell into that classification. And while the central Mexico crossing looked more like a road than a trail on the maps they had purchased in the States, more than one man had a pang of doubt brought on by the smart question the guy who stayed home had asked: "Why's this fellow selling you a map and a guidebook to a gold mine? Seems to me if it was all that easy he'd be picking up gold in California and not wasting time drawing maps and writing books about how to get there."

But if these travelers of the central crossing never struck it rich in California, they did leave a fortune in their recollections about this crazy journey. Their stories interweave like a strange design for a madman's patchwork quilt. For these were the men of the trail, and they saw things in their own special way. Sometimes they looked through fevered eyes, sometimes through fear, exhaustion, or a vision of endless trekking, and sometimes through sheer curiosity and joy.

## TRUE TO THE BREED

If ever a man qualified as pioneer stock, as a man true to the breed, his name was Albert Maver Winn. Born in 1810 in Virginia, young Winn was thirteen years old when he helped drive the family's livestock across the Allegheny Mountains to Ohio.

When he was twenty years old Winn married a girl from Zanesville, Ohio. During their first year of marriage he took his pregnant wife, three apprentice carpenters, and a load of lumber aboard a flatboat. The honeymoon voyage, such as it was, took place on the Muskingum, Ohio, and Mississippi rivers. By the time the flatboat reached Louisville, Kentucky, Mrs. Winn gave birth to their first son.

At Vicksburg, Mississippi, Albert Winn gave all the signs of settling down to a town life. He sold the doors and window frames he and his apprentices had fashioned out of the lumber during their river trip, and he sold his flatboat. He became a resident of Vicksburg and set up shop as a carpenter and builder. As the first years passed, Albert Winn became involved in local politics as a Jackson Democrat, joined the First Regiment of Mississippi Militia, and by 1845 had become a colonel. He was an election judge ". . . when Jefferson Davis was elected Colonel of the First Mississippi Regiment of Volunteers for the Mexican War." [1]

By 1849, Albert Maver Winn was thirty-nine years old, a solid family man, well established in business, and a local political leader. He appeared to be a most unlikely candidate for a gold rush. Yet with the American call to adventure in the air, Winn couldn't resist. Vicksburg was home and success, but it wasn't El Dorado. And the call to strike out for California had come from a man much like himself. It had appeared as a newspaper ad placed by that empire builder of the Texas Gulf Coast, Henry Lawrence Kinney.

Kinney had no intention of making the trip to California, but he was a first-rate promoter anxious to funnel emigrants into his newly dredged harbor at Corpus Christi. His motives were anything but altruistic, but he was not a flim-flam man. The ad he ran in his own newspaper, the Corpus Christi *Star*, and ones he ran in other newspapers from New Orleans to New York, called for a group of men who were willing to travel to California as members of a company called "Kinney's Rangers." The route outlined for their trip was to go from Corpus Christi to Mier, presumably following the plowshare mark that Kinney had paid some traders to make in December, 1848. Beyond Mier the trail followed the roads and paths to Monterrey, Saltillo and Parras. After Parras, the plan for "Kinney's Rangers" was to head northwest through the States of Chihuahua and Sonora to the junction of the Gila and Colorado rivers.

John Peoples, editor of the Corpus Christi *Star*, claimed this route was through a thickly settled country. But either he told a whopper of a lie, or he was completely ignorant about the violent land ahead. Yet even if Albert Winn had known the hardships he would have to face on the journey ahead of him, it is doubtful he would have remained in Vicksburg. He had already become more of a settlement man than his background had prepared him for. It was time to move beyond the limits of towns and cities, time to cross another frontier.

On St. Valentine's Day, 1849, he kissed his wife and family good-by and sailed down the Mississippi to New Orleans. Here he joined 100 other members of "Kinney's Rangers" on board a chartered steamboat. They had an easy trip to Corpus Christi, but that was only the beginning.

At Corpus Christi, Winn and the other men met Captain Walter Harvey, who was going to be their leader. But Harvey didn't take that simple road described in the newspaper come-on. The men who made up "Kinney's Rangers" soon found they were in Comanche country, where a man could easily lose his scalp and his life. And if the Comanches didn't kill him, there were plenty of other ways to die. The ground seemed to be crawling with rattlesnakes. There was a constant lack of water, and after Parras they hit the Bolsón de Parras and found that a lack of forage was typical of this dusty, barren basin country. If this was the easy trail to California that Kinney advertised, it would be hard to imagine what a tough trail might be like.

Long before reaching Chihuahua City, much less the junction of the Gila and Colorado rivers, the company began to break up. Maps were consulted. Distances calculated and considered. Supplies and livestock checked. Then Colonel Winn and about one-half of "Kinney's Rangers" split off from the company. They headed south toward Durango. From there they figured to cross the Sierra Madre to Mazatlán and catch a ship to California.

## THE MAN WHO KNEW DANIEL WEBSTER

Unlike Colonel Winn, who simply passed through Corpus Christi as a member of "Kinney's Rangers," Joseph Wyatt McGaffey was accorded preferential treatment. Perhaps it was because McGaffey had been a classmate of Daniel Webster's at Dartmouth College that he was wined and dined so well by Henry Lawrence Kinney. The empire builder of Corpus Christi had once courted Daniel Webster's daughter, and it may well have been this slim connection that brought about the attention he gave to this New Hampshire man on his way to California. Whatever Kinney's reason, Joseph McGaffey not only dined at the Kinney home in the latter part of March, 1849, but also was invited back to tour the ranch and to attend a party at Warren Kinney's home.

Altogether, Joseph McGaffey and his companions of the Essex Company stayed eight days at Corpus Christi. Then, on April 2, 1849, they gave up what they considered a pleasant but monotonous routine and headed for California. Their company consisted of "... two large government wagons, one drawn by five mules, and one by four; one small wagon drawn by two mules, four pack mules, and twenty-eight mounted men. ..." [2]

They were headed for Mier, Mexico, and the road to Monterrey. Their plan was to follow the eastern flank of the Sierra Madre Oriental until they reached the road that climbed from Monterrey to Saltillo and on up to Parras and the Central Plateau. During the first three days of their journey they traveled through a beautiful, rich, prairie land that had plenty of grass and water, groves of mesquite trees, an abundance of wild flowers, flights of beautiful birds, herds of deer, and large herds of wild horses. One of these herds that McGaffey saw had about 500 animals. "As they came in sight," he wrote, "they looked in the distance like a train of rail cars, the clouds of dust rolling back resembling the smoke of the engine." [3] Except for rattlesnakes, everything about their journey was almost too good to be true.

Four days later they left the flower-covered prairie and entered a dry land of whirring and buzzing insects. Now the dangers of the trip became clear when their favorite dog, Watch, was struck by a rattlesnake, and they had to kill him. The same day they were overtaken by a party of Texans who informed them that they, too, were taking the Lower Road through Texas in order to avoid the cholera epidemic raging in Mexico. Then and only then did McGaffey and his party find out that they had been traveling in the wrong direction. They were not headed for Mier. In fact they were only 40 miles away from Laredo, Texas. Still they could be thankful that they had avoided the cholera. Besides, they could head south into Mexico once they reached Laredo.

But their good luck had run out. Two days after their Friday the thirteenth arrival in Laredo, the first of their party had died of cholera. Between that day and their arrival in Parras on May 17,

175

1849, the Essex Company buried eight men. Their journey from Laredo to Monclova, Mexico, and through the eastern edge of the Bolsón de Parras was an unbelievable nightmare. While men died of fever, those who feared they might be next suffered from heat and exhaustion. All their drive to get to California had been vanquished by the drive to stay alive. To help them stumble through this hostile land they hired a Mexican guide and his servants for $5 per day though McGaffey was certain that the guide didn't really know his way, for he observed that the guide obtained all his information from his servants. Yet whether the man or his servants knew the route didn't really matter. What mattered was that McGaffey and his companions were led through the wilderness of the Sierra Madre Oriental to the town of Parras, where there were green trees, roses in bloom, grapevines lining the meadows and growing up the dry hills as far as irrigation ditches would reach. Beyond the vines, the hills were almost barren except for the sage-colored brush that flourished in the gray-tinted soil.

In Parras, that hub for trails crisscrossing northern Mexico, McGaffey and the others met more Americans who were on their way to California. Then as in all such meetings the talk was about the trail.

"We come down from Laredo."

"How was it, pilgrim?"

"Pure hell. We lost eight men."

"Cholera?"

"What else?"

A man might shake his head slowly from side to side, then offer a drink of Parras brandy. After a toast to the dead, he'd say what was deep inside—that special knowledge that only men of the trail could ever share.

"Pilgrim, this country's got more ways to kill a man than a dog's got fleas. If cholera don't get you, the Comanche or Apache might just do you the kindness. Then there's going without water too many days in a row, putting your hand down for a stick to kill a goddamned rattler only to grab on to its cousin, falling off your horse and landing on your neck, or maybe having the horse fall on top of you, catching a slug from some *ladrón's* pistol, or maybe getting a knife between your ribs. And that ain't all. Oh, hell, friend, there's food poisoning, bad liquor, sunstroke, or a little disagreement that turns into a shooting."

"You sound discouraged."

The natural laughter of men who had been there and lived to joke about it would follow. "Impossible to be discouraged any more. All I have to do is think about going back the way I got here. Maybe it's rough ahead, but it ain't going to be any worse than what I've already seen."

"Which way you headed?"

"I hear the Chihuahua Trail ain't bad."

"That ain't what I hear. Fellow I met says they're offering money for Apache scalps. That don't sound like any easy bet to me."

"How's the trail to Mazatlán?"

"I don't rightly know. They say the Sierra Madre's a steep son-of-a-bitch, and a man might have some trouble getting a ship once he gets to the Pacific."

Out would come the maps. The brandy bottle would go the rounds again. Tattered guidebooks would be consulted. Somebody would try to find out from a Mexican. If he got any advice, it would be confused by neither man's knowing the other's language, and by the fact that the Mexican hadn't even been to Durango, much less Mazatlán.

Parras was a place to make a decision, but a man wouldn't know if he had made the correct one until it was too late to make another. In and out of this place of grapevines, beautiful roses, and graceful cottonwood trees moved the gold seekers of 1849 and 1850. They came from the northeast curve of the Gulf of Mexico; from Galveston, Port Lavaca, Corpus Christi, and Brazos Santiago. They crossed the Río Grande outside Roma, Laredo, and Eagle Pass, Texas. On their way they buried friends who died of cholera, accidental gunshot wounds, knife wounds, a Comanche lance, a Lipan Apache's arrow, and all the other killers of the trail. Yet even in Parras they did not escape death. Some got that far, came through that much hell only to be buried in this place of the vines.

Two letters from William R. Glover—American Consul in Monterrey, Mexico, during August, 1849—illustrate the anonymous quality that death in this foreign land often carried for Argonauts. The dead man referred to in the official correspondence was James O'Reilly;

but in the final analysis he became no more than some monetary facts. The dead Mr. O'Reilly was worth $59.71½. But his funeral cost $33.50, and the *alcalde's* fee was $12.50. All of James O'Reilly that ever reached home was an impersonal $13.71½. But then, he had not reached El Dorado.

Other men had better luck than O'Reilly. For them Parras was a place for resting, buying supplies, replacing worn-out mounts, picking up a few bottles of Parras brandy, and hurrying on their way toward Chihuahua City or Durango. Parras was a pleasant place, and men felt secure there, felt the pull of pleasure, felt the temptation to stay a little longer. But Parras wasn't California, and they *were* on their way to California. And one of the trails beyond Parras was the lonely road to Durango.

---

## THE LONELY ROAD TO DURANGO

---

When the Philadelphia physician rode out of Parras in the predawn hours, it was May 27, 1849. Yet Dr. Lewis C. Gunn was chilled. Here on Mexico's great plateau, it seemed to him that nature was involved in some scheme, some universal test to be applied to all men who dared to live on this land. Six weeks earlier, when they had crossed the Río Grande at Matamoros, they had passed towns, villages, and ranches that were filled with the dying, the dead, and the terrified. Dr. Gunn estimated that in Matamoros alone, cholera had killed at least a fourth of the population. The whole land had the stench of death about it.

To hurry through the stricken coastal area, Gunn's party sold their wagons and purchased horses and mules. Though they knew the cholera was spreading, they felt safer once they were beyond Matamoros. As they rode toward Monterrey their spirits picked up. They shot wild turkeys and deer to change their diet. Then, near Monterrey, they entered a country of rich agriculture, a country of rare beauty. And now, as Gunn shivered and hunched his shoulders, as the hoofbeats of the horses and mules were muffled in the gray, dusty soil of the Bolsón de Parras, he longed to be back in Monterrey.

Here in the *bolsón* he saw no fertile and well-cultivated fields, and no spectacular beauty as the first light of day broke. There was nothing like Monterrey's Saddle Mountain and Miter Mountain. There were only humpbacked gray hills with ancient beachmarks from a time when the endless flat basin had held a large lake. For this was a dead land, a land left over from another time. To make things even more foreboding, banks of dark gray thunderheads were gathering in the west. Then, as the sun rose higher in back of them, Gunn felt his chill give way to warmth. Very quickly the cold of dawn changed into a sultry day. A warm west wind picked up the ash-like soil and blew a steady dust cloud at them, and even though they covered their faces with bandanas, they felt the sting of the pulverized sandstone.

Mile after mile they traveled on like men riding through some torture that even Dante had not thought of for his Hell. Twenty, then twenty-four miles passed. Still there was nothing in sight except the thunderheads, which were now much closer. Lightning lit up the sky, and the long, rolling sound of thunder echoed across the *bolsón*. Suddenly the men were pelted with hailstones ranging in size from a walnut to a chicken egg. Their horses and mules panicked and the pack animals stampeded, taking all the baggage with them. When it was all over, the company camped for the night, and Gunn described what it had been like after the hailstorm:

> Rain fell in torrents and all the road was overflowed, so that we walked in water up to the calves of our legs, and the melting hail made it cold as ice water. Half an hour before it had been very sultry. We were thoroughly wet, and it grew dark while we were still looking, with partial success, for our horses. After trying for half an hour, we succeeded in kindling a fire. We drank some brandy and lay down wet as we were for the night. The next morning went in search of our horses and found them all with all of the baggage, very sore from the pelting of the hail.[4]

The next day broke clear, but it took the Gunn party until two o'clock that afternoon to get moving. They needed time for drying and repacking their baggage. But the old saying that trouble comes in sets of three proved to be true for these emigrants. Three days later they ran into their second crisis.

They had stayed overnight at a *rancho,* and were late in starting.

They rode slowly on their way, and thirty minutes later found themselves surrounded by a Comanche raiding party. As though they had simply materialized from out of nowhere, these graceful horsemen were all around them. Somebody said they had come from behind one of the humpbacked mountains, riding in pairs. Gunn was aware of the tense situation they faced as he looked at these horsemen holding their shields and bridles in one hand and their spears in the other. The Comanches outnumbered them, and they were too far from the *rancho* to try making a running fight. Gunn quickly took all this in, and gave orders for his men to cock their guns and be ready to shoot. This show of strength, of willingness to fight, saved them, for the Comanches waved a white flag at them and rode off, vanishing so quickly that it was as though they had dropped into some secret passage underneath the earth.

Three days after this confrontation with the Comanches, the Gunn party had its third brush with disaster. They had been on the road to Durango for eight days, and this was well within a normal schedule to cross between 200 and 250 miles of this tableland. But on the seventh day they drifted through a *poblado* where the residents told them that soon after leaving their village they would come to grassland and would have easy traveling the rest of the way to Durango. Instead of grass, though, they moved from the dreary gray wasteland into a rough lava area of stones varying in size from a pebble to a boulder. While riding through this formation they arrived at a fork in the road. Here they took the wrong turn and headed southeast toward Zacatecas instead of southwest toward Durango.

Once again luck was with the Gunn party. They had traveled no more than three hours in the wrong direction when they came to a *hacienda*. While they stopped here for water they learned about their error, got proper directions, and backtracked to Rancho Santiago where they halted for the night. Three days later, on the sixth of June, they rode by vendors' stalls on the outskirts of Durango where travelers could buy drinks, chickens, soup, and fruit. The rest of the way into the city the road was lined with a stone wall on each side, and the fields were well cultivated. By four o'clock they had arrived in the city, and they "... took quarters at the Mesón de San José, at fifty cents for two rooms, and 6¼ cents for each horse per day, allowing three horses free to each room." [5]

## Barrancas and Playas: The Central Crossing

Of their three episodes of near-disaster, the most dangerous for Lewis Gunn's party was their brief encounter with the Comanches. If Gunn and his men had not put up a show of strength and a willingness to fight, their scalps would have been hanging from Comanche saddles in a matter of minutes. Just how violent these warriors of the plains could be was witnessed by members of another emigrant party under the leadership of Canadian William Perkins.

This company of Argonauts had completed a three-day lay-over in Parras in order to have their wagons repaired and their mules shod. Samuel McNeil, a rustic cobbler who didn't like Perkins for what he considered his "snooty ways," wrote in detail about a Comanche attack they had seen. The emigrants had crossed the *bolsón* and were near the silver-smelting town of Cuencame, or about 100 miles from Durango, when the attack took place. The Comanche raiders struck a Mexican pack train of about thirty men who were transporting a load of silver. The Perkins party made no real effort to help the Mexicans. Instead, they simply watched while the Indians ran them off, dumped the silver on the ground, and drove away the mules. It wasn't until a wounded Mexican tried to escape that the *gringos* made a move to help. When they did, the Indians killed the man, and then galloped away with the mules as their booty.

When Captain Perkins and his men rode into Cuencame, the people begged them for help in fighting the Indians. They even offered to pay $50 per man if they would lead an attack against the Comanches. But the gold seekers refused. As McNeil, the shoemaker, put it: "... we concluded not to interfere as it might afterwards hinder our journey and endanger our lives, should those Indians hear of our interference." [6]

The desperate citizens of Cuencame went ahead without the desired help, and the *gringos* watched the battle as though it were a spectator sport. The fight was short and without quarter. Five Mexicans were killed, and twelve were wounded. One Comanche lost his life, and a Mexican tied a rope around the dead warrior's ankles, dallied the other end around his saddlehorn, and dragged the body through the streets of Cuencame as though he were Achilles pulling the dead Hector behind his chariot as a final insult to his foe.

Brutality was common to both sides in this constant hit-and-run war between the Indians and the Mexicans, though most emigrants never witnessed an actual conflict. What they usually saw was the aftermath of such battles. The sight of burned-out *haciendas*, and scalped Mexicans with turkey buzzards tearing away their bloated flesh and ants and flies crawling into their bulging eyes, was quite enough to discourage most Argonauts who were considering the *easy* money for Indian scalps. Furthermore, the barren land presented enough problems. There was no sense in compounding the difficulties of passage on the lonely road to Durango.

---

## DURANGO: GATEWAY TO THE SIERRA MADRE

Shoemaker Samuel McNeil had mixed feelings about Durango during his stay there in April, 1849. He was impressed by the fact that this was one of the oldest and largest cities in Mexico, and the gold and silver ornaments within the cathedral struck him as the zenith of religious wealth. Yet McNeil was bothered by the bishop's behavior both in and out of church. Protestant McNeil didn't fancy the idea of a man of God drinking wine and having people doff their hats and kneel in front of him; nor did he consider it proper for the bishop to attend the bullfight on Sunday afternoon. As McNeil summed up the bishop's behavior, he found it incomprehensible that a representative of God would even permit, much less attend, such a barbaric spectacle.

Along with his distaste for the bishop, and for the spectacle of the bullfight, McNeil didn't think much of the houses. To him, the dwellings looked ". . . like prisons, the doors and windows being plentifully supplied with iron bars, as if to prevent the beaux from carrying off the ladies or the Indians from capturing the whole family." [7]

On the other hand, William Perkins had a different view of Durango. He commented on the city's paved streets, its gardens, its *alamedas,* and its fine bull ring, which he ranked as the number-two bull ring in all of Mexico. Though it is difficult to know how much Perkins was influenced because of the preferential treatment accorded to him by the Governor of the State of Durango, General José Urrea. Not only did the Governor visit the Perkins party, but he also invited him and his friends to dinner. This affair ranked high in what Perkins remembered about Durango, and he wrote that he and his companions ". . . were regaled with *nineteen* courses, and drank English porter out of champagne glasses." [8]

To Samuel McNeil the concept of drinking "porter out of champagne glasses" was not within his realm. While all this was going on, while Perkins and a few friends were dining in style, McNeil was defending his honor against B. F. Finefrock, who had accused him of stealing some boiled beans he had purchased but was unable to eat because he had diarrhea. As it turned out, another member of the party had stolen the beans, and the proof of his theft came out when the man got sick and threw up the beans in front of Finefrock and McNeil. Along with this, McNeil believed that Perkins and a few others had ". . . palmed themselves off to Gen. Urrea as very wealthy gentlemen, travelling only to see the country, implying that myself and a few others with their escort or servants." [9] Then, in a final venting of his contempt for Perkins and the others, he wrote that the men who had dined with General Urrea were really traitors because Urrea had murdered straggling American soldiers during the war with Mexico.

Other Argonauts who passed through Durango during these gold-rush years were much more interested in this foothill city than they were in their own personal feuds. After their hard journeys from Parras in the east, or Chihuahua City in the north, they were ready to relax and see the sights. At this gateway to the Sierra Madre, this vital link between the Central Plateau and the Pacific Coast ports of Mazatlán and San Blas, these gold seekers got ready for the final push to the sea. And even if they didn't know that Durango had once been called Guadiana when it was the capital of Spain's Nueva Vizcaya, they did know it was a very old city. How old it really was would have amazed them. It had been founded in 1563, by Don Francisco de Ibarra and named after Durango, Spain.

When Joseph Wyatt McGaffey neared Durango on June 1, 1849, he was impressed with its beautiful setting at the base of the Sierra Madre's eastern foothills. Far in the western background were the jagged peaks of the *sierra*, all golden in the morning sun. Below them, the gold gave way to shadows as the outline of the mountains dissolved into great barriers of darkness where the morning sun hadn't penetrated. Immediately behind the city were the foothills with the mule trail to the Pacific Coast plainly etched in a series of snake-like switchbacks. Where the trail disappeared from sight, McGaffey saw a thin line of evergreens near the edge of the brown foothill slopes. On the outskirts of the city two strange mountains stood high above the plain and isolated from the Sierra Madre. One was the flatiron shape of Cerro del Mercado, a mountain noted for its iron ore. The other was Cerro de Nuestra Señora de los Remedios, or Mount of Our Lady of Remedies. Atop this mountain was a glistening white church with a tapering spire that stood out like a fireless torch against the blue of the sky.

Lowering his vision to the nearby fields, this classmate of Daniel Webster observed rich, agricultural land that was irrigated by a system of canals and ditches bringing water from the Río Tunal. After crossing the wasteland between Parras and Durango, to ride by orchards, vineyards, melon patches, and vegetable gardens was a miracle.

This wasn't a small, pleasant village like Parras. This was a city of size and beauty, a city surrounded by gifts of nature as well as gifts of man. It was easy for McGaffey to see why Durango was the trade center for the other cities of northern Mexico. It was the gateway to the Pacific. It was at the crossroads for men headed north to Chihuahua City and Santa Fé, east to Saltillo and Monterrey, and south to Zacatecas and Mexico City. Then to add to its desirable geographical position, Durango's citizens had made their metropolis a place of beauty.

As McGaffey got closer to Durango, he saw ". . . numerous church spires, each one containing some ten or a dozen bells of different size and tone. . . ." [10] Then, during his four-day stay at Durango, he took time to thoroughly examine this high plains city. Some of the homes he saw were mansions by any standard. They were two and three stories high, constructed of adobe and fieldstone, and solidly braced by handhewn timbers. The roofs were either tiled or covered with heavy shakes. Windows were high off the ground level and protected by grillwork of iron bars. The walls of these homes faced the street, but McGaffey peered through entryways to inner courtyards. He saw magnificent fountains, well-kept gardens with a profusion of roses, and tall elm trees that extended well above roof level to provide a natural umbrella for filtered sunlight. But these were the homes of the rich. The homes of the poor were rude adobe huts or primitive *jacales* that offered very little protection against the elements.

McGaffey even took time to visit Durango's shopping district, where he counted more liquor stores than anything else, but he also went into a few dry-goods shops where he saw fine foreign and domestic fabrics. The churches of Durango also attracted him, and he thought they were very beautiful. His only objection to them was that they were forever tolling their bells. He strolled the *alameda*, taking his turn in the evening promenade around the plaza with its thick shade trees, its beautiful rosebushes, and the hand-carved stone benches that lined the walk and were mostly filled with older people who watched the spectacle and chatted with friends. Beyond the downtown area McGaffey found a splendid park of eight or ten acres in the suburbs. He took time to inspect one of the elementary schools, for he was most impressed by the fact that most persons he met had enough education to be able to read and write—a fact which simply wasn't true north of the Río Grande. Finally, like all Argonauts who passed through Mexico's cities, he attended a bull-fight. Again, like his countrymen, he stayed throughout the whole *corrida*, described it in gory detail, but proclaimed it a ". . . most cowardly and degrading exhibition. . . ." [11]

Two days after Joseph McGaffey rode out of the city and started on the mule trail to Mazatlán, Lewis C. Gunn and his party arrived. Dr. Gunn didn't describe his quarters at the Mesón de San José, but that wasn't strange, as such accommodations were never fancy. *Mesones* were usually constructed in a quadrangular form. All the rooms opened into the corridors around the enclosed courtyard. As for the rooms, they fell into two classes. At worst, they were dark, dirty cells where a man either hung his own hammock or had to sleep on a dirt or stone floor at the mercy of scorpions, fleas, ticks, and mosquitoes. At best, such rooms had one or two beds, which consisted of a wooden frame and tightly stretched strips of rawhide or rough boards to serve as a mattress. Along with the beds there might be a crude table, and a worn bench that was scarred, nicked, and defaced by knife throwers, nervous whittlers, and travelers who felt it necessary to carve some indication of their having been there.

In addition to the crudeness of Durango's *mesones* the *fondas* or restaurants were not noteworthy either, even though the surrounding country provided plenty of beef and a good variety of vegetables. Two 1853 travelers described their dinner as one consisting of stewed and roasted meat, and *frijoles*. Not happy with this bill-of-fare, they

called for a greater variety. This resulted in some sweetmeat, and
nothing more. Then, in a moment of daring, they asked the hostess
for coffee. She looked at them as though they had ordered a rare
brandy, shrugged her shoulders, and opened a locked cupboard.
From the depths of the cupboard "... she produced a cobwebbed
bottle, held it against the light, and satisfied herself and us that it
contained a dark, ominous-looking liquid. Warmed and steaming, it
was then brought in for our consumption. One sip sufficed: the name
of coffee was never mentioned for days subsequently, by either my
friend or me, without an involuntary shudder...." [12] Such were the
joys of dining at a *fonda*.

The population of Durango when Dr. Gunn stopped there was
between 20,000 and 30,000. He thought it the most civilized place
he had seen in his journey across Mexico, and he was aware of considerable wealth and a definite aristocracy. On his second day in the
city he saw the citizens of Durango turn out in large numbers for
the celebration of Corpus Christi.

> The bells were rung all day, the churches open and high mass cele-
> brated; magnificent music mingled with the singing of birds caged
> in the churches. Prisoners were sprinkling and sweeping the streets
> for the procession. The priests, bishops, and the mass of the pepole
> walked in the procession, and in the afternoon they had a bull fight
> in honor of the celebration—quite apropos for a religious festival! [13]

Five days after the festival of Corpus Christi the Gunn party was
ready to cross the Sierra Madre. They had rested, purchased supplies, and, most important of all, had hired the service of an *arriero*
or muleteer. Dr. Gunn left Durango just in time to avoid another
cholera epidemic, for when the Perrysburg Company of Ohio arrived
in Durango in July the city was devastated by it.

The Ohio men had come to Durango from Chihuahua City
through some of the hottest weather they had ever endured. The
temperature ran as high as 120 degrees in the shade. It was so hot
they found that the only way to make the journey was to travel at
night and try to sleep during the day. They stayed five days in
Durango, but these were days of fear. As many as 500 persons died
of cholera each day. The church bells tolled constantly, and the
people who could afford it headed into the mountains to try and
escape the plague.

## Barrancas and Playas: The Central Crossing

Like the Gunn Company, the Ohio men also had hired an *arriero*. Few *gringos* crossed the Sierra Madre without the aid of these transportation experts, and wisely so. These muleteers were a tough, self-reliant breed of men. They knew every move of their pack animals, knew just how to cinch the *aparejo*, or pack saddle, knew if the *aparejo* was slipping and about to make a sore on the mule's back, and knew when to sting a loafing animal with a pebble or a switch, and when to calm a tired or frightened mule with a few soft words.

In town muleteers were sometimes rowdy, sometimes drank too much *aguardiente*, and sometimes got into brawls. But on the trail they assumed a different posture—a posture that said, "This is my country, my business. Look, *gringo*. Look at me. Follow me, and we'll both drink together in Mazatlán."

Along the trail these men walked or trotted on muscular legs behind their pack string. They watched the surrounding country for signs that were not normal; bird calls that didn't sound just right, or no bird calls at all; tracks and droppings of other mules and horses that might show how many days or hours it had been since such animals had passed that way; signs that only Indians might make— unshod horses, an arrowhead beside the trail; signs that the *ladrones* might make—an empty shellcase, a broken bandolier. The muleteers knew how many miles their animals and their charges could make in a day, and they knew where to stop for water and where to camp for the night. In town they were the rowdy carriers of news from other places, but on the trail they were quiet men in the midst of their environment and trade.

Only a fool or another muleteer would think of making the trip from Durango to Mazatlán without an *arriero*. Between these two cities the country belonged to these men of the trail. The Argonauts followed their hired muleteers out of the city in the gray-blue hours before dawn. They rode mules or horses, and all their gear was stowed away in *aparejos* on the string of mules interspersed between the riders. Before they had covered the distance to the first line of evergreens they felt the warmth of the early morning sun on their backs. At a pull-out on one of the switchbacks, gold seekers stopped, and took one last look at Durango. They saw its dark outline highlighted by the sun's rays striking the spires and steeples. Then they moved back onto the trail. Only 200 miles ahead was the Pacific Ocean, and soon they would be standing on long, sandy *playas*, watching the breakers roll into the coast of Mexico. But long before that most of them became convinced that either their maps were inaccurate, that their *arriero* had lied about the distance, or that an entirely different system was used to measure mountain miles.

## AN OCEAN OF MOUNTAINS

After the last view of Durango the Argonauts stared in wonder and almost disbelief at the mountains ahead. The Sierra Madre Occidental loomed like a region of no return, a final wilderness where the passing of man could leave no more than a faint track that would vanish with the next wind, the next thunderstorm. As the morning mist lifted, as a cloud blew away, more mountains became visible. This was not an ordinary mountain range.

As far as a man could see the mountains were stacked on top of one another in an endless confusion of ridge after ridge, each one higher and steeper than the one before it. These mountains looked like some angry and long-forgotten ocean from another time, an ocean that had rolled into Mexico with a pounding surf that had come to a sudden halt before breaking and had turned into earth and stone.

"Somewhere," the gold seeker thought, "somewhere up ahead there must be a trail through this maze.

"But is there?" he asked himself. "Is there really, or do these men of the mules guide miners just beyond the view of Durango to murder and rob them?"

There was a thought to boggle the mind, and the gold seeker dismissed it. Dismissed it and told himself, "Don't be a fool. They do their work, no more than that. Keep going, horse. Keep up with the rest of them. The *arriero* is almost out of sight!"

Then, at that moment, the rider's horse groaned, grunted, and stopped to let out air, to pause and rest. It was a natural thing, a thing the Argonaut became accustomed to before he reached Mazatlán. But that happened later. Now the rider became frantic and kicked the mount sharply in the ribs.

"Move, you four-legged bastard!" he shouted. "Keep going, you lop-eared son-of-a-bitch, or we'll get lost. Move or we'll both become buzzard bait!"

Samuel McNeil of the Perkins Party didn't voice such concern as he rode beyond Durango on the first steep stretch of trail. McNeil was a practical man, a man whose pragmatism only gave way to expressions of two kinds of emotion when he wrote his journal: his distaste for Perkins and his friends, for they were not practical men according to McNeil's view; and his tendency to include quotations from poems, references to history, and Biblical allusions as though he were trying to prove that it was possible for a shoemaker to have knowledge that went beyond his workbench. But no matter how hard McNeil tried, he could not escape his penchant for detail, his attention to practical matters.

At one steep point at the beginning of the mule trail, McNeil was quite critical of another man who wasn't riding his mule but driving it ahead of him. "My courage and skill in riding up and down the precipices," he wrote, "showed his fearfulness in a rediculous light, so much so that he advised me to do as he did, only riding on the levels on the summits of the mountains." [14] However, the real thing that bothered McNeil about this man's not riding his mule was that the man was paying $1 a day for the use of the animal. "I told him that if he was willing to give $1 per day for the privilege of driving a mule up hill and down, he might do it, but that for myself I had given $1 per day for my mule for the privilege of riding when-ever it suited my convenience, and that was all the time." [15]

A dollar spent is a dollar to be used. So would say the practical man, and McNeil was so practical, so filled with self-virtue, that he equated an excess expenditure with vice. But virtue and vice both begin with the letter "v," and on the trail across the Sierra Madre there were places where it was better to indulge in a little vice, to lose a dollar for the practicality of insuring another day of life.

McNeil's antithesis, William Perkins, was well aware of the virtue of monetary waste in the interest of longevity. Perkins looked at the deep *barrancas*, the granite and slate palisades, and saw the country for what it was. "It is like the Chinese Wall," he wrote, "running butt up to almost inaccessible mountain fastness; scaling dizzy heights, dashing through torrents and burying itself from daylight in the cavernous valleys." [16] No more than 2 miles out of Durango the

189

possibility of disaster became apparent to Perkins as they reached a slippery granite face which the mules got across by making strong leaps. It was so steep, Perkins ". . . had some difficulty in scrambling up on foot." [17] Yet this was only the beginning. Beyond here the Argonauts traveled through country where great faces of granite and slate lined *barrancas* that were fantastic cracks in the earth, *barrancas* that looked like the work of monstrous machete slashes. In these places the narrow path had been cut out of the cliff to make a hanging-wall trail.

Here it was far better to waste one dollar than to risk one slip. A slip meant but one thing: a last, echoing scream by animal and man as they fell for a thousand feet and smashed against the rocks. In these narrow shelves men usually were silent. If they talked at all they spoke quietly—almost at a whisper. Here and there along these stretches of the trail the gold seekers saw little piles of stones supporting a small wooden cross. As their *arriero* passed such mounds he added another stone, paused, crossed himself, then continued on. One dollar, one *peso*, it didn't matter. In such places it was far better for a man to walk. The dollar or the *peso* could be replaced at another time.

It was cool when the Perkins Party reached the high country, for this was only April. In the morning hours as they all crouched around the campfire for warmth, they talked in wisps of steam. They shivered as they ate some *frijoles* and *tortillas* and burned their hands on tin cups filled with hot coffee. The dawn seemed to come late in this country, and the first light of the sun carried very little heat, while the wind that blew through the *barrancas* had the bite of snow in it. The men looked at the higher peaks above timberline and saw lingering patches of snow. When they crossed streams during the day and filled their canteens, the water was so cold to drink that it hurt a man's teeth.

Even two months later, when Joseph Wyatt McGaffey rode the mule trail across the mountains, the weather was cool and stormy. His first day out of Durango, he was drenched by a rain- and hailstorm. But the same thing happened to Lewis C. Gunn and his party traveling only a week behind McGaffey. Yet Dr. Gunn and his companions were fortunate. They stopped at a *rancho* during a storm and were able to rent a room for the night. Though he wrote that all of them and their baggage were put in one room that was so small ". . . we could not lie down at night. I was bent nearly double and of course could not rest." [18]

A month later the weather was warmer in the Sierra Madre, but it wasn't hot. The Perrysburg, Ohio, Company enjoyed their crossing. They were happy to get away from the cholera-stricken Durango, and for the first 100 miles they rode in style with 500 members of Durango's richest families. These people were heading into the mountains because they thought that by removing themselves from the city they could escape the cholera plague. The Ohio men were delighted to ride with these rich Mexicans. "We lived high," wrote one Ohioan, "as they divided with us. They had boxes and boxes of roasted spring chicken and everything that was good. We were sorry when they left us." [19] Along with the good food and company of the Mexicans the Ohio men also enjoyed the scenery. They liked the forests of pine and cedar, the mountain meadows filled with wild flowers just in bloom, and the spectacular mountains and canyons.

Of the many parties who crossed the *sierra* between Durango and Mazatlán during 1849 and 1850, the journal keeper from Perrysburg, Ohio, was one of the few to mention the heavy use of this trail for trade purposes. He saw pack trains that had as many as 100 mules; and in the narrow, one-way stretches the *arrieros* signaled that they were about to enter such paths by blowing bugles. The sound of the bugle served notice that a pack train was on its way. This gave other mule trains, coming from the opposite direction, time to bunch their pack string at a wider portion of the trail, or at one of the side tracks built for such problems.

Thomas B. Eastland and his son Joseph of Nashville, Tennessee, felt much the same about the beauty of the Sierra Madre country as the Ohio men. No small wonder, either, for the Eastlands had come a long way, and had been on the move for months. They had taken leave of their Nashville home in the third week of April, 1849, but they didn't reach the high country of the Sierra Madre until November. They had made their biggest error, the one that had cost them time and suffering, by traveling as far as El Paso del Norte with Colonel John C. Hays's group. But at the Pass of the North they left Hays and headed south to Durango and the Mazatlán trail.

At Durango the Eastlands fell in with yet another band of Texans who had just finished a stint as scalp hunters for the State of Du-

# THE EL DORADO TRAIL

rango. They traveled with these hired killers into the Sierra Madre. To the Eastlands the company didn't really matter after the trip they had already made through southwestern Texas and Chihuahua. All they wanted was to get to Mazatlán and catch a ship to California as quickly as possible. However, the elder Eastland was taken with the beauty of the high mountain country—a country he considered more beautiful than anything he had ever seen in the States. He mentioned the narrowness of the trail, and pointed out that, in places, long use of this trail had created deep channels that were "... barely wide enough for a single mule to pass...."[20] Even so, the Eastlands were thankful to be in a country of trees, a land of rivers, and most of all they were happy to be well on their way.

It took the Eastlands only nine days to cross the Sierra Madre, and this was very good time compared to other parties that took anywhere from eleven days to two weeks. For most of the gold seekers the time was lost on the initial climb from Durango's elevation of 6,200 feet to the actual summit of 9,200 feet. If the professional packers made the journey by themselves, they took no more than four days to reach the summit, which meant they averaged 26 miles per day. Parties of gold seekers simply could not keep up this pace. Most of them took between seven and eight days to reach the summit alone, and from there to Mazatlán it was a journey of from three to four more days. When the Eastlands made the whole journey in nine days, they were keeping pace with the *arrieros*.

While the *arrieros* preferred a faster pace over the mountains, the slower pace of most *gringos* meant more money for the muleteers. The going rate for the services of an *arriero* was $4 per day, and they charged $1 per day for the use of any of their animals. Yet the muleteers hurried the Argonauts over the Continental Divide as quickly as they could. The best season for crossing the Sierra Madre was short, and during that season these proud men of the mules wanted to get as many parties across as possible.

Pride was a major factor, but safety in rapid movement also played a key role. The *arriero* knew from experience that the more time he spent on the trail, especially the eastern slope of the Sierra Madre, the more he was open to an attack from Indians or *ladrones*. On the eastern side of the mountains, once a party left Durango there were few places of safety, few places one could call a settlement. There were scattered *ranchos* such as El Salto, but such places were subjected to frequent Indian raids and sometimes were hangouts for *ladrones* who made a business of robbing silver pack trains, Mexican businessmen, and an occasional band of Argonauts.

One of the survivors of the Parker H. French Expedition, Michael Baldridge, wrote about the *ladrones* whose activities on the Durango to Mazatlán Trail made it necessary for government troops to accompany the silver pack trains. Baldridge and his party met a party of Mexicans who had been attacked by *ladrones*. "Two of the best mules had lost their packs, and one of the *vaqueros* had an ugly saber cut across the breast, from which he was bleeding profusely." [21] Shortly after meeting this stricken party, Baldridge and his companions came upon the *ladrones* in a mountain meadow. There were about twenty-five or thirty men, and they were going through the goods they had taken from the Mexican party. One of the Baldridge party, Lieutenant Hare, spoke fluent Spanish, and he parleyed with the leader of the bandits, who proclaimed they were Mexican troops defending travelers of the trail. The outcome of this meeting resulted in the *ladrones'* riding off to look for more prosperous victims, for they apparently considered this party of Argonauts too poor to be worth the battle to steal their goods. Still, the meeting with these robbers convinced Baldridge that it was best to get across the mountains and down to the port of Mazatlán without wasting any time.

While an attack by *ladrones* was to be feared, an attack by Indians was the ultimate in terror for any traveler in the Sierra Madre. When the Indians struck, they came with the intent to kill. If they robbed at all, the robbery was only an afterthought. An 1853 traveler of the trail reported that he and his party came upon the remains of a large, well-armed Mexican party that had started a day or two ahead of them in the trip from Mazatlán to Durango. The Mexicans had made it to Los Mimbres, a day's ride from Durango. But here in this lonely, mountain canyon they were ambushed and killed by Indians. Twenty-nine of the thirty men who had started the trip were sprawled on the ground. Their bodies had been pierced by lances and arrows, and their scalps had been cut from their heads. "It seemed to us," the traveler wrote, "that they were killed without much resistance on their part, as many of them had carbines still loaded in their cold grasp. . . ." [22]

There were many good reasons for hurrying across the Sierra

Madre and the *arrieros* knew all of them. But the chance of a violent death was a major incentive to push animals and men to their maximum, to reach the *poblado* of Los Banos near the summit, and to begin the rapid descent of the western slopes into the State of Sinaloa.

For the Argonauts the descent of the western slopes was much more than a crossing of the mountain barrier. On this side of the *sierra* they entered an entirely different world from any they had ever known. This wasn't arid country similar to the plains of Texas, nor was it a country of pines and firs. Switchback after switchback took them farther and farther south of the Tropic of Cancer and into a semi-tropical land. Most of the evergreens were gone after the first hour or two of descent, giving way to oaks, which in turn soon gave way to ferns, cacti, and then to dry, bush-like trees with rickety limbs. And as they neared *poblados* and towns, they saw small limbs cut, gathered, and packed high on a burro—so high, that to see a burro moving along with such a load was to see a burro with its private brush pile.

To most of the Argonauts this descent through the western slopes was a thing of magic. "The road," William Perkins wrote, "led through groves of cocoa-nut trees, banana orchards, date and other palm-trees, immense cacti and *cereus*, five and twenty feet in height, interspersed with trees of all dimensions, covered with parasitical flowers as big as a dinner plate." [23] But this tropical country with its western exposure also suffered from the dry season. Where the *barrancas* offered no protection from the late afternoon sun, where there was no water for irrigation, the land cried out for rain. A man riding through this country could look about him and see that it was tinderbox land, kindling land. All that would be needed was a spark, a single spark, and wildfire would run the hillsides with astounding rapidity as the fire picked up speed with the westerly wind from the Pacific. No wonder, the gold seekers must have thought, no wonder there were firebreaks around Santa Lucía, Panuco, Copala, Chapaderos, and San Sebastián. These towns know what the dry season means. They know the danger of fire, how easily it can start, how fast it can move.

After the summit of the Sierra Madre the gold seekers moved rapidly. From every ridge they could see the Pacific Ocean, and they knew Mazatlán was not more than three or four days away. But keepers of journals like Lewis C. Gunn continued to make their entries. On June 18, 1849, he wrote: "At San Lucias we were treated exceedingly well. Had some fowls roasted at 75 cents each. Eggs were 12½ cents, corn 37½ per almo." [24] The next day Dr. Gunn passed many silver mines between Santa Lucia and Copala. At Copala he noticed that the "... houses were well built of stone and brick, with tile roofs." [25] One day beyond Copala Gunn had lunch at San Sebastián and early the next day they passed through old Mazatlán. By two o'clock in the afternoon the ocean surf was in view.

*They had reached Mazatlán!* Those were the magic words. As Joseph McGaffey entered in his journal that same June, "... our eyes were gladdened by the joyful sight of Old Ocean and the long wished for port of Mazatlán." [26]

From old Mazatlán to new Mazatlán the gold seekers had about 15 more miles to travel. But after their trek across the Southwest, the Central Tableland of Mexico, and the Sierra Madre Occidental, what was another 15 miles? It was no more than a dance across the sand with relief from the tropical heat in the form of the westerly wind—a cool wind carrying the odor of salt water, kelp, and fish. Somewhere just ahead was what they had been watching from the mountains: the blue Pacific with its long, curving white beaches, or *playas,* as their guide had called them.

"Sí, *playas, señor.*"

"Sí, *señor, es muy hermosa.*"

"Oh, *sí, señor,*" the Argonaut thought, "it's damned beautiful all right, you just bet your last *peso,* and I'll tell you, it's the most beautiful ocean in the world. And with luck, *señor,* there'll be a ship in the harbor. And with a little more luck, I'll be aboard that ship and on my way to San Francisco before another day passes."

Then, as they rode on, as the pounding surf became audible, as they rode onto the peninsula, they passed through the town to look at the Pacific Ocean even before they'd found a *mesón* for the night. They topped the last knoll; looked beyond the harbor businesses scattered along Olas Altas—the beach of high waves; looked at the far horizon of the ocean, and thought, "By God! I've made it to Mazatlán!"

# THE EL DORADO TRAIL

## MAZATLÁN AND OLD OCEAN

Way before the Argonauts appeared, the peninsula belonged to nobody. There were the wild animals and semi-tropical plants, but man wasn't there to see any of it. From out of the north came the first men. They settled here, became accustomed to the warm, humid climate; and enjoyed the fresh western breeze that seemed to come up from the depths of the big water offshore and rattle the palm leaves in the late afternoon. These early settlers were the Totorame Indians. They liked this place and prospered here. They speared fish, snared bright-colored birds, cracked shellfish with rocks, and shot deer with arrows. There were so many deer they named this place Mazatlán, or "Land of the Deer."

For a long, long time the Totorame were the People of this place. To the north, to the south, and in the mountains to the west there were other people they traded and fought with sometimes. But the Totorame were the People of Mazatlán. Then from the south came news of yet another people. They were very different. They were not brown; they were the color of sand or of an old bone. It was said that they walked on two legs sometimes and on four legs at other times. They carried a square tree with two limbs, and could kill with a stick of thunder and fire.

As news of these strange creatures got nearer and nearer, as it took less and less time to hear about them, the Totorame became very uneasy. Then the unthinkable happened. These strange men with the bone-colored faces, the faces with hair on them, appeared. It was true what had been heard about them. Sometimes they did walk on two legs; other times they even seemed to be two animals in one and walked on four legs. In sounds of war, these people held high the square tree with two limbs. The Indians shot arrows at them, and saw their brothers drop beside them in death as the thunder sticks spoke out.

The leader of these strange men was Captain Nuño Beltrán de Guzmán, and it would have been difficult to have chosen a more inhuman monster to be the first Spaniard to encounter the Totorame. Nuño de Guzmán was a scripture-quoting, sadistic, twisted personality who was driven by his hatred and jealousy of Hernán Cortés. Guzmán's one goal in life was to prove himself a greater conqueror than Cortés. In pursuing his dream, Guzmán proved only one thing: that he was a bloody butcher who enjoyed the sordid arts of torture and murder.

Wherever Nuño de Guzmán and his troops went they left a wake of bloodshed and misery. The "Land of the Deer" was not an exception. With unbridled cruelty this psychopath and his army slaughtered and defeated the Totorame in 1531, claimed Mazatlán for Spain, and moved north to found the outpost of Culiacán—the place where Coronado later started his expedition in search of the Seven Cites of Cíbola. While all this took place, the home of the Totorame became a northern seaport for the Spanish movement into the Sea of Cortés, Baja California, and the northern reaches of the Sonoran Desert.

Year after year Mazatlán saw more and more men heading north. Some searched for gold. Some searched for souls. They walked, rode horses and mules, and sailed their ships into Mazatlán's shallow harbor. Silver, not gold, was found in the mountains; and the souls of the Totorame and the other tribes were slowly found and changed. But as the Indians changed, the pale men from the south also changed. They married Indian women, and their sons and daughters were not the color of a fish's belly. The invaders were also changing. They learned to love the white beaches, and the high rolling waves that swept into shore and broke against the jutting, rocky promontories with a wild burst of salt-water spray.

Gradually Mazatlán became a busy seaport. Like all seaports it became accustomed to different men and their ways and to different goods from other lands. Yankee whalers stopped to buy fresh fruit and to see a woman for the first time in two or three years. Chinese ships sailed into the harbor, and their masters traded fine silks and porcelains for silver taken from Sierra Madre mines. Then, two years before the Argonauts appeared, the people of Mazatlán, who now called themselves Mexicans, were involved in a war with the *gringos*.

*Gringo* ships sailed into the shallow harbor, found that nobody fired at them, and that the troops had moved out of the city to the presidio at Old Mazatlán. Business continued as usual. The citizens of Mazatlán were accustomed to strangers coming into their harbor. There was no need to start shooting within the city. If men wished to shoot at one another, there was plenty of wide open country for that. Besides, the seaport had become international. English, French, German, and Chinese merchants operated flourishing businesses. War was not for them. War was for the generals and politicians. The *gringos* found only two adversaries: the constant turmoil of waves in the shallow harbor that rolled a ship back and forth, and the sea worms in the water that could reduce a ship's planks ". . . to an almost impalpable powder. . . ." [27] On shore, *gringos* found the city and the people to their liking except for their internal strife. For, like the rest of Mexico, Mazatlán was caught up in a struggle between citizens who were for their government and revolutionaries who wanted a change. Still, the *gringos* enjoyed themselves until the time came for them to sail away and become another phase in Mazatlán's past.

This, then, was the city the Argonauts came to in 1849. It was a city of the sea, a city that was not surprised when the gold seekers rode down the Sierra Madre mule trail and followed their *arrieros* to the Pacific. To the citizens of the "Land of the Deer," the appearance of another wave of invaders was nothing unusual, nothing to become excited about. But to Joseph Wyatt McGaffey, Mazatlán was the next to the last leg in a long journey. He was overjoyed to see it. When he rode into town on June 13, 1849, McGaffey and his party had been on the trail for seventy-four days since leaving Corpus Christi. The sight of the bright blue Pacific Ocean and the sound of rolling breakers crashing on the sand and on the rocky points with a wild rush of white-topped waves was a sight he would never forget.

In his journal McGaffey wrote: ". . . Old Ocean is what gives charm to the place. The heat of the sun is very much mitigated by the refreshing sea breezes, and here also is a fine opportunity for sea bathing." [28] Yet McGaffey's feeling about Mazatlán was not shared by all Argonauts. Many men remembered only the muggy, summer weather—the days when the only relief from heat was an afternoon tropical cloudburst that left the ground steaming.

Where the Indians had once lived in their villages there now was a town built ". . . partly on the foot of a steep promontory, partly on a sandy bank which encircles an extensive lagoon." [29] It was a well-built town with a mixture of flat-roofed adobe buildings, thatched huts, handsome shops and business houses, two small plazas, and street lamps.

Gold seekers saw the crescent shape of Olas Altas, and the long, curving beach extending to the north. They saw the rocky promontories jutting into the high rolling waves; the sugarloaf peak at the southern tip of the peninsula; the rocky twin islands just offshore from Olas Altas and the three larger islands in the north end of the bay. They watched Indian fishermen go to sea in dugouts that seemed to vanish beneath the swells as though pulled down by a giant squid, only to reappear and slowly make their way to shore with the day's catch of red snapper, flounder, sole, sea trout, bass, squid, and sea perch—some still flopping with the last gasp of life. Not far from the beach of the fishermen was Cerro de la Nevería, or Ice Box Hill. This hill within pistol range of Olas Altas, this dominating feature shaped like a giant's decapitated thumb, was where Mazatlán stored its ice on the sawdust-covered floors of tunnels—ice that was brought by ships all the way from San Francisco.

By the time most gold seekers reached Mazatlán they were trail-weary, saddle-sore, running short on money, and becoming terribly impatient. All they really wanted was to board a ship and get on with the quest. First, though, they had to sell their horses and mules. Some *gringos* claimed the Mexicans took advantage of their situation. Others, like Dr. Lewis C. Gunn, believed they had fared very well. "In an hour after we had reached our destination," he wrote, "my horse was sold for eleven dollars, while they offered me only seven in Durango." [30] William T. Sayward of Maine brought out another side to the selling of horses at this seaport. He complained that he and his friends had made a mistake in not buying American horses instead of Mexican mustangs to ride on their journey. They had been told that the larger American horses would not be able to make the hard trip. To Sayward this was a sorry mistake, for the two American horses they did take along got fat, and they were able to sell them for four times their cost. In fact, they would have made a considerable profit if they had brought only American horses, as "... they would have sold at Mazatlán for five or six hundred dollars." [31]

After the sale of horses and mules the gold seekers rented rooms in *mesones* for about 50 cents per day. Such rooms were infested with fleas, offered little in the way of comfort, and hardly made a weary traveler feel at home. On the walls of these rooms, the emigrants left markings of their passing. An 1853 traveler wrote that the art work ran all the way from crude figures to "... a clipper in full sail, with stars and stripes, and General Jackson for a godfather." [32]

The Argonauts also wrote some of their gripes on the walls of their rooms. Some men complained about the delay in getting passage aboard a ship, and about the cost of a voyage to San Francisco —it ranged anywhere from $60 for deck or steerage to $100 and up for a cabin, if one were available. Some men, such as Andrew Steele, who already had had the misfortune of having been a member of the Parker H. French Expedition, complained about having to pay $2.50 to an official in order to get a passport signed before boarding a ship. But as one would expect, the general complaint voiced by almost all the men was that they were tired of the food served to them in the *fondas*. They were tired of a steady diet of *tortillas*, tough meat, *frijoles*, eggs, and chili-pepper sauce. Thomas B. Eastland was one of the few emigrants who found a good place to eat. He located a Chinese *fonda* where a dish of food only cost 12½ cents. But he did have a complaint that far outstripped daily gripes about *mesones* and *fondas*. An old friend had got into a fight with a Mexican soldier and killed him. For this the Kentuckian was sentenced to one year in jail. Eastland thought this completely out of line, as his friend had only killed in self-defense. But he was unable to get him released, and received no help from the American consul.

The Kentuckian wasn't the only American who got into trouble at Mazatlán. Others who had made the long trip from the Gulf of Mexico also had difficulty. They seemed to take out all the weeks and months of hardship on the city while they awaited passage to California, and this caused trouble. William Dunphy and his friends fell into the hands of the law and were kept in the local jail for almost a week for shooting their pistols into the air at one of the *playas*. Altogether, about forty men were arrested and imprisoned over this affair by "... two hundred and fifty infantrymen ..." [33] who had been told that the *gringos* were attacking the city.

Not long after Dunphy and the others had been released from jail, a group of ex–Texas Rangers and their companions got into a brawl in a gambling house over a game of monte. When the fight was over a Mexican was dead. Troops were called out, and the

Americans holed up in their *mesón*. The soldiers lined up in front, aimed a twelve-pound cannon loaded with grapeshot at the door, and demanded that the Americans surrender or face the consequences. W. Augustus Knapp later wrote that if they had surrendered, they believed there would have been a mass killing. A group of the rangers managed to get out of the *mesón* and between the soldiers and officers. During the excitement ". . . they quickly plugged up the vent hole of the cannon, this preventing the soldiers from using it on us until all the Americans were free to get together for protection."[34] Once outside, the Americans quickly took possession of the cannon and rolled it into the ocean.

Not all Mazatlán adventures turned out as well for the Argonauts. Gambling-house brawls and incidents with the Mexican police never approached the degree of danger the men faced within the bay. The harbor was shallow, and its water churned in a steady thunder of rolling breakers whenever the wind blew. Under these conditions the rocky points, offshore islands, and lack of depth were potential death traps for ships. During a heavy storm on August 19, 1849, all the conditions for disaster ran together and focused on the French ship *Roland.*

One survivor of this disaster, H. O. Harper, later described what happened when the ship broke its anchor chain about two o'clock in the morning while the ". . . wind was blowing a hurricane . . ."[35] and each thunderclap seemed to flood the deck with more and more rain. The minute Harper felt the ship floating loose and rolling from side to side he tried to find the captain, only to discover he wasn't even aboard. Then, during the height of the storm, the crew deserted the ship without any warning to the passengers. Even though Harper was an experienced seaman, he couldn't handle the vessel by himself. Almost before he realized it he saw the ship heading into the churning and foaming surf breaking over a rocky point on one of the islands. The vessel rammed the rocks with a splintering of wood, and Harper was knocked off his feet. In a matter of minutes the ship began to break up, and he was afraid he would be crushed by the falling masts. He waited for a high wave to come over the deck, jumped with it, and swam for shore. He was under water most of the time, and just as he thought he could no longer hold his breath he was carried ashore like a piece of driftwood.

George McKnight was another of the lucky survivors of this shipwreck. Like Harper, McKnight also managed to swim ashore. But twenty-nine men ended their journey to El Dorado within two or three hundred yards of Mazatlán's white, sandy beach.

"I lost everything I had," McKnight said, "except what I had on, and my watch and $30 in money." [36] As for the others, most of them were drowned, crushed by falling timbers, or smashed to death on the rocks. Among the dead was a seventy-five-year-old cousin of President Zachary Taylor. According to McKnight of the Perrysburg Company, the man's last words were: "My God! have I come to this?" [37]

While men of good will and good intention made it as far as Mazatlán only to die in a shipwreck, a gunfight, or to finally become a victim of cholera, one of the most infamous of the Argonauts drifted in and out of Mazatlán in 1850 in fine shape. This was none other than one-armed Parker H. French, prince of the flim-flam men. He had been delayed for a time by the loss of his right arm, but that wasn't all. French and his gang had been caught outside Durango after they had robbed a mail coach. While awaiting execution in Durango's jail, French convinced a priest that he and his men could be put to much better use in helping to protect the Mexicans against Indian raids. He told the priest that he had been an orphan while yet a small boy, that he had fallen into evil ways without parents to guide him but that he was "... a man more sinned against than sinning." [38]

Not only was French released—though the sentence of execution hung over him—but the Governor of the State of Durango actually put him in command of Mexican troops as well as French's own men. When the "... first favorable opportunity presented itself, he and his small band of freebooters and Indian fighters deserted ..." [39] and turned up at Mazatlán.

Logically, someone should have killed Parker H. French at Mazatlán, for he ran into a number of men he had swindled. Yet, in his usual manner, he was able to convince most of them that what had happened had not really been his fault at all.

Looking even smaller now that he had only one arm, French smiled and talked his way back into favor. Many of his former victims even believed him when he said that he was every bit as much a victim as any of them. He had been a "victim" of Mexican injustice, and had barely escaped with his life. And now, he was offering to help any of the men who were short of money.

Three of French's former company were not taken in by him this time, and they tried to warn the others but had no success. Young Baldridge, who had been French's secretary when they left New York, wrote that his former employer knew that some of the men had borrowed money from other Argonauts, and Baldridge saw what the flim-flam man was leading up to.

French told the men that he intended to charter a vessel to get to San Francisco. All he needed was some capital. He told them he was willing to "... take the eight hundred or a thousand dollars they could raise on account, and take their notes for the remainder, payable after their arrival in California." [40] Once again French proved he was a superb confidence man. The men put up the money. French took it and had sailed out of the harbor before they could get their hands on him.

Little did these fleeced Argonauts realize that they had not yet heard the last of Parker H. French. By 1851 he was District Attorney in California's San Luis Obispo County, and by 1854 he was elected to the California State Assembly and was appointed a member of the Ways and Means Committee.

Mazatlán had seen pirates before, but it is doubtful that any ever surpassed the incredible Parker H. French. Yet of all the men who passed through that port city during those hectic years, French was the nearest thing to the embodiment of the spirit of the gold rush. He sang the siren's song of unbelievable riches, of a Mother Lode where nuggets were scattered on the ground in a golden blaze of pebbles waiting to be picked up. And while he was a scoundrel and a swindler, he could not have been such a superior flim-flam man if he had not keyed his come-on to the very golden dream that had aroused the world.

All during 1849 and 1850 men came to the "Land of the Deer." They came by foot, by horse and mule, or up the coast by boat. They came, stopped for a short time, and caught a ship heading up the Pacific Coast. They were not like the first invaders of the home of the Totorame, for they were not in search of souls as well as gold. So, while they carried the latest Samuel Colt model in thunder sticks, none of them carried square trees with two limbs, nor did they talk

THE EL DORADO TRAIL

about the Man on the Cross. To these invaders Mazatlán was important because it meant the end of a hard, overland journey. After
Mazatlán, all a man had to do was put his money down, take a
chance with Old Ocean, and get ready to stake a claim in El Dorado.

## THE TAMPICO TRAIL

The Reverend Daniel B. Woods set aside his search for souls, walked
away from his pulpit, and joined a group of gold seekers called the
Camargo Company. On February 1, 1849, they boarded the Baltimore brig *Thomas Walters* and set sail from Philadelphia. They were
bound for Tampico, Mexico, south of the Tropic of Cancer. There
they planned to take the southern fork of the central Mexico route
to the Pacific Coast seaports of San Blas and Mazatlán.

Once Woods had decided to high-tail it to El Dorado, he dropped
his clerical title, opened his journal, and began to keep a record of
his journey. The trip from Philadelphia to Tampico took twenty-one
days, and Woods and his companions were "... happy to exchange
the monotony, the junk and other salt provisions, and the green waves
of sea life, for the pleasing variety, the delicious fruits and vegetables, and the beautiful fields of a tropical climate." [41]

From the deck of the *Thomas Walters* as it lay at anchor in the
harbor Woods saw that Tampico was built upon a promontory overlooking the Gulf of Mexico. The northern border of the city was the
Río Panuco, which cut through a tangle of palms, banana trees, and
mangroves. The southern border was a lake that appeared to be in
a constant state of movement because of the flights of water birds
either taking off or landing on its surface.

As Woods and the others stepped ashore they were notified that
they had to present their passports to the *alcalde,* and secure another
passport to cross Mexico. However, the Camargo Company was in
good shape with regard to such requirements thanks to the foresight
of Edwin Allen Sherman [42]—an ex-journalist and one of the company's organizers. Sherman had secured passports from Secretary of
State James Buchanan before leaving the States, and he had obtained

"... permission from Rosas, the Mexican Minister at Washington to bear arms through Mexico. ..." [43] Because he had taken care of such details Sherman was able to tell Woods and the other company members that they could enjoy Tampico as preparations were made for their overland crossing.

While the Camargo Company entered Tampico with a minimum of red tape, other companies were not so fortunate. Thomas Sayre— an unsophisticated and non-learned gold seeker—wrote that he and his friends had to present themselves to the Collector of the Port, who checked their passports to enter the country and issued them another one for their crossing. In his diary Sayre entered a complaint about this system: "... all contractes must be made on Stamped paper the partys paying 16 Dollar for the privelege. ..." [44]

Yet Thomas Sayre wasn't the only foreigner to point out the confusion of government regulations that faced travelers who crossed Mexico during the gold rush. Englishman R. H. Mason even took time to make a considerable list of all aspects of passports and penalties that Mexican officials had access to for causing delays and charging fees.

Mason pointed out that the captain of any foreign ship putting into Mexican ports had to make a written declaration as to the number of passengers aboard his ship, where each passenger was from, what his trade or occupation was, and where he had boarded the ship. "The penalty for neglecting to comply with this regulation, or making a false statement ... was 100 dollars; and an additional fine of 20 dollars for each passenger omitted in this report." [45] In addition, there were rules and duties regarding the importation of goods; absolutely no Spaniards were allowed entry into Mexico; and all other foreigners were granted a passport that was good for one month. At the end of a month foreign travelers were required to report to a government office and apply for a *carta de seguridad,* or letter of safety. The *carta de seguridad* was good for one year, which gave Argonauts more than enough time to cross Mexico and board a California-bound ship. But many men refused to get such passports. In Yankee tradition, they did not believe a man should have to submit to such personal indignity. Others who did get the required documents sometimes found they were only good within the borders of one state. When they crossed into another state they were badgered about getting yet another document and paying yet another fee. Altogether, the whole business of passports and penalties was a kind of bunko game in which the timid were taken, and the bold were bluffed but finally ignored.

Daniel B. Woods and the Camargo Company were quite obviously well prepared for the passport game, and as a group they were bold enough to stand up against bluff. Yet Thomas Sayre was incensed but taken at Tampico; and the English traveler R. H. Mason was too much of a gentleman to do anything other than follow all the rules to the point where he felt it necessary to list them in his journal.

Except for humidity, heat, and insects most Argonauts thought Tampico a pleasant place. While it had its share of thatched huts, it also had quite a number of well-built adobe homes, a few large plazas, and a considerable group of Americans among the permanent population of about 7,000 people.

The American Consul at Tampico was Franklin Chase, and ex-Reverend Woods wrote that Chase took the men of the Camargo Company ". . . to the spot where his heroic wife raised the American flag, and maintained it in spite of the threats of the Mexicans." [46] Then, as though in payment for this glimpse of a patriotic scene where American womanhood had challenged and stood-off the enemy during the Mexican War, the gold seekers performed ". . . the celebrated farce, the California Gold Diggers. . . ." [47]

While Woods and his friends were entertaining the American settlement with their little drama, Thomas Sayre and a group of men from another company saw a cockfight. As Sayre remembered it, the fighting cocks were two different colors. The Mexicans called the lighter-colored ones Americans; and they called the red cocks Mexicans. While Mrs. Chase had managed to keep the Stars and Stripes floating in the Gulf Coast breeze, she hadn't been able to change the attitudes of cockfight fans with regard to *gringos*.

In addition to cockfights, melodramas, and gambling there were other diversions that occupied the Argonaut's spare time as he got ready for the overland journey. Some men speared fish in the Río Panuco. Some went deer hunting or shot ducks and geese, and a few tried the local sport of shooting alligators. But all these things were only temporary amusements. They did not keep mosquitoes, chiggers, fleas, and ticks from biting a man; nor did they hide the fact that Tampico's climate was ideal for any kind of fever.

Tampico was a good place to hurry through, an unusual place to write home about, but it wasn't healthy to stay there for long unless a man had already built up some natural immunity to fevers and developed a tolerance for the swarms of insects. For the gold seekers, the novelty of the hot country wore off very quickly. They were anxious to get on their way to the gold country. After a few days of playing tourist, they moved on their way up the Río Panuco toward the Sierra Madre Oriental.

Between 18 and 20 miles west of Tampico was the first major stop for the California-bound men. This was Laffler's Hacienda. Laffler was an Ohio man who had settled in Mexico, and during the gold rush he did a profitable business with Americans taking the Tampico Trail. At Laffler's a man didn't have to know any Spanish to do business, and it was possible to buy good horses for twenty dollars and fine mules for thirty-five. Additional supplies also could be purchased, and a man could ask Laffler about the best route to San Blas and Mazatlán.

Inevitably, the answer to any question about the trail was to keep moving west across the flatland beyond Laffler's ranch to the foothills of the *sierra*. After crossing the Río Tamuin, all a man had to do was follow the road to Ciudad Valles, continue from there into the cloud-covered mountains, and cross over to the Central Plateau. Once a man reached the tableland, it was not more than a day's ride to San Luis Potosí. From there everything was supposed to be easy. All a man had to do was follow the road on into Guadalajara, drop down the Sierra Madre Occidental to Tepic. A day or two after that he'd be swatting mosquitoes and chiggers at San Blas while he looked at white beaches, tall coconut palms, and listened to the constant roar and crash of high rolling surf.

"I talked to Laffler," one Argonaut would tell another, "and he says it's no more than a day's ride to this San Luis place, once we get through the mountains."

"That's just dandy, but how many days will it take?"

"To what?"

"To get through the mountains."

"He says something like seven or eight days."

"What do you mean by *something like*?"

"I mean it all depends."

"On what?"

207

"How the hell do I know?"

"Goddamit! You're the one who talked to him. Didn't you ask him what he meant?"

"Jesus Christ! Sure, sure. I talked to him, but I didn't ask him one damned fool question after another. All I did was try and get some idea about the lay of the land, about how long the trip might take."

*About how long the trip might take* depended upon the men who were making it. From Laffler's ranch to Ciudad de Valles was easy traveling, and it took no more than three to five days. Here in this town the Spanish had established as Villa de Santiago de los Valles de Oxitipa in 1533, the Argonauts were in the first foothills of the Sierra Madre Oriental. Beyond the roofless and collapsing cathedral, beyond the plaza, the stone and adobe houses, and the palm thatched bamboo huts, the gold seekers could look up at the cloud-topped mountains and the dark creases marking the deep *barrancas*.

The seven or eight days of hard traveling it was supposed to take to get across the Sierra Madre to the Central Plateau was a correct estimate for men who knew their way and were accustomed to a long day's ride through rough country. But even though the Argonauts hired *arrieros* at Tampico to guide them, this didn't take care of another major factor. Most of these *gringos* were not hardened to the saddle, not capable of a full day of riding. Most of them were sore and stiff by the time they reached Ciudad de Valles, and here the tough part of their journey was just beginning. This lack of conditioning plus their inability to carry out assigned duties with speed and know-how all added to the length of time it took them to climb upward through the mountains to the tableland and the road to San Luis Potosí.

Seven or eight days became ten or fourteen, and this caused great concern among the *arrieros*. The Sierra Madre Oriental was a vast hiding place for *ladrones* and revolutionaries. And neither of these groups approved of what the *arrieros* were doing. As far as these men of violence were concerned, the *arrieros* were traitors to Mexico for hiring out as guides for these *gringos*. The muleteers hurried the gold seekers as much as they could, and constantly told them that the longer they remained in the mountains, the greater were the chances for all of them to be killed.

Daniel B. Woods and the Camargo Company crossed the *sierra* in good shape, dropped down through the foothills on to the straight chute of Mexico's Central Plateau; and by March 22, 1849, two weeks after leaving Laffler's, they crossed the parched and dusty tableland and entered San Luis Potosí. On the same day, Thomas Sayre and his companions straggled into the city, but they were in bad shape. They had lost three horses, and the rest of their animals were worn out. One man had been lost for twenty-four hours before they found him. Another man had fallen off his horse and sprained his ankle, and two others were on the sick list: one with a bad fever, and one with a broken arm.

Despite injuries, illness, and exhaustion, the Argonauts who rode through the lime dust of the tableland knew they had completed the first leg of their Mexico crossing. They had made it over the Tampico Trail. Ahead of them was a city of considerable size and beauty. And beyond San Luis Potosí was the road to Guadalajara.

## THE ROAD TO GUADALAJARA

After their journey from Tampico, the Argonauts were amazed with what they saw at San Luis Potosí. Not only was this a city of between 25,000 and 30,000 people, but also a place of wealth and beauty. The Spanish had built this city in the late 1500's as a center of civilization near the rich silver mines of San Pedro Mountain. And though the residents cursed the *gringos* who came across the *sierra* and passed on through, this didn't prevent the admiration of the gold seekers for this colonial city.

When Josiah Gregg stopped at San Luis Potosí in December of 1849, he was delighted with the city's beauty. He commented on its architecture and the very good granite used in the construction of the city's major buildings. But more than the buildings interested this Santa Fé trader and physician. He was quite awed with the size of what the natives called the *órgano* cactus. He saw it planted in rows for fencing that ranged in height from ten to thirty feet, and looked like the pipes of an organ.

Most gold seekers were not as acute in their observations as Josiah Gregg, nor did they possess his facility with the Spanish lan-

guage. Yet even an uneducated man such as Thomas Sayre saw the
beauty of San Luis Potosí, but his short stay there was marred by
the open hostility of the citizens. He didn't need any command of
Spanish to know he was not liked or wanted. Furthermore, the
Mexicans knew enough English to be able to call him a "son-of-a-
bitch and a damned American." Still, considering that San Luis
Potosí had been the starting point for General Santa Anna's fatal
march to the battlefield of Buena Vista, it is something of a wonder
that the only complaints of Argonauts passing through this part of
Mexico were that they were cursed, plagued by petty thieves, sometimes forced to pay fees of passage by revolutionaries outside the
city, and faced two dangers that respected no nationality on the
road to Guadalajara—Indians and *ladrones*.

From San Luis Potosí the Argonauts had a three-day ride to Ciudad Lagos (now Lagos de Moreno). The first part of this trip was up
a switchback mountain grade into the four-corners country where
the boundaries of the States of Guanajuato, Jalisco, Zacatecas and
San Luis Potosí meet. Then as they neared Lagos, they saw crops
under irrigation with water drawn from wells and the Río San Juan
de los Lagos.

Most travelers who visited Lagos found it an interesting city.
When Lieutenant Wise of the United States Navy passed through it
in 1847, he thought the town was ". .-. extremely pretty—a remark-
ably handsome church faces the Plaza—the houses elegantly adorned
externally in fanciful frescoes, with designs of flowers, wreaths, gardens, and mythological figures. . . ." [48] The young naval officer also
pointed out that the Río San Juan de los Lagos flowed swiftly
through the center of the town, was lined with trees and willows
and was divided into two channels by a narrow ridge of pebbles
and sand. On this beach Wise saw ". . . hundreds of little nude boys
and girls, and women nearly so, bathing and washing in the pools
along the shores." [49]

Lagos also appealed to Thomas Sayre when he saw it in March of
1849. He calculated its population at about 10,000 people, and most
of them seemed a good deal friendlier than the residents of San Luis
Potosí. Much of this difference in attitude was probably due to the
fact that Lagos was on the major Mexican road from Mexico City
to Guadalajara, Durango, and other northern cities. As a result, the
citizens were accustomed to the comings and goings of outsiders.

During his overnight stop Sayre saw and talked to other Argonauts who had come to Lagos from the south. These were men who had caught ships to Vera Cruz, and followed the National Road to Mexico City. At the capital, they purchased seats on *diligencias* (stagecoaches) bound for Guadalajara, hired *arrieros* and two-wheeled *carretas*, or came north on horseback with their goods on pack mules. But like Sayre, Woods, and the other Tampico men, these *norteamericanos* also were headed for the ports of San Blas and Mazatlán.

Lagos was a crossroads town where gold seeker met gold seeker. Here on the road to Guadalajara, these Argonauts exchanged tales about their experiences, traded information about the trip ahead, and sometimes watched the Mexicans carry out brutal acts of violence against captured *ladrones*, rebels, and Indians.

In Lagos, New Englander J. A. Perry watched a squad of Mexican soldiers as they brought thirty captured Comanches through the town. All the warriors had their hands tied behind their backs, and they were being pulled by a long rope held by the laughing and boasting cavalrymen. If an Indian stumbled and fell, he was dragged across the cobblestone streets until he managed to get back onto his feet or until he passed out. The people of Lagos watched this scene without any protest, and many of them followed the stumbling captives so that they could watch the soldiers line them up in front of a firing squad and carry out a public execution.

Cruel and barbaric as this scene appeared, J. A. Perry saw the motivation for it when he and his companions rode out of Lagos early the next morning. As the country grew wilder, there were numerous roadside crosses. "I counted nine," he wrote, "within a gun-shot of each other, all temporary crosses stuck up where people had been murdered." [50]

Shortly after seeing the crosses, J. A. Perry saw that an attack by *ladrones* could be just as horrible as a Comanche raid. They came upon two Mexicans who had been robbed and assaulted. One man had been "... very badly mangled with a sword, and the other so nearly gone there appeared no chance for him to live." [51]

Outside Lagos the gold seekers traveled as quickly as possible. Stories of violence and shocking examples encouraged them to waste no time in between settlements. Following the same road on which Lieutenant Edward Fitzgerald Beale had made his famous ride with news of the discovery at Sutter's Mill, the Argonauts hurried on their way. Roadside crosses, tales of Indians and *ladrones*, and the possibility of being attacked by disgruntled followers of the defeated rebel chief, General Mariano Paredes, were excellent reasons for haste.

After Lagos the next safe stop was some 30 miles west at San Juan de los Lagos—the site of Mexico's great annual fair. This deep valley, where the Río San Juan de los Lagos had cut its way through the surrounding high mountains, was where Lieutenant Beale and his Mexican guide had been forced to swim their horses across the storm-swollen river, and then in the dark of night work their way up the mountain grade while watching out for falling trees and mud slides.

As the gold seekers rode along the narrow streets of this colonial town, they noticed its fine houses, plaza, and beautiful church. But while Thomas Sayre took time out to visit the church, other gold seekers overlooked its aesthetic qualities because of their anti-Catholic bias. J. A. Perry was a good example of such an attitude. For even though he heard the church bells tolling and saw people uncovering their heads and kneeling on the sidewalks and streets to pray, he kept on riding and refused to remove his hat for the Church of Rome.

Perry's behavior caused an unnecessary incident as the angry citizens began to throw stones at his head. In what he considered to be a case of self-defense, Perry quickly drew his pistol and threatened to shoot if the rock throwing didn't stop. Fortunately, what could have developed into a violent and dangerous affair for the innocent townsfolk and the intolerant New Englander never got beyond an exchange of a few rocks and mutual insults. Yet what happened was typical of the type of meeting that often occurred between the Protestant Yankees and the Catholic Mexicans.

Beyond San Juan de los Lagos were fifty of the most dangerous miles on the road to Guadalajara, for there was no real safety until one reached the village of Tepatitlán. As the road climbed upward again, there were a few scattered *ranchos* and an occasional *poblado* that was barely hanging on. In general, though, the country was very thinly settled. Worse yet, those who lived in this no man's land were a people of fear. For them the next sound of horses on the move might very well mean a band of Comanche raiders or a gang of *ladrones*. There was good reason to fear either one, and such fear was infectious, and the gold seekers tried to make the long journey to Tepatitlán in one day. But few of them managed to do this. Usually they were forced to stop over for one night somewhere along the way. When this happened they tried to stay at some *rancho* or small settlement for mutual protection.

Such steps rarely offered much in the way of accommodations or food. If the weary traveler got some jerked beef, *tortillas,* and *frijoles,* he considered himself lucky. Then if he got a stiff shot of homemade *pulque* to ease his tiredness, he really had the best that could be offered. It was only in the cold light of dawn that reality made itself much too clear as a man looked around at his surroundings. New Englander J. A. Perry described what a meal was like in one of these poor stopovers:

> The next morning, while the woman was making some tortealiers, she laid her dough on the stone where she rubbed her corn, and while she was engaged in cooking some jerk beef, quite a number of fleas pounced upon the dough, and it being wet, they stuck fast, and soon the poor things were mixed in and baked on a hot stone. It is astonishing to see how hunger will alter one's palate and destroy his prejudices.[52]

Between their flea-seasoned breakfast and Tepatitlán, Perry and his company passed through the *poblado* of La Venta, which had been plundered just two days before by *ladrones.* Here they also met a Mexican woman who asked them if she and her two servants and three pack mules of merchandise could ride along with them for protection. The Argonauts agreed, and it was fortunate for the woman that they did. For not too many miles west of La Venta they came upon a stagecoach that had just been robbed. Then as they proceeded with caution up a series of mountain switchbacks, they rounded a turn and encountered the *ladrones.*

Perry counted twenty-five horsemen, and all were carrying carbines and swords. The company's muleteers quickly stopped, and told the Americans that they were afraid to go ahead. Realizing that to stop or to retreat would be disastrous, the gold seekers ordered the muleteers to show no fear, get all weapons ready, and form a double file. In this fashion they rode right up to the bandits, stopped in front of them, and waited for them to make a move. Both sides looked each other over. Then the leader of the *ladrones* asked the company if they had seen any robbers, for they were hunting for some men who had robbed the stagecoach.

In a very sarcastic tone, Antonio—the head *arriero*—replied that the company had seen *ladrones*. Then for good measure he added: "That we saw more or less every day—that we asked no odds of them and that we were prepared to give them their just deserts at any time." [53]

The *ladrones* turned down this obvious invitation to a fight. They again proclaimed their need to try to capture the bandits who had robbed the stagecoach, and rode away without causing any trouble. With great relief, Perry and all but one of the company watched them go. One dissenter had been all for opening fire on the bandits, but the hothead had been stopped by Colonel Stone—the party's leader.

When they rode out of Tepatitlán the next day, the would-be gun-slinger saw what could have happened to him if they had fought it out with the *ladrones*. They met another company of Americans who were carrying a wounded man. When the New Englanders asked what had happened, they were told that the man had dropped behind the party in order to buy some fruit. As he was riding to catch up to his companions, he had been dry-gulched. The rifleball had shattered the stock of his double-barrel shotgun hanging in a saddle scabbard and had ricocheted into his thigh. Not only did it leave him with a nasty wound, it also broke his femur. The sight of the injured man ". . . in a litter of blankets slung between two poles . . ." [54] with a mule behind and one ahead was a sobering glimpse of how the unexpected moment of violence was more than a casual threat on the road to Guadalajara. There was no need to court disaster, but there was a very real reason to be cautious and avoid any move that might swing the odds in its favor.

Party after party of gold seekers learned this lesson as they traveled from Tampico or from the Vera Cruz–Mexico City route. This was a violent land. Much could happen in the normal course of events, and fate needed no prompting. A wise man wasted no time in between *poblados* and *ciudades*. Though the distance from Tepatitlán to Guadalajara was 50 miles, Argonauts and *arrieros* tried to make the trip in one long day. The most time any of them cared to spend in this last stretch on their way to the Valley of Atemajac was two days.

Finally, when the weary riders or stagecoach passengers heard church bells, when they had their first view of this high plateau capital of the State of Jalisco, it was like topping a ridge, rounding a bend and discovering a lost kingdom. In the distance loomed the tall peaks of the Sierra Madre Occidental, serving as a backdrop. Above was a clear blue sky that made a man's eye's squint. Alongside the road were the reflected pieces of blue sky in the vibrant flowers of the jacaranda trees. After the gray and brown tableland, after the clouds of lime-dust, here was the kingdom of color. Here was Guadalajara where the sky and the earth ran together, where the desert was barred by a barrier of flowers and fountains, and where the face of fear was vanquished by the face of laughter. Guadalajara was everything a man could wish for plus all the things he hadn't even thought about.

---

## GUADALAJARA: KINGDOM OF COLOR

---

All during the first two years of the gold rush the Argonauts passed through Guadalajara. They wore their rough, heavy clothing, they were unshaven, unwashed, and grimy with trail dust. They came on horseback with an *arriero* to guide them, and they carried their goods on pack mules or in two-wheeled *carretas*. Some even traveled by stagecoach and then bought horses and mules from one of the great *haciendas* of Jalisco. They came with a dream in their minds, a vision in their eyes, but they couldn't overlook Guadalajara.

Some were Tampico men. They had crossed the Sierra Madre Oriental, and the dry dusty Central Plateau. They had stopped at San Luis Potosí where the memory of the Battle of Buena Vista was too fresh in too many minds to tolerate another wave of *gringos*. So they had hightailed on their way until they saw the first vendors and the first jacaranda trees.

*You rode this way, Thomas Sayre. You rode into the city on April 2, 1849—the same day as ex-Reverend Daniel Woods and the Camargo Company. You kept a record in your primitive English, Thomas Sayre. And what did you first notice as you approached the Kingdom of Color?*

". . . among the varietys of the markit as we past in the town was

215

wattermellons tobe Seen for Saile . . . it may be called the citty of the cross and Soldere . . . there is several bublic Squires and fountains which supplys the inhabitantes with watter as well as ornament." [55]

Some men came by way of Vera Cruz, Mexico City, and up the Central Plateau to Lagos. At Lagos they headed west to the Valley of Atemajac. Some on horses, some in stagecoaches, and some carrying their goods in *carretas*.

*You came this route, Daniel Wadsworth Coit. By normal standards, at sixty-one, you were too old for the adventure. Yet gold rushes do away with normal standards. So, you overlooked retirement and the rocking chair. You and your party arrived in Guadalajara with* carretas *loaded with coins to trade for gold dust in that coinless El Dorado. But you also carried your sketch pad and notebook, and you wrote letters to your wife who waited for you at the family home in Norwich, Connecticut. What was it like for you, when your body no longer had that morning bounce-back of your youth?*

"We arrived at Guadalajara pretty well jaded out, and the two or three days required for obtaining pack mules to prosecute our journey was very acceptable for resting and recruiting. As to accommodations, however, we did not fare much better here than on the road. These Spanish or Mexican towns (except in the capital) have miserable *posadas*, or inns, worse bedrooms, and no beds at all. They give you a dirty room with a stone or tile floor, no furniture, and on this you are expected to extend your own *catre* (bedstead), or spread your own blanket, as the case may be." [56]

*But what of the city, what did you think of the second largest city in all of Mexico?*

"These were the accommodations, if it be not an abuse of the term, which our party had to submit to in this fine city, myself being the only exception, inasmuch as I had a nice, portable, jointed iron bedstead, with sacking bottom, which folded up in a trunk." [57]

*But what did you think of Guadalajara, Mr. Coit? Weren't you at all impressed with this Kingdom of Color?*

". . . I did get rather a striking sketch of the public or principal square, embracing the palace, cathedral, fountain, with orange trees, etc." [58]

Former Santa Fé trader Josiah Gregg took an out-of-the-way route to Guadalajara. His driving curiosity to explore new territory, to see different peoples, to catalog animals and plants he had never seen before, and to study the geology of another part of the American West were forces he couldn't resist. In the latter part of April, 1849, he left Mexico City and headed northwest across the Sierra de Las Cruces. With him on this mule trail to Morelia were two Irishmen, two Germans, one Scotsman, another American, and a Mexican servant. These men rode through some of Mexico's beautiful mountain country, passed the eastern shoreline of Lake Chapala, and at noontime on Friday, May 17, 1849, entered the capital of Jalisco with pine needles still clinging to their gear.

*You were a keen observer, an amateur naturalist on the verge of professionalism. You spoke fluent Spanish, Josiah Gregg. Mexico was no strange land to you. After the war you had become a physician at Saltillo. Then came your trip to Mexico City and the old curiosity that sent you on your way to California. What about you, Dr. Gregg? What did you think of the city that mirrored the sky?*

The physician from Saltillo thought that the Kingdom of Color was located in a splendid valley. And in his typical manner, he made inquiries. From the governor he learned that Guadalajara was founded in 1531 and was the second largest city in Mexico. He was told that the city was noted for its manufacturing, pottery, cotton mills, and nearby silver mines.

*But what of the city, Dr. Gregg? What did you really think of it? Did you notice the profusion of flowers: the roses like gaily colored cabbages; the bougainvillea like some strange stigmata against the glare of whitewashed adobe? And the fountains, Dr. Gregg, did you see that clear water shooting skyward, water that you would have given almost anything for on your long treks from Santa Fé to Chihuahua City?*

Dr. Gregg noticed little for a man who usually saw so very much. He commented upon the nightly, brilliant illumination in the *plaza pública*, the bands of musicians giving concerts, and he complained about the terrible *mesón* in which he stayed and of the scoundrel in charge.

So little to say, so very little, yet when most Argonauts reached Guadalajara they were anxious to press on. A few, like New Englander J. A. Perry, noticed quite a few French and English had settled in the city, and owned factories that manufactured cotton goods. But Perry was also interested in the entertainment the city had to offer. He and his friends attended a *corrida* at the *plaza de toros*, watched a cockfight, and observed the men and women playing monte at the gaming tables. The *corrida* and cockfights were exhibitions of cruelty to Perry, but the female monte gamblers disgusted him even more. "I have seen them lose their last cent," he wrote, "and then pull off their chemise and pawn it, and when they have lost that they will get up and walk away as indifferent as though they had been lookers on." [59]

Like most of the Americans who came through Mexico during the gold rush, Perry didn't hesitate to watch with fascination and jot down the details of what he saw. For in his role of vicarious participant he enjoyed both the pleasures of sin and the self-righteous smirking of a moral do-gooder.

Of all the Yankees who passed through Guadalajara in those years between the close of the Mexican War and the end of the frantic rush to California's Mother Lode, a young officer of the United States Navy saw Guadalajara for what it truly was. This was Lieutenant Henry Augustus Wise, and two years before the Argonauts arrived he stopped in the capital of Jalisco as he rode to Mexico City with the news of Lower California's surrender to the United States.

Lieutenant Wise and his Mexican guide had traveled by ship from Mazatlán to San Blas. From there they had made a wild ride through the tropical jungle, up through the deep *barranca* country of the *sierra* and into the temperate climate of Guadalajara. After this hard and difficult ride, Guadalajara was almost unbelievable to young Wise. This was more than a city. It was very much a Kingdom of Color, a pleasure capital beneath the clear blue sky and—most of all—a passionate state of mind.

Everywhere that Wise looked he saw something of beauty. The streets were broad and tree-lined. The houses were "... solid and imposing ... painted outside gaily in frescoes...." [60] There were beautiful plazas and fountains, magnificent churches and public buildings, and "... crowds of well-dressed pedestrians ... thronged the streets and squares ... all gave the air, even at a rapid glance, of great ease and opulence." [61] Then, unlike the complaining Argonauts, Wise had good quarters, good food, and walked the marble-paved paths in the main plaza until he and a friend found a seat on one of the marble benches where they could sit and listen to the band concert. Here Wise lit his cigar, leaned back against the cool marble, and watched the women of Guadalajara. Never in his life had he seen so many beautiful women gathered in one place. If ever any town in the whole universe deserved acclaim as the home of beautiful women, that town was Guadalajara.

Unlike Lieutenant Wise, the anxious Argonauts took very little time to observe the women of Guadalajara. These men of the trail were too absorbed by their quest to do more than pause for a day or two in Jalisco's beautiful city. And during those hours they asked about the trail to San Blas and Mazatlán; sold equipment that couldn't be carried through the *barranca* country; inquired about *ladrones* who might be lurking on the trail; and got on their way as soon as possible. Beautiful women and the magnificence of the Kingdom of Color would simply have to wait until another time. The gold seekers were caught up in a golden dream that became more and more intense as the end of their Mexico crossing drew nearer. From Guadalajara it was only a matter of crossing the *barranca* country of the Sierra Madre Occidental and dropping downward into the hot jungle land. Beyond that were the long white beaches of the Pacific Ocean. One week or maybe two weeks away was the ship just waiting in the harbor.

"What about the *barrancas*?" a worried traveler would ask.

"Hell," another would answer, "we're on our way to El Dorado. Why worry about the *barranca* country?"

## THE BARRANCA COUNTRY

And none of the Argonauts worried too much about the *barranca* country until they got to it. Instead, these men rode out of Guadalajara in a fine mood. The trail was good. It had to be good. After all, there was that advertisement in Disturnell's guidebook that said: "The State of Guadalajara is making a great effort to establish a carriage road from that city to Mazatlán and to San Blas. It is expected that both roads will soon be finished." [62] If both roads were soon to be finished, what was there to worry about? The thought ran through their minds that the *barranca* country was of the imagination. The real threat to their lives was the possibility of being attacked by *ladrones* who plagued the trail to Tepic and San Blas. All a man had to do was ask any *arriero* what was the greatest danger on the trail, and the muleteer's answer was always the same: "*¡Ladrones, señor!*"

As to the threat of these bands of *ladrones*, it was very real. When Lieutenant Edward Fitzgerald Beale and his guide had traveled this route with the news of the gold discovery in 1848, they not only saw the deadly aftermath of a bandit raid on a Mexican party but also were chased by a gang of these cutthroats. However, in between Beale's ride and the coming of the gold seekers, Mexican soldiers had greatly reduced the threat of these bandits.

A day's ride northwest of Guadalajara, three bodies dangled by their necks from a roadside gallows for all to see. Josiah Gregg saw these human scarecrows in May of 1849, and asked local residents if the men had just been executed. When he was told they had been killed almost a year before and had been left as a warning to others, he rode closer to the bodies to examine them. To his amazement, he discovered corpses that had dried into mummies. Above the skulls of these dead *ladrones* was a warning sign that stated that this was the punishment for robbers and assassins. This sight impressed the gold seekers, and practically every keeper of a journal or diary devoted space to the gruesome trio.

Punishment was final in the *barranca* country. In this wild region man accepted violence as part of his life. The big difficulty for gold seekers who traveled this route was to avoid being caught up in such violence. Not all of them managed to do so. One month before Josiah Gregg saw the mummified *ladrones*, Daniel Wadsworth Coit made this journey; and in a letter to his wife he told her how violent action had taken the life of a young American who was with a party no more than a day or two behind him. The Argonauts had got into a dispute with an innkeeper over a bill. Harsh words were exchanged. The American threw the money on the ground, but the innkeeper refused to pick it up. At this point, the *alcalde* ". . . interfered and ordered the man to dismount and pick up the money. This he indignantly refused to do." [63] The *alcalde* ordered his soldiers to open fire, and when the shooting ceased, an innocent member of the party had been shot through the head and killed. Except for one man who escaped and caught up to the main contingent of Americans, all the others were made prisoners until the head of the company, Captain Hutton, convinced the *alcalde* that there would be serious trouble with the United States government if he did not let his men go.

The constant threat of violence was not the only hardship on the trail to San Blas. Contrary to the advertisement of the stagecoach company, this route showed no signs of soon becoming a road. W. C. Smith had come all the way from Vera Cruz on Mexico's National Road; and when he left Guadalajara in March of 1849 he soon saw that ". . . all traces of a wagon road disappeared, leaving nothing but a mule trail, full of rocks. . . ." [64] Still, a rough trail didn't stop the steady rush of gold seekers; nor did it prevent their appreciation for the beauty of the country.

From the Kingdom of Color the trail wound down the western flanks of the Sierra Madre Occidental. The Argonauts rode by cattle herds, and near the end of the first long day out of Guadalajara they saw fields of green bayonets. These were the cactus-like *maguey* plants, and there were fields and hillsides covered with them. At the end of the day, the travelers came to a bowl-shaped valley at the base of an extinct volcano. Here was the town of Tequila, surrounded by *maguey haciendas*. Josiah Gregg was fascinated with this plant. He said that practically nothing else was cultivated in this fertile area. The town was famous for its superior *mescal*, and he watched the whole process for making *tequila*: the roasting and crushing of the plant's onion-shaped bulb, the fermenting in skin vats, and the final distillation into liquor.

The town of Tequila had a very good business going, for most of the emigrants didn't limit themselves to a scientific interest in the manufacture of *maguey* liquor. At many places along the route to Tepic and San Blas there were trailside *jacales* doing a booming business in selling *tequila* to the *gringos*. While Gregg looked with disgust at the picture presented by drunken, noisy Americans who gathered at such places, the success of these grog shops clearly indicated that many gold seekers found a shot of *tequila* a welcome luxury as they crossed the *barranca* country.

Beyond Tequila the trail dropped sharply downward, and the riders crossed a ridge of almost pure black obsidian. A horse did very well to avoid slipping and falling on the shiny volcanic glass. A few miles farther on the emigrants came to their first overnight stop after Tequila. This was the village of Magdalena, built near the shores of a fine mountain lake. From this place to Tepic was a three-day trip of about 75 miles, but most of those miles were either going up or down the sides of deep *barrancas*. It was a tough trip even for the *arrieros*, who had made it countless times. Yet nobody wished to travel at a slower pace through this country. For while the soldiers claimed they had killed all the *ladrones*, stories that travelers heard hardly gave credence to what the soldiers wished people to believe. On the contrary, the region known as Plan de Barrancas was still notorious as the land of the *ladrones*. It was not territory suited to peaceful observations, and the gold seekers pushed themselves and their animals to the maximum in order to get through this stretch of the trail as quickly as possible.

When J. A. Perry of New England came through this country in March of 1849 he thought it was one of the steepest and wildest areas he had ever seen. He found that most of the trail would not permit the passage of two horses abreast. It was single-file on a hanging-wall path cut into the side of the canyon. When Perry looked straight down it made him feel dizzy. To add to his uneasiness, he could see the broken bodies of dead mules and horses splattered on the rocks far below. This was enough for Perry and his party. They got off their horses and walked. Yet the same month that they led their horses up and down this zigzag trail another group of men from New York and Vermont took small wagons through here.

W. C. Smith was a member of the wagon party, and he later recalled that they had worked like mules in order to get their wagons in and out of the *barrancas*. One place that he could never forget had a sheer cliff face that dropped 2,000 feet to the bottom, and at this place they had to take their wagons apart and slowly lower each individual piece to the bottom, then put the wagons back together again and continue on. In other places they even had to gather stones and build roads so that they could move the wagons ahead.

All Argonauts who took the trail through the Plan de Barrancas remembered it for the rest of their lives as one of the wildest places they had seen in all of Mexico. In their descent to the bottom of the deepest *barranca*, the gold seekers dropped from a temperate climate to a tropical one. Poplar and elm trees were replaced by banyan and banana trees. Wild turkeys seemed to be everywhere, and the trees were filled with parrots of all shapes, sizes, and colors.

In the midst of this deep *barranca* the emigrants came upon a *rancho* where they could stop for the night. The owner had been catering to the *ladrones* who hid in the craggy vastness of this country, but he welcomed the additional trade of the gold seekers. While his accommodations were crude, they did offer some protection. The food was passable, the *tequila* excellent, and the bananas unbelievably good and cheap as he sold them for as little as three to five cents per dozen.

After the long and hard climb out of the Plan de Barrancas most of the emigrants stopped overnight at the village of Ixlán del Río. From here to Tepic it was a little over 50 miles, but the steady climbing up and down in the *barranca* country took most of an emigrant's get-up-and-go. When he left Ixlán del Río, he usually didn't make it all the way into Tepic the next day. Instead, most men did very well to travel the next 20 miles to Santa Isabel, a very ancient *poblado* on the northeastern side of an old lava flow called "Black Pass."

A night's rest at Santa Isabel got a man back on his feet for the next day's long ride. Starting out of Santa Isabel at dawn, the Argonaut rode between ten and twelve hours. Then just before nightfall he entered a magnificent mountain valley, and at the foot of the extinct Sángagüey volcano was what he had been waiting to see ever since he had left Guadalajara. There, surrounded by cotton and tobacco fields, outlined by tall poplar and elm trees lining the *alamedas*, was Tepic—a seaport town in the mountains.

---

## TEPIC: A MOUNTAIN SEAPORT

---

A seaport city without a sea might have seemed strange to the Argonauts if they hadn't come to Tepic from such places as Tampico and Vera Cruz. But they had seen friends die of fever, or become so sick they had to be shipped back to the States. They had tried breathing hot, humid air that was like steam. They had battled swarms of buzzing and droning insects. And they had had their fill of the tropics. To these men, a seaport that was 50 miles from the ocean, over 3,000 feet above sea level, and situated in a temperate valley surrounded by hills and tall mountains except for a narrow western pass was not strange. Tepic's mountain location made perfect sense.

They rode into the city on the broad, clean, tree-lined streets. And they laughed as their *arriero* said, "*Señor*, in Tepic the streets are so clean you can eat off them." For indeed, the streets were clean— a good deal cleaner than most *fondas* the men had ever seen. But J. A. Perry discovered that clean streets didn't automatically mean clean *fondas*.

After having walked past "The Rum-shop of the Virgin Mary" and "The Inn of Christ," Perry and another man of his company selected a likely-looking *fonda* and stepped inside. As they sat down and ordered dinner, it must have occurred to them that it might be cleaner if they did eat their dinner off the streets. They watched with fascination as the cook searched her hair for lice while she prepared dinner, and they knew they were going to be served another vermin-spiced meal. When the meal was served, Perry decided he didn't want to eat with his fingers, and asked for a fork. The woman looked startled, but managed to find a fork for him. Then just as she was somewhat pleased with herself for having helped the fussy *gringo,* Perry asked her to wash the fork for him. She looked disgusted, but took his fork, dipped it in water, and wiped it with a dirty rag. When Perry took another look at the fork, he decided that ". . . it needed cleaning with a piece of twine, as you would clean a dirty comb . . .," [65] so he put it aside and used his jackknife.

All things considered, though, New Englander Perry had a knack for finding the dirtiest *fonda* in town, no matter where he stopped while crossing Mexico. Other gold seekers who passed through Tepic never complained about such things. On the contrary, they were highly pleased with this mountain seaport. No doubt part of their pleasure was due to the fact that they were within one day's ride of San Blas and only had to wait until they were notified by one of Tepic's shipping offices that a vessel was in the harbor and space available for California passengers. But gold seekers who were bound for Mazatlán and still had a week's ride up the coast once they left Tepic also felt that they were much more welcome here than they had been in other Mexican towns and cities. While some of the goodwill the men felt was the result of the business they brought to shipping firms, *fondas, mesones,* and *cantinas,* another reason for such friendly treatment was the response of a large number of Europeans who lived in Tepic.

Many of these foreigners were connected with various mercantile houses "...doing business through Pacific ports...," [66] but these men lived in Tepic rather than San Blas for reasons of health and comfort. Other Europeans were involved in such businesses as the import and export trade, the operation of distilleries, the management of cotton, rice, sugar, and tobacco plantations, and in the case of the English firm of Barron, Forbes & Company—the operation of an extensive cotton mill.

While waiting in Tepic the Argonauts walked the balcony-covered sidewalks in the business district. They visited the city's magnificent cathedral with its twin Gothic towers. They sat on a bench and watched the evening promenade around the plaza. A few men attended the theater. Others went to the bullfights if they were in season. Many of the men went to the horse races, and a few went hunting for ducks and geese at the marshy lakes about a mile and a half east of the city. But for all the men their greatest pleasure was the knowledge that they were near the end of the trail, and they sat and talked about the various gold-mining techniques they had heard or read about.

Men like ex-Reverend Daniel B. Woods, who had made the Mexico crossing from Tampico with the Camargo Company, New Englander J. A. Perry, who had come all the way from Vera Cruz, Daniel Wadsworth Coit, who had traveled from Mexico City with his load of coins to trade for gold, and all the others knew that at Tepic they could relax. Even men who were going on to Mazatlán—men like Josiah Gregg, Thomas Sayre, and Edwin Allen Sherman—knew that their Mexico crossing was fast becoming memory. One week more and the Mazatlán men would be walking on the crescent *playa* and watching the high rolling breakers rush into Olas Altas with a roar. One day more and the San Blas men would be swatting mosquitoes, sweating in a humid, hothouse climate, walking the coconut-palm-lined white *playa* or trying to get cool in the surf of the Pacific Ocean. And with luck these men of the trail knew they would soon be aboard a ship that was sailing to California.

## THERE'S A SHIP AT SAN BLAS

It would begin like this: an Argonaut with his heavy wool clothing, an Argonaut with long hair getting near his shoulders and with an untrimmed beard that made him look much older than he really was, would rush out of a shipping office in Tepic, give a wild shout, and walk the streets like a town crier.

"A ship's at San Blas! A California ship!"

Another gold seeker, perhaps a man resting in the sun, a man writing a journal entry, or a man marveling at the fair and beautiful women of Tepic, would suddenly realize what he had heard, and say, "Are you sure?"

"Yes, yes I'm dead certain!"

"Is she booked tight? Does she have any space?"

"She's still got space, but you'd better hurry. The line's already getting long."

This was how the last rush to San Blas began. The line at the shipping office formed in a hurry. Passenger space was quickly sold. Then the Argonauts learned that they had to be in San Blas within a day, or their space on the ship would be sold to another who was already waiting on the beach.

Daniel Wadsworth Coit was content to rest at Tepic. He had been invited to stay at the home of George W. P. Bissell, the American Consul and the agent for Howland & Aspinwall. And after the long trip from Mexico City, Coit was happy to sleep in a good bed, be waited on by servants, and eat good food. But it lasted for only two days. On the third day, even before Coit was out of bed, a servant handed him a letter that Bissell had sent from San Blas telling him that the steamer *Oregon* had put into port and that he had to be in San Blas by seven o'clock that evening if he ". . . expected to secure . . . passage in her." [67]

With the aid of Mr. Forbes of Barron, Forbes & Company, Coit was able to hire *arrieros* and pack mules and get out of Tepic by nine-thirty that morning. Twelve hours later he was swatting mosquitoes at San Blas. While he hadn't made the seven o'clock dead-line, the steamer had been detained for a day, and his passage space had not yet been sold to someone else.

The trail Coit and the other Argonauts took from Tepic to San Blas wasted no time in getting out of the mountains. A few miles outside Tepic it began to drop from the temperate climate of Tepic's mountain valley. As riders looked below and to the west, they saw a thin, blue haze. Many emigrants thought this was the sea, and that the high land shooting up here and there were islands. Then when they asked their *arrieros*, these men of the trails would smile and explain that what they really saw was the rising warm air of the hot country.

After the view of the blue haze, the trail dropped sharply through a series of *arroyos* and small *barrancas*. Then it passed through an area of small farms. Beyond this fine, cultivated land, gold seekers followed the trail across the ridge of a steep hill. From this ridge they saw a jumble of mountains on both sides. Then the trail de-scended even lower, and the wool-shirted Argonauts felt as though they suffered from fever and were wrapped in heavy blankets. Next they came to Guaristempa, a *poblado* the Spanish had established in the eighteenth century as a halfway station between Tepic and San Blas. After Guaristempa the trail switchbacked upward again to the summit of a tremendous hill. From here the emigrants saw the Pacific Ocean for the first time.

The first view of the ocean was also the last until the men had almost reached San Blas, for the trail wound its way down from the summit of the last mountain onto a hot plain that was almost bare of trees except for a few palms that seemed to be growing in the glare of the hot sun as though they were the last of an ancient and dying forest. It was a short and hot ride through this area where the sun seemed to reflect off the ground and make a man's eyes squint and burn—a short ride that took the Argonauts into a region of jungle-covered foothills that the *arrieros* called La Puerta, or the Gateway.

From this point on, Coit and all the others who rode this trail to San Blas passed through a tropical forest that was almost impassable except for the road the Spanish had cut through it. The predominant color was green, but it was highlighted with bright warm colors that might have been painted by Paul Gauguin. The tall coconut palms formed an umbrella of green over this color, and below them were wild banana trees in bloom—their flowers as scarlet as a cutlass wound. From broad-leafed banyan or wild fig trees came the screech of strange birds calling. There were bright green parrots, variegated hummingbirds that were like large bumblebees, macaws with bright yellow beaks and a loud squawk, and pheasants that took off in a blur of color and sound that spooked horses and mules. Added to the scene as moving dots of color, flitting among the tangle of vines that tied the trees together, were butterflies of every color and size. An English traveler who came through La Puerta in 1850 wrote that he was astounded by ". . . those gorgeous blue butterflies which are nearly as large as the crown of one's hat." [68]

But the tropical life of the trees and vines was not the only thing which fascinated the men who traveled this road. Iguana lizards also were unusual, and W. C. Smith found that these reptiles that looked like something from another period of the earth's history were not allowed to go to waste by the natives, who considered sliced iguana a rare delicacy. "One day," Smith said, "some of us bought at a roadside place what we thought was cold fried veal, and splendid eating. . . ." [69] Then when their interpreter agreed it was quite good but that it was iguana and not veal, Smith and his companions stopped eating. They simply could not cope with the idea that a lizard was something that a person could eat.

Once the Argonauts crossed through La Puerta, they passed by large salt beds on an old Spanish road that convicts from Guadalajara had constructed out of stones, thin tree limbs, sand, and broken oyster shells that were bigger than a man's hand. From these salt beds on into San Blas, the gold seekers entered an area of swampland where the Río Santiago often overflowed its banks and covered the road with water. This was the land of waterfowl. Great flocks of ducks, geese, egrets, and birds the men couldn't identify were in constant movement. At times it appeared as though the swampland had been caught up by the rhythm of movement and was shifting back and forth with the varied flight patterns of the birds.

A few miles west of the salt beds the road terminated at an estuary. Here the Argonauts and their supplies were ferried across in dugout canoes, while the horses and mules had to swim. As the men crossed, they got a good view to the south of a thick jungle area of mangrove trees extending to the banks of the estuary. The *arrieros* explained to the gold seekers that on the trees next to the water it was easy to get oysters that attached themselves to the roots and trunks at high tide; then at low tide all a man had to do was paddle along in a canoe—watching out for alligators and water snakes—and simply pick oysters off the trees the way he picked oranges and bananas.

On the western side of the estuary the gold seekers stepped ashore near the foot of the squared-off bluff called Cerro de Basilio. Looking upward, the men saw the remaining portion of old San Blas, the San Blas the Spanish had built between 1773 and 1781 as their base for operations in northwestern Mexico and Baja California. As the gold seekers passed by the old town they saw crested iguanas darting in and out of stone walls. They saw the chapel and fort built of lava boulders and the ruins of the well-planned town that was slowly giving way to the encroaching jungle. William Carpenter visited San Blas in 1848, just shortly after Lieutenant Beale had passed through with the news of the gold discovery, and Carpenter described the old town on Cerro de Basilio:

> . . . it appeared . . . like the ruins of some ancient castle, situated on a high hill. We soon entered it, and found that it was almost as ruinous as it looked when we first came in sight. It was regularly laid out, and had once been of considerable importance. . . . But at the present time it is nearly deserted, and many of its public buildings are a mass of ruins. Complete solitude appeared to reign throughout the place.[70]

When J. A. Perry arrived at San Blas in the spring of 1849 he thought the old town should have been kept in better shape; for he considered the new town down on the flat to be nothing more than ". . . a miserable village of sticks and mud and flags." [71] But he did go down to the beach to take a swim, and there he found many men and women getting ready to go into the surf. To his surprise, he also saw that both men and women thought ". . . nothing of stripping naked on the beach, and in this manner they go into the water to bathe." [72]

The gold rush had brought new life to San Blas, and it was no longer a sleepy and forgotten village. The harbor saw the comings and goings of Howland & Aspinwall's steamships, of sailing vessels, and of anything else that might possibly be able to sail up the Pacific

Coast. Day and night the old Spanish seaport did a booming business serving both California-bound men and those who were already returning with their pile or with a belly full of the mining business. *Fandangos* were all-night affairs. *Cantinas* were jammed with men who wore red worsted shirts, trousers tucked into their boots, swatted mosquitoes and gnats, gambled at the monte tables, drank too much *tequila*, and sometimes got into fatal fights over women. Some of the W. C. Smith party got involved in such a brawl, and before it ended four or five Mexicans had been killed and several of the Americans were wounded. J. A. Perry also wrote about one of these violent affairs in which a Mexican struck an Argonaut on the head with a sword. While it was a glancing blow and didn't do too much damage, the Americans quickly pulled out pistols and began to shoot. They killed the sword-swinger and wounded several others at the *fandango*. Then the Americans went to their rooms, thinking that the fight had ended. But the Mexicans returned, and were armed for battle. The Americans barricaded their room, and when the shooting stopped, several *gringos* were wounded; but four citizens of San Blas were dead.

Despite such moments of violence San Blas welcomed its new prosperity. But *cantinas, fondas,* and *mesones* were not the only businesses that made a profit out of the gold rush. Supplies of all kinds were needed in California, and many items were shipped from San Blas. Vegetables and fruits were the major export products, but mules, decks of cards, and even fighting cocks were sent to San Francisco. One of the biggest money-makers was the onion business. "When I left San Blas," wrote an English traveler, "onions were selling at a dollar and a half per pound in the market at San Francisco." [73] At this rate it was highly profitable to buy and sell onions even though a percentage of them would spoil on the voyage. Yet the profit in onions was small compared to the coin business that attracted Daniel Wadsworth Coit. For until California got its own mint it was terribly short of coins in a society wildly jumping in population growth. In this situation a man with coins for sale was able to purchase gold worth $16 per ounce for as little as $8.

However, the most profitable export of all that passed through San Blas during the first two years of the gold rush was the Argonaut himself. And nobody was more aware of this than men who owned anything that might conceivably carry these gold seekers up the Pacific Coast to San Francisco. Passage from San Blas to California generally cost between $150 for steerage to $300 for a cabin during 1849. During 1850, the average dropped $50 in each category as a result of the increasing number of ships making runs from San Francisco to Panama and back.

Conditions aboard many of these ships left much to be desired in the way of comfort and safety. Captains crowded as many passengers aboard as they thought the ship might hold, had a tendency to put everybody on short rations, and seemed to think they'd sail the distance without running into bad weather. As a result of such conditions, more than one ship went down; and more than one passenger got off a risky vessel as she stopped at Mazatlán or Baja California.

Even the King of the Sandwich Islands, King Kamehameha III, entered into the business of transporting Argonauts to California. He had purchased an old condemned whaler called the *Mary Frances* which he had been using as his "warship." But when he heard about the gold rush migration, he sent the ship to Mexico to pick up passengers. One of the men who sailed out of San Blas on the *Mary Frances* was W. C. Smith, who had come all the way from Vera Cruz by way of Guadalajara where he joined the emigrants from Tampico. According to what Smith said, the *Mary Frances* had "... no fixtures save the bare, oil soaked decks, old oil barrels for water tanks, and as a cooking range two try kettles in a furnace, just as left by the whalers—our quarters and food were both pretty rough. To each of us was allotted and marked on the main deck with chalk a space of about four by eight feet, where we were expected to keep all our belongings and to sleep." [74] Bad as she was, though, the *Mary Frances* was far better than many vessels that were employed in a service for which they had never been designed. At least, the *Mary Frances* did make it to San Francisco even though Smith and some of the other passengers left the whaler when she put into the harbor at Cape San Lucas, Baja California, and walked the rest of the way.

Like the whaler *Mary Frances*, San Blas had seen better days. For years the old Spanish seaport had been suffering from neglect. She was not really ready for the great migration of 1849 and 1850. But ready or not, there was no denying that these bearded, sweaty and noisy *gringos* who had come down out of the *barrancas* and were nervously and impatiently walking the *playa* had the jingle of coins in their pockets. Though the merchants, gamblers, and whores had forgotten many things during the quiet years, they had not lost their knack for picking up *pesos*. So, while some citizens of San Blas joined these *norteamericanos* in their rush to California, others lit more punks in their business houses to help fight off the mosquitoes, gnats, and chiggers and cashed in on the gold rush by mining the miners.

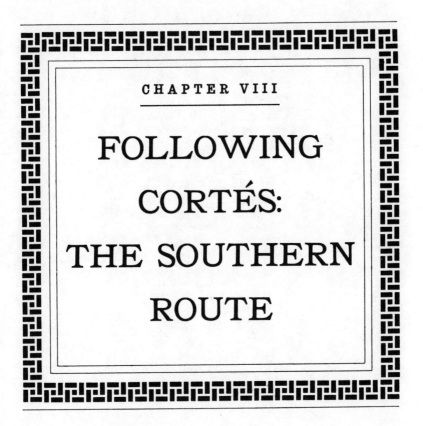

CHAPTER VIII

# FOLLOWING CORTÉS: THE SOUTHERN ROUTE

# A HELMET FULL OF GOLD

It was Holy Thursday, April 21, 1519, when Cortés and his fleet dropped anchor at the port of San Juan de Ulúa. On Good Friday they established their camp on the sand dunes. An altar was set up for Mass; wood and brush were gathered for the construction of huts; the artillery was placed in a commanding position, and the horses were safely picketed.

By Saturday, representatives of Montezuma's government approached the camp. They brought food, and some gifts of jewels and gold. They explained to Cortés that on the next day a governor named Teuhtlilli would arrive to confer with them.

The Aztecs were very curious about the faces of these strangers—faces that were the color of the moon and had hair that extended from their heads and formed a line of brush like a jungle growth. They were also astounded by the strange four-legged animals that the bone-colored men were able to become a part of, by the loud barking thunder sticks, and by the funny tree with two straight arms that these men worshipped. So when Cortés and his officers greeted Teuhtlilli on Easter Sunday, the Aztecs had brought artists with them. Then while the representatives of the two nations broke bread together, the artists painted portraits of Cortés and his men, so that Montezuma might know what they looked like.

Cortés was quite polite, and made all the proper signs of friendship as he thanked Teuhtlilli for the gifts of food, jewels, and gold. Then he told the Aztec governor that he wished to visit Montezuma. Along with his request for an audience with the Aztec ruler, Cortés presented Teuhtlilli with some gifts: glass beads, a carved armchair for Montezuma, and a medal with the figure of St. George on horseback busily slaying the dragon. Then, at the request of the Aztecs, he gave them a soldier's gilded helmet.

Six or seven days after this first meeting, Teuhtlilli returned to the camp of Cortés on the beach that would one day be the waterfront of Vera Cruz. With him were over a hundred men. These men carried more gifts for these strange visitors to Montezuma's land. Among these gifts were some items that astounded Cortés and his men.

> . . . a wheel like a sun, as big as a cartwheel, with many sorts of pictures on it . . . the whole of fine gold . . . another wheel . . . of greater size made of silver of great brilliancy in imitation of the moon with other figures shown on it . . . and the chief brought back the helmet full of fine grains of gold.[1]

Nor was this all that the Aztecs presented to the men from Spain. There were twenty golden ducks, golden dogs, golden jaguars, golden lions, and golden monkeys. And there were gifts of cloth, food, and semi-precious jewels. But of all these wonderful treasures, it was the soldier's helmet filled with free gold that was the final invitation for conquest. For Cortés was interested in more than gifts. He wanted the source of the treasure, and reasoned that if these people had free gold in such quantity they *had* gold mines.

Three hundred and thirty years later, the harbor at Vera Cruz was once again filled with gold seekers. This time, though, no Aztecs came forth with a helmet full of gold. This time the people of Mexico sent forth their customs officers to meet this new migration of pale strangers.

## THE PREVAILING INFECTION

George Holbrook Baker was an up-and-coming young art student at the National Academy of Design when he was stricken with gold fever. While he loved his work, the excitement of the moment, combined with the fact that he was tired of having to put up with the accepted artistic standards, were all that he needed to break the pattern of his life. To Baker, the gold fields of California presented an opportunity for adventure and a chance to get rich. "Accordingly," he wrote, "I caught the prevailing infection, and dropped my brushes. . . ." [2]

He returned to the family home in Boston, bade everyone farewell, and joined eleven other men to form the New England Pioneers. On January 8, 1849, this company of Argonauts left Boston. The snow was eighteen inches deep, and Baker remembered the jingle of sleighbells on their way to the train. This was not too surprising, in that his mother's family—the Holbrooks—were noted bell makers.

The New England Pioneers rode the train to Washington. Here they obtained passports to enter Mexico, gathered the latest news about California, and sailed on the steamer *Powhatan*, which had to break its way through the covering of ice on the Potomac River. But this was almost the last cold weather these Easterners would feel. South of Washington they left the Potomac and traveled southwest by train and steamer to New Orleans. There they purchased deck passage aboard the schooner *Nancy Bishop* bound for Vera Cruz. On January 30 she set sail on a morning that was so foggy her captain had to keep a man aloft to sing out should he see the mast of another vessel. Without being able to take a last look at the States, the New England Pioneers sailed down the Mississippi River and into the Gulf of Mexico.

During their voyage the passengers were seasick for the first part of the trip, and terrified for the last two days when the schooner was hit by a norther and tossed about like a bobbing cork. Baker never forgot this experience. The ocean appeared ready to engulf the ship as they dropped into a trough and saw waves towering higher than the schooner. Then, just as they were certain of their doom, the ship would shoot upward and ride the crest of a wave. At times the storm struck with such fury that Baker and the others had to lash themselves to the spars to avoid being washed overboard. But the *Nancy Bishop* rode the storm in good shape even though her passengers did not, and the morning after it was all over, the day broke clear; and the schooner was in full sail and within sight of the coastline of Mexico.

As Baker and his fellow passengers strained their eyes for a first glimpse of the Castle of San Juan de Ulúa and the city of Vera Cruz, far above and in back of the city, they saw the morning sun's rays give a golden hue to white thunderheads gathered over higher mountains than they had ever seen before. Then the wind shifted the clouds momentarily, and they had their first glimpse of Mount Orizaba jutting over 18,000 feet into the air. The wind changed directions again, and Citlaltepetl, or Mountain of the Star, vanished from their view. By early afternoon the *Nancy Bishop* sailed into the open harbor facing the walls of Castillo de San Juan de Ulúa. The ship's captain proceeded without a pilot, and before they dropped anchor they almost rammed the bark *Eugenia*. She was out of New York and carrying 130 gold seekers under the command of Captain Hutton. His party was destined to have one man shot to death on the trail from Guadalajara to Tepic.

After the close call with the *Eugenia*, the captain of the *Nancy Bishop* dropped anchor, and the New England Pioneers and the other passengers prepared to go ashore. But the Captain of the Port did not come aboard to check the ship right away for its cargo, number of passengers, crew, and their health. Consequently, nobody could go ashore until the port official got around to his job.

With an afternoon and an evening to spend aboard ship, Baker had time to examine the harbor and the outline of the city from the deck. "The harbor," he wrote, "is open from the north, but on the south and east protected by a long range of coral reefs terminating at its northern point with the renowned castle of San Juan d'Ulloa. This latter, although a fine castle, did not come up to my ideas of the Gibraltar of America, as it has been styled. . . ." [3] He also saw the Isla de los Sacrificios, which the Aztecs had used for bloody religious services. Then, as Baker looked toward shore, he saw the city's irregular outline with its church spires dominating the skyline. He saw the battered sea wall with great shellholes in it from the American bombardment during the Mexican War. In the still, tropical evening he heard the tolling of church bells, and tried to determine the type and size. Automatically, he compared the quality of these bells to the ones his grandfather made.

In the morning the New England Pioneers were allowed to go ashore. They hired some of the many small boats that were clustered around the *Nancy Bishop*, and for a few *pesos* they were rowed to a stone breakwater. Here they were checked by Mexican customs officers who examined their passports and gear. Baker didn't care too much for this, but he did credit the officials for their politeness and mild concern as they gave his trunk a cursory inspection. Such treatment, though, varied considerably. In great measure what took place between the individual customs officer and the individual Argonaut depended upon their respective attitude toward each other. In Baker's case things went smoothly, but other *norteamericanos* had difficulty.

Some difficulties came about for a variety of reasons, but the usual cause was disrespect. Either the Yankee considered the Mexican nothing but a greaser, and let him know it; or the Mexican considered the American a *gringo* who was directly responsible for the Mexican War, and let him know it. Another New Englander, J. A. Perry, had the kind of unpleasant experience typical of such mutual disrespect.

Perry and his party sailed to Vera Cruz by way of Havana, and had left there feeling that wherever Catholicism was the basic religion the society would be one of bigotry, cruelty, and dishonesty. With this idea firmly entrenched in their minds, Perry and his friends approached the customs officers with a haughty air of superiority. They had picked up their passports from the Mexican consul in New York, and had been told that would be all they needed to get through Mexico. But the officers at Vera Cruz sensed their attitude, or were out to make some extra money. The passports were called for, and a notation was made on the back of them. This cost Perry and the others 75 cents each. Then they were ordered to take them to the governor, who placed his seal on them. This not only took time but also cost $1 per man. All of this convinced Perry that ". . . either the Mexican Consul at New York lied to us, or the Mexican government at Vera Cruz swindled us, and they may have it the way that suits them best." [4]

This initial experience with the customs officers quite frequently set the mood for the Argonaut and determined the nature of his trip. If he got the kind of treatment that Perry received, he usually carped, complained, and found fault with everything all the way across Mexico. But if he was accorded the kind of treatment that Baker received, then his Mexican adventure frequently became one of the most important experiences in his life.

## VERA CRUZ: CITY OF INVASION

Vera Cruz began as a beachhead for invasion. When Hernán Cortés
needed a legal base to show the Crown that he was acting within the
law, he established ". . . the municipality of Villa Rica de la Vera
Cruz, which thereupon elected him Governor and Captain-Gen-
eral. . . ." [5] By doing this, Cortés had perfectly legitimate grounds to
do whatever was necessary in defense of this Spanish municipality.
He established the notion that this new Spanish settlement was
threatened by Montezuma's realm, and began his march to the Aztec
capital. After the fighting was over Cortés silenced potential critics
of the moment who might question his distorting legality by pre-
senting the Crown with *all* that gold. The only justification for ac-
cepting such gifts was to recognize the legal acquisition of them as
something taken in a defensive war. In this fashion Cortés and the
Conquistadors were not only the first wave of invaders to land at Vera
Cruz, but also its first "legal" settlers.

Following in the wake of the Spanish were the English pirates.
They became involved in the business of selling African slaves to
Spanish settlers of the West Indies. Then, after they had sold a
shipload of slaves, they preyed upon the Spanish treasure fleets.
Once again Vera Cruz saw an invasion force near its shore. The
year was 1568, just forty-nine years after Cortés had landed. This
wave of invaders was not successful. John Hawkins and his pirate
fleet were trapped by the Spanish Navy off the coast of San Juan
de Ulúa, and suffered a severe defeat. Many of the pirates were
killed in battle. Others were captured, tortured, killed in public
spectacles, or forced to become loyal Spanish Catholics. But two small
tenders of the English fleet managed to escape and make their way
to England. The biggest prize of all for the Spaniards, John Hawkins,
escaped in one of these tenders.

The next major invasion of Vera Cruz took place in the latter part
of November, 1838. Once again it was over gold. This time the
French had come to collect money that Mexico owed them. They
blockaded the port, but stayed beyond shelling range of San Juan

de Ulúa—the foreboding, quadrangular stone fortress built by the Spanish on Gallega Island, a coral reef about one-half mile offshore. While the French sailors and marines stared at the whitewashed, heavy walls protecting the base of Castillo de San Juan de Ulúa's tower, their admiral sent an official message to the Governor of Vera Cruz telling him to pay the debt or suffer the consequences. This bit of gunboat diplomacy got nowhere with the Mexicans, who considered San Juan de Ulúa invincible.

In a furious artillery battle on the afternoon of November 27, 1838, the French cannons hit the magazine on one of the fort's bastions. The explosion that followed was the major blow of the battle. As darkness ended the first day's engagement, the Mexican generals went all to pieces and sent word to the French that they were willing to surrender. But before they could, General Santa Anna arrived and quickly took command. He had the surrendering generals arrested, and opened fire on the unsuspecting French.

Bitter at the loss of an easy victory, the French decided to capture Santa Anna. Before dawn on December 5 they landed a force of marines. These men managed to spike the cannons guarding the port, but failed to capture the wily Santa Anna. Yet they did get part of him. For as they withdrew and Santa Anna and his men charged, he was wounded in one leg. What followed was a comic-opera finish to the attempted French conquest of Vera Cruz. The only victory the French would really claim as they sailed out of the harbor was that they had spiked the cannons of the Mexican Gibraltar. On the other side, General Santa Anna, who was still smarting from his defeat by Texans at San Jacinto, was once again Mexico's true hero. The loss of a leg was worth all the pain and suffering for his new popularity as the man who defeated the French at Vera Cruz.

Nine years later, though, General Santa Anna suffered a crushing defeat at the Battle of Buena Vista outside Saltillo on February 22–23, 1847. Then, on March 9, an American army of about 12,000 men under the command of General Winfield Scott landed in the surf at Vera Cruz. It was an all-day operation that required ferrying the troops ashore in sixty-seven whaleboats that were under constant fire from the batteries of Castillo de San Juan de Ulúa. In this manner the siege of Vera Cruz began, but the shelling of the city was held off until March 22 because the steady blowing of northers made it impossible for the artillery to land.

General Scott called for the surrender of the city, but the Gover-

THE EL DORADO TRAIL

nor, General Morales, refused. What followed was sheer hell for the
citizens. Day and night American artillery and rockets struck all
parts of Vera Cruz. The hospital in the church of Santo Domingo
was hit many times, and patients, doctors, and nurses were killed or
wounded. Then the hospital was moved to the church of San Francisco, and this was also blasted. By the twenty-sixth the Mexican
forces were almost out of ammunition, but the real horror was the
death and destruction the American shelling was bringing to the
city right around the clock. Consuls of foreign governments within
the city pleaded with General Scott to stop this bombardment. His
reply was that it would cease when the Mexicans surrendered. But
General Morales grimly hung on. Then, at midnight of March 28,
General Landero relieved Morales of his command. Landero saw
that there was only enough ammunition for about three more hours
of battle, that Vera Cruz was filled with the dead and the dying,
and that the city was being reduced to rubble. There was no other
choice that made sense. General Landero surrendered.

When the American troops entered Vera Cruz on the twenty-
eighth they were stunned by the results of their bombardment. As
one man with the troops put it, ". . . our army had thrown 3,000 ten-
inch shells, 200 howitzer shells, 1,000 paxihan shot, and 2,500 round-
shot, weighing on the whole about *half a million of pounds!* Most
effective and most terrible was the disaster and destruction they
caused within the walls of the city, whose ruins and mourning
attested both the energy and sadness of war." [6]

Following in the footsteps of Cortés, General Scott and his troops
moved through Vera Cruz and headed for Mexico City. But they
were marching against a nation near the brink of collapse. General
Santa Anna's crushing defeat at Buena Vista had been the final
proof that Mexico was truly defeated from within. The country had
been too poor for too long. Its leaders were consumed by personal
hatred and old feuds. The citizenry who might have rallied to the
country's defense was apathetic and indifferent. For the Halls of
Montezuma were plagued with the sickness of despair, and many
Mexicans welcomed the American invasion as an event that might
cause the collapse of a corrupt society.

Yet no matter how much the Mexicans disliked their leaders, they
disliked defeat and occupation even more. This was a fact of life
that the Argonauts discovered when they landed at Vera Cruz in

1849, just two years after the city had been devastated by American artillery. To the Mexicans it seemed as though the American troops had just sailed away. Now here was another invasion of *gringos!* Only this time they were not shelling the city. Why bother? Most of the old wounds were plainly visible.

This new army of *gringos* had different uniforms. They wore wide-brimmed, soft hats; rubber or leather boots that reached to the knees; wool trousers that were tucked into their boots, and red flannel or wool shirts. And they carried different equipment: ". . . tin pans for washing out the gold, shovels, picks, spades, crowbars, camp-kettles, frying pans, tin plates, tin cups, daguerreotypes, locks of hair, Spanish books, a few patent gold washers, musical instruments . . . rifles, carbines, shot-guns, revolvers, and bowie-knives. . . ." [7]

Among these gold seekers were men who had invaded Vera Cruz with the forces of General Scott. Only this time they had a different viewpoint regarding the city from the one they had on that day when they had jumped out of a whaleboat into the surf and waded ashore. This time they saw things they hadn't noticed before because of the shooting and the dying. But there were also reminders of that time of violence.

Colonel Daniel E. Hungerford had landed with General Scott's troops and had marched and fought his way to Mexico City. At that time he had noticed that Vera Cruz was built up on the shore with the ocean washing against the foundations of some buildings. And he had paid very close attention to the sandy plain that stretched for 2 miles behind the city and terminated in high sandhills. He remembered how he had felt when he first looked at that open ground, and it hadn't been a good feeling. He knew that crossing the plain of sand would be slow going, and that his troopers would be wide open to rifle and artillery fire. Most of all, he remembered he had thought of how anxious the Mexicans would be to punish the Americans after the fall of Vera Cruz.

Now, in February of 1849, nearly two years after that time of invasion, Colonel Hungerford moved in and out of Vera Cruz in three hours. It was as though he didn't wish to linger, as though he wished to get through a bad memory as quickly as possible. For in a letter he wrote during the war Hungerford said that it ". . . was a horrible sight to behold the unburied bodies. The buildings in ruins . . . their

243

dilapidated condition being the havoc made by the shells from our batteries. . . ." [8] And reminders of that bloody siege were all about the city. The beach was littered with the wreckage of whaleboats that had landed troops. U. S. Army wagons seemed to be everywhere, and caissons and artillery carriages were scattered along the waterfront like piles of strangely shaped driftwood. Many walls of buildings bore pockmarks of rifle bullets, and there were great shattered sections caused by artillery hits. Everywhere Hungerford looked it appeared as though the war had just ended. Spent shells and empty shell casings lay where they had fallen, or where some child had rolled or kicked them. A thriving scavenger business in abandoned military supplies was being carried on with the same thoroughness turkey buzzards displayed in picking clean the carcasses of dead animals.

But Colonel Hungerford wasn't the only gold seeker who hurried through Vera Cruz, nor was he the only one who noticed the leavings of war. J. A. Perry saw what the American bombardment had done, and was horrified by what he saw: the remains of a hospital with its few standing walls stained by blood; a church reduced to rubble; and nearby a common grave for the 130 men, women, and children who died in what they thought was a sanctuary—a grave where ". . . parts of human limbs were visible . . .," [9] and the stench was sickening except to the great flocks of turkey buzzards still contesting for what little rotten flesh remained.

The role of the turkey buzzard in the life of Vera Cruz was not overlooked by the government. Perry pointed out that it was strictly against the law to kill these birds. He also agreed that in this tropical climate, the health of the population depended in great measure upon the existence of these black, winged eaters of offal.

But even the beneficent buzzards failed to reduce a man's chances of coming down with yellow fever as he moved in and out of Vera Cruz. Ponds of stagnant water were all around this southern seaport during the non-rainy season, and such ponds were natural breeding places for the small, dark-colored mosquitoes that carried the yellow fever virus. Even though gold seekers wore heavy woolen and flannel shirts to protect themselves against fever, they did not know that the small mosquitoes they were constantly cursing and swatting were the real carriers of the disease the Mexicans called *vómito*.

Yet threats of tropical disease, violent clashes with *ladrones* or bitter Mexican patriots, fatal fights among their own parties, and crippling or deadly accidents failed to hold back the rush of men who landed at Vera Cruz during the first two years of the gold rush. There were many reasons for selecting this route across Mexico, but most of these came down to either one or more of the following factors. Men came this way because they had been here with General Scott's invading army; because they had been talked into it by ex-soldiers or by sellers of the dream; and because they had read about this "short and easy" route in one of the popular guidebooks of the time. Whatever their reasons, they came to Vera Cruz in small and large parties from all over the States. They came, and most groups usually passed through this city of invasion in one day.

A few companies of Argonauts did stay over for two or three days while they waited to catch the next *diligencia,* or stagecoach. Some men took a little more time to purchase horses and mules, buy wagons, and hire *arrieros.* Then there were others who stopped in the city because they were ill or because they had become discouraged early in the game and decided to catch the next ship homeward bound. These various groups usually behaved like typical tourists. They strolled around the city, looked at everything, and if they kept a journal or knew how to sketch, they recorded their impressions of this seaport.

Most of all, two things about this city of invasion fascinated men who stayed for any length of time: the residue of the Mexican War and the poor quality of the *mesones.* That self-styled expert on poor *mesones,* J. A. Perry, conceded that the hotel he had taken a room in for the night rated as one of the best in the city. Yet there wasn't a bed in the place. Worst of all, Perry was ushered into a communal room where a few early arrivals had managed to crowd together on the room's one table. All the other overnight guests were sprawled out on the floor.

Perry looked around, shrugged his shoulders, and began to spread out his blankets. His movements flushed out two lizards resting in a corner, and they scurried in among the blankets of the sleepers.

A man who was awake assured Perry that the lizards were absolutely harmless. But his attitude was much too casual, and didn't put Perry at ease. Yet Perry was a practical man, and decided to make the best of the situation. He settled down on the hard floor, twisted and rolled until he found a position of comfort, and started to go to sleep. At that moment somebody lit a piece of candle, and its small flame seemed like a lantern in the dark room. Perry sat bolt upright and looked around. What he saw ended his night's sleep:

> . . . upon the wall was one of the largest spiders that I ever beheld. We tried to kill it, but it fled to the corner where we had started the lizards, and made its exit into a hole. A few feet from this hole we killed a scorpion. This aroused several, and another huge spider was seen and killed, which proved to be a santipee, whose bite is more poisonous than that of the rattle-snake. I now took up my blanket, wrapped it about me, and sat down on a trunk, preferring to sit up and sleep, rather than to lie down with scorpions and santipees.[10]

While Perry went into detail about his lodging for the night, other journal keepers wrote about the city in general. These men visited the churches, admired the tall towers, but considered the interiors to be a display of Catholic vulgarity. They walked along the cobble-stone streets that were washed and swept every morning, and toured the residential area. They looked at thick adobe walls fronting the streets, windows barred with iron grillwork and set well above the reach of a passing horseman, and at the red tiled roofs. Entrances to these homes were either through thick, carved hardwood doors, or stout iron gates that allowed the passage of carriages into court-yards where there was usually a fountain, and always a profusion of bright-colored flowers.

In the business section of Vera Cruz the gold seekers ambled along on sidewalks shaded by floors of second-story balconies that were supported by graceful columns and arches. Here the *norteamerica-nos* ate dinner in *fondas* of varying quality. In the best of these places meals generally consisted of soup, fresh fish from the Gulf Stream, *carne asada*—tough, stringy, highly spiced beef that was roasted until it was almost like jerky—*frijoles, tortillas,* a bottle of very bad wine, and a cup of coffee or chocolate. Close to the *fondas* were the offices of the stage and freighting companies. Some of the flush Argonauts purchased tickets to Mexico City for $50. If they were bound for San Blas or Mazatlán, they paid a fare of $110 just for the trip to Guadalajara, and then had to buy a horse or mule for the rest of the journey. Neither of these fares included any meals or lodgings along the way, and all passengers were told to carry fire-arms in case the stagecoach was attacked by *ladrones*.

## Following Cortés: The Southern Route

Travel by *diligencia* was much too expensive for most gold seekers, so they bought horses and mules for their trip across Mexico. Prices varied considerably, depending upon the quality of the animal but it usually ranged between $25 and $40.[11] A few companies of miners also bought abandoned U. S. Army wagons which they planned to take as far as Guadalajara if they were headed northwest, or as far as Mexico City if they were on their way to Acapulco.

No matter how they traveled, the beginning stretch of the National Road was tough on animals and men. First, gold-rush companies were hit in the pocketbook by a vacillating policy that sometimes charged emigrants as much as $3 per wagon to gain admittance through the Vera Cruz gate to the National Road. Second, most companies did very well to travel 10 miles on the first day to the *poblado* of Santa Fé. For a few miles along the hard-packed sand of the shoreline the going wasn't bad at all, but then it headed through deep, heavy sandhills that continually shifted and covered the road.

Alongside the road were many different kinds of cacti, matted and tangled shrubs, vines, gray chaparral brush, stunted and spindly trees, and some tall palms that swayed with the slightest breeze. If a man traveled this route in the spring, each cactus, shrub, vine, bush, and tree added its bright and colorful flowers to the otherwise dull landscape. But travelers who came this way during the season of drought saw only a world where everything blended into a gray wasteland.

After Santa Fé, where the houses were thatched huts, the road passed across an area where there was easier traction, more trees, and tremendous flights of birds. There were ". . . parrots and birds which seemed to be the toucan—about the size of the great woodpecker of the United States with an enormous bill—great numbers of wild pigeons, doves of two or three varieties, small birds similar to the oriole of gaudy plumage . . ."[12] and a continuous movement of waterfowl. Beyond this region of birds lay the slopes of the foothills.

The first summit on the National Road was the crest of a small ridge. From this point, on a clear day, the Argonauts were able to see the high, distant, glistening white snow on the cone of Mount Orizaba. This was the real start of their Mexico journey. Here men looked back and saw the sandhills, the sandy plain, the outline of

Vera Cruz, and the Gulf of Mexico. Ahead they saw the zigzag line of switchbacks cut into the earth and rock of the Sierra Madre Oriental—switchbacks leading into a jumble of intertwined ridges, *barrancas,* and cloud-covered peaks. Yet the way ahead didn't require any trail blazing. For this was the National Road, and much of the route followed the old trail of conquest.

---

## TRAIL OF CONQUEST

---

The Manhattan-California Overland Association arrived in Vera Cruz aboard the bark *Mara* in the latter part of February, 1849. There were 200 men in this company on the day it landed. But 50 gold seekers took one look at Vera Cruz, listened with horror to lurid descriptions of what *ladrones* sometimes did to travelers on the National Road, and promptly purchased return passage on the next ship sailing back to New York.

The remainder of the company stayed in Vera Cruz a day and a night. On the following morning they bought horses and mules, loaded their gear into packs, and made the short ride to the *poblado* of Santa Fé. They camped here for one night, and discussed their situation.

While they had already broken their company into four smaller units even before reaching Mexico, one major problem remained. The flim-flam man who had organized the entire venture and who claimed to be a veteran of Mexican travel was not with them. In the last-minute rush at New York he had managed to miss the ship, and the trusting greenhorns didn't even know their leader wasn't with them until they were well at sea.

On the voyage to Vera Cruz the men tried to remedy this by dividing into four companies which elected their respective leaders. But this didn't satisfy them once they had stepped ashore in Mexico and had to face up to a strange language and a country that only the Mexican War veterans among them knew anything about. All of them felt the need for a more military-like organization headed by one major officer. So, at their Santa Fé camp they elected journal keeper A. C. Ferris as their over-all commander.

At this camp the company also divided into messes for convenience. They purchased and slaughtered a beef, and began their life on the trail. When they left here, after the one night, Ferris was completely aware of the responsibility he had accepted. In his recollection of this journey, he described the appearance of this company of gold-hungry greenhorns:

> The first camp-fires, the cooking, the saddling-up, the loading of baggage and equipments on the vicious, kicking, biting mustangs and donkeys, and the final mount were altogether beyond description. Besides the rider, they had to carry two blankets, his mining tools, coffee-pot, camp-kettle, and frying-pan laid on or hanging from his saddle, and his bag of tin cups, spoons, and tin plates, and his gun, rifle, or carbine slung on his back, and a variety of other articles supposed to be essential. Don Quixote and Sancho Panza joined to Falstaff's regiment would not have presented half so motley a group.[13]

Yet the Manhattan-California Overland Association wasn't the only "motley group" that moved out of Santa Fé and began the upward climb toward Mexico City. In the first few months of 1849 many Yankee Argonauts traveled this route. During this period J. A. Perry and his party were on the move. W. C. Smith reported that his company left Santa Fé after a noon meal of ". . . what the boys pronounced jackass meat."[14] The large New York party of 100 men headed by Colonel Hutton passed this way in February of 1849, and so did the dozen men of the New England Pioneers. George H. Baker, the journal keeper among the New England men, was amazed at the country he saw as his company left the sandy plains and moved into the foothills of the Sierra Madre Oriental. Tropical birds fascinated him, and he was impressed with the great variety of trees— the lofty palms, the broad-leafed banana trees, the papaya, orange, and lemon trees. It seemed to him that the country was a lush garden that grew without any work at all. Here there was free food for anybody. All a man had to do was pick it. After the cold New England countryside this was an uninhibited paradise that advertised itself with colors that ranged from the subdued green of ferns to the brilliant hues of tropical flowers.

As he stared at this wonderland, there was a steady stream of traffic going in both directions on the National Road. Along with the westbound parties of Argonauts there were eastbound ". . . trains of mules loaded with goods bound for Vera Cruz."[15] Some of these

# THE EL DORADO TRAIL

mule trains had as many as 200 heavily laden animals being led along their way by tough but friendly *arrieros*. And it was not an easy road, for "... the heavy artillery of the Americans in passing over it ... destroyed it, and rendered it almost impassable to travel...." [16]

Two days after the Santa Fé camp, Baker and his friends were in a country above the tropics and nearing Jalapa. In this region they crossed deep *barrancas* on bridges made of native limestone, saw pines and oaks intermingled with banana and papaya trees, went past fields of maize and tobacco, through small *poblados* where houses were more like strange plants than creations of man, and topped hogback ridges and were always astounded at the view of tall white mountain peaks that seemed to have a constant swirl of clouds around them.

At the deep *barranca* where the fast, clear water of the Río Antigua rushes toward the Gulf of Mexico, the New England men crossed to the western cliffs on the National Bridge where the invading American forces had fought a furious battle during the Mexican War. The bridge impressed all the men who crossed it on their way to Mexico City. But it wasn't the mixture of limestone and cement and the graceful arches of the span that made it stick in men's minds. Even more than the bridge, it was the setting that men remembered: the long drop to the river, the roaring sound of the water, the great masses of rock that might have been chopped by a clean stroke of a mighty machete, the rich foliage of trees and ferns, and far in the background the brooding heights of Mount Orizaba. Then to add even more to the memory there were the signs of the raging battle that had taken place at this spot. They saw "... the wreckage and the unburied bones of that battlefield..." [17] where Colonel Harney's dragoons had climbed the heights in the face of Santa Anna's open field of fire. The dragoons lost many men in this battle, but they kept moving, pulling themselves forward by hanging on to bushes until they reached the Mexican artillery batteries, captured them, and turned the cannons at the men who had fought to defend the heights.

Twenty miles beyond the bridge, the men from New England—and all others traveling this route—passed by or camped at another famous battleground of the Mexican War. The fight at Cerro Gordo had been even more intense than the one at the National Bridge. Many Argonauts had fought in this battle. Others knew someone who had, or had lost a relative or friend where General Santa Anna's forces put up their most stubborn resistance. Baker wrote that ". . . testimonials of the Americans were found on the road in the shape of grape and cannon shot." [18]

When the Manhattan-California Overland Association reached Cerro Gordo during the same month as the New England Pioneers, they stopped there for a noon break. Their leader, A. C. Ferris, described what they saw as they kindled their fires and got ready to cook.

> . . . dipping water from . . . sunken pools covered with slimy green vegetation, we drank our coffee under the shade of the same trees where the desperately wounded lay to die, glad of the luxury of that stagnant pool to quench their thirst. . . . All around us lay scattered uncoffined bones, and ghastly skulls looked down upon us where in mockery they had been secured among the branches of the trees, and everywhere earth and trees and broken armament gave silent witness of the awful struggles. . . .[19]

At Cerro Gordo the gold seekers were about 3,000 feet above sea level and still moving upward on the twisting National Road. In the next 15 miles they slowly climbed another 1,000 feet and stopped to rest near El Encero—one of General Santa Anna's *haciendas*. Most of the men thought "Santy Anny" had built a place of grand luxury. Not only were the buildings of his ranch admirable, but so was the location. The valley provided good soil and natural grass. There was plenty of water. The nearby mountains were a' handy source of timber, and the climate was ideal.

Yet 10 miles farther ahead and 500 feet higher in the mountains the Argonauts came to a valley which had even greater beauty. In a location that travelers never forgot was the city of Jalapa, the capital of the State of Vera Cruz. All around this valley the tall, cloud-reaching mountains dominated the scene with their incredible size and shape. But the chill from these snow-covered peaks blended with the warm air rising from the tropical plain near Vera Cruz to create a happy mean where both tropical- and temperate-zone plants and trees grew side by side, and where the threat of the dreaded *vómito* was not present.

A. C. Ferris even picked up a saying about Jalapa that wrapped up everything in one neat statement: "See Jalapa and die." See Jalapa and die was what it all amounted to in the end, for here was a garden world of beauty and peace, a place to escape the extremes and to live out a tranquil life.

W. C. Smith looked at the magnificent mountains, the fertile valley, and took particular notice of the fruit trees: orange, lemon, banana, and apple. To Smith this was the Garden of the World, as so many called it.

George H. Baker noticed the wonderful gardens too; but he also thought it a quiet city, a place where all the quick movements of an American city were not present. Here people took time to savor the world about them.

Yet the city of Jalapa didn't impress these gold seekers. It was like Vera Cruz, but on a smaller scale. They rode along the narrow, cobblestone streets and felt they were passing by the back walls of buildings or were traveling through a chute of blank adobe walls topped by flat tile roofs. There was no feeling of life and warmth, just a feeling of being an unwelcomed guest. Only in the plaza, the cathedral, and the marketplace did these men have any real contact with the people. Only in these very public places did they rid themselves of the illusion that they were passing through a deserted city where the air was filled with the odor of flowers.

But the perfume of all the flowers in Mexico couldn't hide one important fact from these Argonauts. In Jalapa there was no love for the *gringo*. The men of the Manhattan-California Overland Association found that the city was so hostile that they were attacked by a mob that tried to knock them off their horses.

German-born Rudolf Jordan, who had been operating a famous and profitable daguerreotype business in Havana, was acutely aware of this anti-American feeling when he passed through Jalapa aboard a stagecoach. He felt that the citizens were so bitter about the events of the Mexican War that the least thing could trigger a violent reaction. To prevent the possibility of any clash, Jordan and his companions agreed ". . . to avoid the use of the English language . . ." [20] during their trip across Mexico to the port of Mazatlán.

After Jalapa the National Road became a series of steep switchbacks as it climbed up toward the Central Plateau. Not far outside the walled city it crossed a rough area of an old lava flow. Then the road wound its way up through oaks, pines, and junipers. As the Argonauts worked their way higher and higher into the *sierra*, many of them began to feel the altitude. They suffered from nosebleeds, lightheadedness, nausea, and at times found it difficult to breathe. About 20 miles from Jalapa the road reached an altitude of about 8,000 feet above sea level at the *poblado* of Las Vigas.

J. A. Perry and the other New England men stopped overnight at this *poblado* in early March of 1849. "This was a small place, of straw houses, situated on the plains." [21] But it offered some shelter against the chill wind that whistled down from the heights and across the flats. Also, it had a corral for their animals, and was not so likely to be raided by a band of *ladrones* because there were enough men there to cost bandits a high price.

From Las Vigas to Perote was just over 25 miles, but during this part of the journey J. A. Perry and his group saw many crosses alongside the road that marked places where persons had died at the hands of *ladrones*. Along this stretch of road there were ". . . miserable huts, where a few oranges, and some cake, with very poor water, together with some bad liquors. . . " [22] were offered for sale to weary travelers. And by this time, travelers were very weary. From Jalapa the trip had been all uphill, and across *barrancas* that were like giant cracks in the earth. Then to make the journey even more difficult, some of the bridges across these *barrancas* had been destroyed by the retreating Mexican forces during the war. In these places the United States Army had cut roads into sheer cliff walls; but these roads dropped anywhere from one to two thousand feet to the river at the bottom, and made a steep climb up the other side. By the time gold seekers saw the squared-off shape of Cofre de Perote they were so tired that few of them even mentioned the chopped-off peak of this volcano that gave it the look of a blockhouse for some giant fort.

As for Perote, practically nothing was said about the town. These Americans on the move were interested in only one thing at this place, and that was Fort San Carlos, situated about a half mile north of the town. This quadrangular-shaped fort was spread out on the plain and surrounded by a moat. It had been built by the Spanish over a four-year period between 1770–1774. But Americans remembered it for other reasons.

One reason was that this grim fort had been a prison for some Texans who had been captured in their ill-fated expedition against Mier, Mexico, in 1842. The prisoners were kept here until General Santa

# THE EL DORADO TRAIL

Anna released them on September 16, 1844, as part of his mourning for the death of his wife. Among the men who walked out of this prison on that day was Texas Ranger Samuel H. Walker who— according to legend—had buried a coin under the fort's flagstaff which he vowed he'd retrieve when he returned as part of a conquering army. And during the Mexican War, Captain Walker ". . . reached Perote after its surrender . . . proceeded to the flagstaff and fulfilled his hope." [23]

The main attraction of Fort San Carlos for the Argonauts, though, was that here was yet another historical site for them to write home about. For some of the gold seekers had served with General Wool's troops when they captured and occupied this fort, and some had lost friends here because of the unhealthy climate of the cold and damp bastion. As one officer put it, "A long line of American graves on the east flank of the castle attests the dreadful mortality that prevailed among our troops . . . Colonel Seymour [Commander of the Georgia Battalion] informed me that about twenty-six hundred American soldiers had died there since he held it." [24]

Like Vera Cruz and Cerro Gordo, the fort at Perote was another landmark of American victory on the trail of invasion; and the Yankees who passed here looked at this site as yet another proof of the Manifest Destiny of the American people. Or if they had been opposed to this unpopular war, they saw Fort San Carlos as another stain of dishonor for the United States.

After Perote the National Road headed southwest toward Puebla. Twelve miles beyond Perote the gold seekers passed by the *poblado* of Alchichica and Lago Alchichica, a lake formed in the crater of an extinct volcano. The going became rougher after this, for the travelers entered the Sierra Negra and an area known as Las Derrumbadas, or the Precipices. To make matters worse, many of the bridges in this stretch of the road had not been rebuilt since the war. Whenever his party reached one of these stretches, J. A. Perry said that they chained their wagon wheels, held back on ropes to keep the wagon from rolling to the bottom, forded the river at the bottom of the *barranca,* then doubled their teams in order to pull each wagon up the other side.

A hard day's journey beyond Las Derrumbadas brought Perry and his party through the *poblado* of Nopalucan and on to Acajete, where they camped for the night. On the next day they traveled by

Amozoc and by noontime they had shown their passports, paid their fees, and entered the beautiful city of Puebla.

Part of the city's beauty, a very dominant part, was its location. Situated in a large valley, this very Spanish-looking city was flanked by four tall volcanoes: Popocatépetl, Ixtaccíhuatl, Malinche, and Citlaltépetl, or Mount Orizaba. To the passing Argonauts, Puebla was a city surrounded by incredible natural beauty; and to men from the East, the height and shape of these volcanoes was something they were completely unprepared to describe. After knowing only the mountains of New England, they had no mental measuring stick by which to gauge the size of these peaks that were hidden much of the time by great banks of drifting and swirling clouds.

But Puebla also impressed these gold seekers with its man-made beauty. The homes were much better than they had seen in Vera Cruz or Jalapa. They thought that the *alameda* was magnificent with its many trees, its statues and fountains. Yet the greatest beauty was in the churches. Facing the small, main plaza was the Cathedral of the Immaculate Conception which had been completed by the Spaniards in 1649, forty-six years after the English had established their first colony at Jamestown, Virginia. The tall, square bell towers were erected in 1678, and it seemed to the Yankees that these two campaniles were trying to outdo the surrounding mountains, as these towers stood well above the tiled main dome of the cathedral. Then to add even more grandeur to this structure, the interior was, as one American wrote, "... richly decorated with the gorgeous, but barbaric taste manifested in the ecclesiastical edifices throughout Mexico." [25]

In Puebla the Argonauts also ran into some fellow Americans. These were men from the San Patricio Battalion, Irish Americans who had deserted from the American Army and fought on the side of the Mexicans and flew a green flag that had the figure of St. Patrick, a harp of Erin, and a shamrock on it. Many of these men had been captured and executed when General Scott's forces took Mexico City, but others had escaped or had been disfigured by the Americans. Such was the case with one of the men that J. A. Perry saw.

Perry only knew the man as "... the famous *Riley,* who was cropped and branded, by order of General Scott, at the time the fifty Irish deserters were hung at Mexico." [26] But Perry never forgot this character. For Riley was not only sociable—he was also an imposing figure. He stood over six feet tall, kept his hair long to hide the marks of the branding iron on his cheeks and the results of fast knife work on his ears, and he carried the rank of colonel in the Mexican Army. Perry was greatly impressed by this American outcast, but in a burst of patriotic balderdash he summed up his picture of him by saying that he was "... but a miserable, dissipated fellow." [27]

From Puebla on, the Argonauts who kept journals were skimpy in their descriptions of the country they traveled through. Yet this is understandable. They knew they had less than 100 miles to travel to Mexico City. They were in a hurry to get to this great hub where all the roads and trails leading to other parts of Mexico fanned out like spokes on a wagon wheel. Still, only 8 miles west of Puebla, the gold seekers passed through Cholula, which had once been an integral part of the Toltec kingdom before Cortés and his men destroyed this religious center to make way for the temples of their Christian God. But this astounding remnant was difficult to overlook. This was Tlachi-hual-tepetl, one of the world's largest pyramids—so large it might well have looked like another hill to many of these men on the move.

Less than two years before the coming of the gold seekers, one American Army officer commented that this pyramid looked very much like a massive mound of earth that had been thrown up on the plain. Then he wrote that along the pyramid's face there were walls built to act as supporting braces for the hard-packed soil. "The adobes or sun-dried bricks were every now and then clearly discernible in layers for short distances, and then would be discontinued. Numbers of horrible-looking little clay images were profusely scattered over the face of the Pyramid, some of which I picked up." [28]

Taking an image, a stone, or an adobe brick was nothing new in the history of this magnificent monument. The Spanish had plundered tons of material from it, and used it for the construction of their own churches in Puebla. Yet all these years of desecration did not remove the fact that outside Puebla was a pyramid that had a larger mass than the great Egyptian pyramid of Cheops.

One of the Argonauts who did mention seeing this pyramid with its truncated or flat top was W. C. Smith, who passed by it in February, 1849. "I remember," he wrote, "that while we were viewing the pyramid with interest and about to ascend it, it was announced that one of the miserable old wagons had broken down and we were wanted in haste to make repairs. So I did not ascend Cholula." [29]

If Smith had ascended this pyramid and taken the time to calculate its size, he would have been as amazed as Alexander von Humboldt was when he saw it in 1804. This scientist did take time to roughly measure it, and found it was even larger than it looked. The base alone covered forty-four acres. The flattened top was almost an acre, and there was a temple on top of it. To add to its grandeur in this valley where towering volcanoes formed the skyline, Tlachihual-tepetl was only a few feet short of being 190 feet tall.

But for W. C. Smith and his friends a broken-down wagon had first priority. They never climbed the pyramid's steep steps, never paced off its measurements, and never got to examine it closely enough to even speculate about why it was there and what it had been.

Most Argonauts were single-purpose men, and they obeyed the semi-military rules of their overland companies. Like W. C. Smith, an occasional man took time out to observe something that was an unusual aspect of the Mexico crossing. But, generally speaking, the need to keep together as a company in order to avoid danger, and the desire of most men to get to Pacific Coast seaports as quickly as possible, limited the amount of sightseeing a man was able to do.

After Cholula the National Road to Mexico City began to climb into the higher mountains. Nine miles west of the great pyramid gold seekers passed through Huejotzingo. The men who took time to look saw one of the first four churches the Spaniards had founded after the conquest of the Aztecs—a church that dated back to 1525. In this town the Yankees were over 7,500 feet above sea level, and the road ahead went upward. The men saw apple orchards that reminded them of home, and they shivered as the cold wind whistled down from the snow-covered peaks.

Not too far beyond Huejotzingo the road went through San Martín Texmelucan, and this was the starting point upon the long grade to the Río Frío and the Continental Divide beyond that. By the time gold seekers reached this cold river they were way above the valley of Puebla. At this high altitude they felt short of breath, and frequently ran into mountain storms.

The Manhattan-California Overland Association felt the fury of such a storm, and A. C. Ferris never forgot it. The whole thing broke about their party as they entered a pine forest. The black thunderheads seemed to settle almost on their heads; lightning danced off the rocks near them and lit up the landscape with blinding blue and white colors that made the horses and mules jump as though they had been struck. Then, just as the men managed to get the animals under control, the sound of thunder rolled with a crashing boom as it echoed from peak to peak. This was followed by a combination of rain, hail, and wet snow that was blown into the faces of the men and their mounts by a freezing wind that nearly bowled them over. They were totally unprepared for such a drastic change in the weather, and Ferris wrote that it had a considerable effect on the men and their animals.

We were drenched through and through, and shook as with ague, and our poor animals, used to the warm plains below, chilled with cold and in terror from fright trembled in every limb and crouched helplessly upon the ground, dazed by the lightning and shocked by the thunder which seemed to discharge at our very sides; they seemed to cling to us for safety.[30]

To add to their troubles after they left the Río Frío, Ferris and his large company were plagued by short-windedness as they made the final push to the Continental Divide and the summit well over 10,000 feet above sea level. Yet even in this high and lonely land their worst enemy was not the altitude or the icy storms spawned in the towering peaks. As their *arrieros* warned them and as the roadside crosses underlined, the greatest danger in this high country was the sudden and bloody raid of a band of *ladrones*.

Tired, suffering from the cold and the high altitude, Ferris and the men of the Manhattan-California Overland Association were badly in need of rest. But this was not the place to let down, and they knew it. They drove themselves and their animals to the limit of their endurance, crossed the summit, and began the descent into the Valley of Mexico. Even under such circumstances, Ferris said ". . . it was a sublime experience to ride down that mountain height— Mounts Popocatepetl and Ixtaccihuatl both looking down upon us, and the great valley and City of Mexico in full view below us, and a thunder shower with its dark nimbus clouds and forked lightning full in the sunshine under us." [31]

From the pass, the National Road dropped to the great valley in a series of steep switchbacks. As the men rode downgrade they felt the jarring movements of their horses as the animals stiffened their legs against the steep grade. They heard their mounts grunt, groan, and let out air. They heard the squeak of saddle leather, and felt their knees being rubbed raw as they braced themselves against the shoulders of their horses.

When they reached the *poblado* of Zoquiapan, the worst part of the downgrade trip was over. At this point the men were very nearly on the valley floor. The rest of the ride to Mexico City was a fast and easy journey across the tableland and through the *poblados* of Santa Bárbara, Ayotla, and Los Reyes. The last stretch on this trail of conquest was across the long causeway between the shallow waters of drying Lake Texcoco and the nearby marshes. Then, directly ahead of them, near the mountains on the western side of the valley on an area once covered by water, was the City of Mexico. Like Cortés and all the others who landed at Vera Cruz and made the journey of some 280 miles inland to what the Aztecs had called the Valley of Anáhuac, or the land on the edge of the water, the Manhattan-California Overland Association and all the other Argonauts looked with wonder and awe at this original Mother Lode of the New World.

## THE WHEEL OF FORTUNE: MEXICO CITY

Beginning with the circular golden sun and silver moon that Montezuma sent to Cortés, the City of Mexico assumed the symbolic shape of a wheel of fortune for the gold seekers. The city's relationship to a wheel was one of the first things that W. C. Smith noticed as he rode in from Vera Cruz. It was February, 1849, as he approached the ancient Sun Kingdom, and he entered in his journal that the city was "... built upon a low, flat island ... only a few inches above the water ... from which causeways radiate like the spokes of a wheel." [32]

And like a great wheel of fortune, Mexico City was a gathering place for gold seekers on the move. Within the city these *norteamericanos* on their way to El Dorado were astounded by what they

259

saw. To men from St. Louis, from a New England hamlet, and from the streets of New York City, here was a remarkable center of civilization. They were impressed with the huge Cathedral, the two- and three-story houses, the government buildings, the aqueducts, the fountains, the tree-lined avenues, and the mixed and picturesque population.

One of the most avid sightseers of these first Argonauts was none other than J. A. Perry, that connoisseur of foul *fondas* and motley *mesones*. His curiosity about the city was insatiable. As always, he gave a thorough description of the poor living quarters and poor food that he had to endure, but this was typical of him. One has to assume that he either was terribly fussy or lacked the money to patronize the better places. But once this New Englander got outside his room and away from the dining table, he looked over the city with an unflagging interest.

At the central plaza a chain gang of prisoners was hard at work planting trees, repairing sidewalks, and constructing new benches. The wealthy drove by in their fancy carriages in the late afternoon, bound for the park to take a turn about the splendid fountains and gardens. In the marketplace Perry saw the poorer people, and was fascinated by the abundance of products for sale at such cheap prices. With his usual eye for females, he described the women and their goods:

> These market women often have the whole family with them. At sunset, they kindle their fires and cook their provisions, and it was quite pleasing to pass through the market-place at early candle lighting, and see them gathered around their dishes, each helping themselves with their fingers. It is not unfrequently that one sees a young woman, with her head trimmed very tastefully, sitting in the market-place selling fruit.[33]

Like most Argonauts passing through Mexico, Perry didn't get to know the aristocracy. He caught but a fleeting glimpse of them as they hurried in and out of business houses, or as the women made a quick appearance in one of the churches. But in his walking about the city, he saw many of the poorer class, and wrote in detail about them. The women did not wear hats. Instead they usually tied a scarf over their black hair. Their skirts were long, coming almost to the ankles. Blouses were cut low. Sleeves were short. And the predominating color was white, but it was highlighted with fine embroidery work. The prevailing costume for men consisted of large, loose-fitting white trousers and a white top or a *serape*. The skin coloration of these people fascinated Perry, as it varied from quite dark to pale white. But most of all, he found them very friendly and sociable—especially the women.

The Halls of Montezuma drew his attention to the sacrificial stone of the Aztecs, to a dress, he was told, that had belonged to none other than Montezuma's wife—a dress made of tanned bird skins with the feathers completely intact, And he also was shown "... the bow and quiver of arrows, war-club, knife, tomahawk, and spear used by Montezuma." [34]

But of all his adventures, the most unusual took place at the Cathedral. Stiff-necked, Protestant Perry went to the Cathedral with a "show me" attitude. While there he was disgusted by what he considered to be the worship of idols. Yet he was attracted back for more than one visit. As he put it, each time he went he saw something he hadn't seen before. But what piqued his curiosity most of all was that the priests moved in and out of several doors where the public was not allowed to go. Determined to find out what was behind those doors, Perry returned to his *mesón* and worked out a plan to get inside.

He had fashioned a cane in the form of a shepherd's crook even before he had sailed for Mexico. There was a cross mounted on the front of it. "Standing two inches above the turn in the centre of the cross is a stone, two thirds of which was red. This stone was set in a brass belt. The whole represented the Great Shepherd of Israel, bearing his cross, while the stone represented the world, and the color on the stone the distance or proportion that the knowledge of the efficacy of Christianity had covered the world." [35]

Next Perry purchased a Mexican hat. Then he walked back to the Cathedral, and saw that people bowed to him as though he were a priest when they noticed his cane. With supreme confidence he marched into the Cathedral and approached the forbidden doors. When stopped by a priest he held up his cane, but in that he could speak no Spanish, this was as far as he could get.

Discouraged but not willing to give up, he developed yet another plan. He went to a French coffeehouse, and asked the landlord to introduce him to a gentleman who could speak both Spanish and

English. He then passed himself off as an American priest, and requested the aid of this gentleman in his problem at the Cathedral. This time Perry had the right combination to get into the closed part. After a conversation with the padres about the difficulties of Catholics in the United States, and about the merits of his cane, Perry was invited to visit the private rooms he had been so curious about. They descended a long flight of stairs into an underground chamber. What followed may or may not have been true, as it reads too much like something from a Gothic novel.

Perry claimed he was invited into an Inquisition room. There he saw "... a young woman, about sixteen or eighteen years old, stripped naked, her ancles fastened to some rings in the floor, her breast resting upon a pile of timber, her hands fastened by cords on the opposite side, and in this stooping position she had been beaten by the monster that held the scourge until the purple gore had puddled at her feet, and her body was scarred in a horrid manner." [36]

When Perry asked what the young woman had done to deserve such treatment, he was told she had falsely accused a priest of a crime that would have sent him to prison. Yet this was only one of a number of women he claimed that he saw undergoing torture of one kind or another.

In contrast to Perry's lurid experience the adventures of Daniel Wadsworth Coit were so different that for all purposes he might well have been in a different country. And in a good many respects this was very nearly true. A cousin of the Howland family of Norwich, Connecticut, Coit had passed his sixtieth birthday when he accepted the offer to be representative for Howland and Aspinwall in Mexico City. He was very well educated, had studied art in Europe, had been associated with a German firm, Frederick Huth & Co., in Chile and Peru, and had made a late marriage to his second cousin, Harriet Frances Coit, granddaughter of Joseph Howland. According to his own self-portrait, Daniel Wadsworth Coit was a gentleman of the world. He was a far better than average-looking man whose features were unforgettable because of his large, long nose, his small mouth, deep-set eyes, high forehead, his full head of wavy hair and carefully groomed mutton-chop whiskers.

Coit's station in life and his knowledge of the Spanish language gained him an immediate acceptance among the upper class of Mexico City. He attended some of the nightly masked balls which were extremely popular at that time; watched the continuous gambling in such places as the Bella Union and the Astor House; walked about parts of the city and rode around other sections in a carriage; and made many fine sketches of what he saw. But most of all he saw a part of Mexico City's society that the general run of gold seeker never had a chance to know. In his faithful, bi-weekly letters to his wife and in his beautifully rendered drawing he left a record of what Mexico City was like during the first year after the war and at the beginning of the gold rush.

After a short stay at the Gran Sociedad Hotel above the Astor House, Coit was offered quarters in the home of William de Drusina, the ". . . owner of the firm through which he carried on his business affairs in Mexico. . . ." [37] Mr. Drusina was a German by birth, had lived in England for a time during his youth, and was fluent in English, French, German, and Spanish. Coit liked him very much and considered him one of the most intelligent, well-mannered persons he had ever known.

Mrs. Drusina was from one of Mexico's prominent families, and commanded a retinue of sixteen servants who saw to her every need. She was, Coit wrote, ". . . rather above the ordinary height, quite thin, with black hair and large prominent black eyes, complexion dark and sallow, with but little animation or conversation." [38] She traveled about the city visiting friends and relatives every day, and rode in a fine carriage accompanied by a coachman and footman.

In addition to the family home within the city, the Drusinas also owned an extensive *hacienda* some 10 or 12 miles from the city at San Antonio. Coit was quite impressed with the *hacienda* and described it as ". . . a great mass of buildings resembling rather a small castle than a private residence . . . including a chapel attached to the house. . . ." [39]

Ultimately, it was Coit's association with William de Drusina that sent him off to California with gold and silver coins to trade for gold dust. For just as Coit was about to leave Mexico and return to the States, Drusina approached him with the proposition of handling this business in San Francisco for a three per cent commission on an investment of $100,000.

So it was that at an age when most men begin to think about retirement Daniel Wadsworth Coit left the good life of Mexico City, temporarily set aside a return to the family estate in Connecticut, and joined the Argonauts. Behind him he left the theater, the strolls through the *alameda* with its beautiful trees and fountains, the pleasant carriage rides along the *paseo* or public drive, country trips to the Drusina Hacienda or to the Tacubaya country home of another of his Mexico City friends. Ahead of him was the long trip up the Central Plateau to Guadalajara, the rough trail to San Blas, and a journey by ship to the frontier city of San Francisco.

One thing that comes out time and again in the letters of Daniel Wadsworth Coit and in the journals of the gold seekers is that none of them could dismiss the City of Mexico as they might some country *poblado* smack in the middle of nowhere. The City of Mexico was far beyond that, and far beyond the experiences of most men who wandered into the Valley of Anáhuac and stared with astonishment in much the same manner as had that earlier band of gold seekers under the command of Hernán Cortés.

Oh, yes, there were complaints to be made about the narrow streets and living conditions of the poor in parts of the city; about the inability of the Mexicans to solve their water drainage problem; about the influence of Catholicism in the daily life of everybody; and about the plague of petty theft that was a constant nuisance. But when it was all said, most Argonauts rode out of Mexico City with fine memories of the *alameda,* the *zócalo* or main plaza, the Cathedral, the National Palace, the Castle of Chapultepec, the massive bronze statue of Charles IV on horseback, the Aztec calendar, and as W. C. Smith said of his *mesón*: ". . . an open court . . . in the middle of which was a playing fountain, a water tank, plants, and blooming flowers." [40] For fountains and blooming flowers were the final touch to impressions of beauty that these gold seekers took away with them and never forgot for the rest of their lives.

And of all the Argonauts who passed through Mexico City in those first years of the gold rush, none left a more detailed account of what he saw than Josiah Gregg. The former Santa Fé trader arrived in the city on January 8, 1849, and he didn't depart until the twenty-sixth of April. During his stay he visited all of the city he was able to see, and made many trips to nearby areas to satisfy his own undeniable curiosity about the botanical and geological features of the region.

Some of his comments concerned topics others wrote about, but as in everything he did, Gregg was much more thorough and scientific in his approach. While he criticized the city's lake-bed location, he suggested that once the Spaniards had conquered the Aztecs they should have had the common sense to have built on the surrounding hills and not on top of the Aztec city and in the partially drained and filled-in lake areas. This, he reasoned, would have prevented the constant fight the Mexicans had to wage against boggy ground that made it necessary to drive timber pilings to a considerable depth as a base for stone foundations. He was also highly critical of the city's suburbs, which he thought exceedingly filthy, of the badly paved streets which ran slightly uphill from the sidewalks and formed a raised spine in the center, and of the Mexican habit of giving the same street a variety of names. The latter custom, Gregg claimed, made it extremely difficult and sometimes impossible for a visitor to locate any address.

Unlike many other *norteamericanos*, Gregg was not pleased with the main public buildings. He did not think that the Cathedral compared in beauty to the one at Chihuahua City, found that the National Palace was an immense structure that occupied a large city block without any particular grace, and that the President's home lacked any architectural elegance.

Gregg was impressed by Molino del Rey, which he called the West Point of Mexico, but even this fort sitting on an isolated hill about 2 miles from the city was not nearly as interesting to him as the cypress grove around it. Here he saw cypress trees that were as much as fifteen feet in diameter even when measured four or five feet above ground level. But he never got a chance to examine the Castle of Chapultepec, for while there he got into trouble. He was barely inside the grounds when he raised a prismatic compass to his eye to take a bearing on the village of Tacubaya some 4 miles away. Instantly an Army captain knocked the compass from his hand, and ordered a lieutenant and a non-commisisoned officer to place Gregg under arrest and put him in a dungeon. All this was a temporary situation, as Gregg's command of Spanish enabled him to talk his way into an audience with the commanding general.

Though he knew he was in no position to threaten the general with the wrath of the United States government, Gregg expressed his extreme displeasure concerning the treatment he had received. The general agreed that this had been a most unfortunate and insulting incident. He apologized for the conduct of his men and for the great inconvenience all this had caused. Then he issued the order for Gregg's release.

Gregg was seething with anger by the time he got back to his *mesón* room. He sat down at a desk and composed a detailed letter of complaint to Nathan Clifford, Minister of the United States of America, in which he requested redress for the gross insults he had suffered. Yet bad as his treatment had been, it was understandable within the framework of what had taken place at the Castle of Chapultepec during the Mexican War. Just prior to the furious battle at this place, General Santa Anna pulled one of his greatest acts of folly. In the face of the approaching enemy Santa Anna withdrew his large force of men because he did not wish to share any personal glory with General Gabriel Valencia, the commander of Chapultepec. This one act of petty jealousy left the defense of Chapultepec to General Valencia's small garrison of the post, and "... the boys of the military academy, the famous Niños Héroes." [41] Only after the bloody battle had ended did the horrified American troops discover that many of the Mexican dead were mere boys.

Disconcerting as his Chapultepec experience had been, Gregg did not let it color his attitude about Mexico City. In contrast to many of his fellow countrymen, he thought the city was fairly safe and peaceful. It was a place where a man could go about his business during the day or night without too much concern for thieves—excluding petty theft—or other troublemakers. In fact, the greatest trouble he had came about through the actions of *gringos*.

Two of Gregg's best mules were stolen by Americans, and he had a strange experience with New Yorker Benjamin Richardson, who, along with his son Joseph, had joined his California party. Gregg had given the Richardsons a free room in his *mesón,* and when the mules were stolen, the thieves also took $100 the New Yorker had left in his room. Then when Gregg and the police were unable to recover the money, the elder Richardson blamed him for the loss! Gregg was astounded by the man's attitude, and decided he did not want to take a chance with such a man as a trail companion and dismissed him from his party.

On April 6, 1849, the Gregg party rode out of Mexico City. It consisted of one other American, two Germans, two Irishman, a Scotchman, and a Mexican servant. This mixed group of gold seekers was bound for Mazatlán, and they were headed west into the Sierra Madre Occidental and on to the seldom used trail through the State of Michoacán. This was a much harder route to Guadalajara and the trail to the Pacific Coast; but Gregg wanted to take it, so that he could collect information about the flora and fauna of that region.

While few Argonauts took this route, there were other choices a man could make after he arrived in the Valley of Mexico. For Mexico City was a true wheel of fortune, and its spokes pointed in many directions. Though most gold seekers hurried through Mexico's major city and hardly took time to look it over, all of them examined the possible roads and trails across the country, and made their choice.

It was a gambler's game. It was put your money and your life down, spin the wheel, and hope the damned thing sent you off on the right path. For the discouraged there was the backtrack on the National Road to Vera Cruz and a case of *vómito,* or passage on a ship back to the States. For the adventurous there was the high mountain trail that Gregg followed. For men in a hurry there was the stagecoach road leading north by northwest up the Central Plateau, through Querétaro with its magnificent aqueduct and its immediate history as the place where the Treaty of Guadalupe Hidalgo signed away almost half (five-twelfths) of Mex's territory to the United States. For men who had heard about Cap' Horn and Panama ships making stops for water and fuel at the old port of Acapulco, there was the China Road leading south by southwest from Mexico City. It was all right as far as Cuernavaca, not too bad from there to Chilpancingo, but a tough mountain trail from there on down the western slopes of the Sierra Madre del Sur to the tropical port of Acapulco.

The selection of a given route, a particular spoke of the wheel, was only the beginning. If a man's luck ran good he made it to a port, caught a ship right away, and landed in foggy San Francisco in a matter of weeks. If his luck ran just fair he missed his connection, had a long and expensive wait along the way, or got off a risky or sinking ship at the lower tip of Baja California and made the long desert hike all the way to San Diego. If his luck ran bad, Mexico was where he cashed in his chips, and became another trailside cross where passing *arrieros* placed a stone, crossed themselves, and then moved their pack string on its way.

## THE CHINA ROAD

Compared to other branches of the El Dorado Trail the route to Acapulco drew a small amount of traffic. There were good reasons for not taking this path, and most gold seekers heard about them in Mexico City.

"What about Acapulco?" one Argonaut would ask another.

"It ain't such a good bet, so I hear tell."

"How so?"

"Northbound ships only stop for water and fuel."

"Long as they stop, that's all that counts."

"Not so, pilgrim. They're mostly loaded to the gunwales, and don't fancy more passengers."

"Well, hell, friend, it looks a damned sight closer to Mexico City than San Blas or Mazatlán."

"I know. I seen the map."

"What the hell, why not give her a try?"

"I told you. Mostly, those ships are a bit shy on space."

"Ain't it going to be the same up north?"

"Not the way they tell it. Seems there's coast ships just making the run to San Blas and Mazatlán, picking up a load, then heading back to California."

"Where'd you hear that?"

"An American who lives here told me that . . ."

"You don't mean one of them crazy Irishman, one of the god-damned Mick traitors? You ain't going to tell me you'd listen to one of them?"

"Hell, friend, you know me better than that. I got the story from a guy in a shipping company."

Usually, this would bring the discussion to an end about the trail to Acapulco, and the gold seekers would head northwest out of Mexico City. If the lack of passenger space aboard Acapulco ships didn't discourage a man, then talk about how bad this route could be might change a man's mind. Or somebody might mention that there were

lots of bad characters—some deserters from the American Army—
hiding out in that part of the country, making a living as *ladrones*.
Finally, there was the worry about running into yellow fever and
other tropical diseases. There was no need to push luck too far.
"Maybe," a man would think, "it'd be better to head for one of the
northwestern ports after all."

Yet a few Argonauts asked more questions about this route. It was
called the China Road—all 283 miles of it.

"But what about the road?" they asked. "What shape is it in?"

"As far as Chilpancingo, *es muy bueno, señor.*"

"And then?"

A shrug of the shoulders, and the information that the rest of
way was a rough trail, but it wasn't a long trip from Chilpancingo,
just rough.

Benjamin Richardson hadn't heard about the China Road, but
after his one-hundred-dollar misunderstanding with Josiah Gregg,
Captain Ben—as he liked to be called—heard about a party of
Americans bound for Acapulco. He and his son Joseph couldn't
leave Mexico City the same time as the group, but they talked to
the leader; and he agreed to take on two more if the Richardsons
caught up to them.

So it was that the Richardsons were riding hard and early in the
morning when they passed through the Gate of Belén at the southwestern outskirts of Mexico City. They passed by Chapultepec, and
took one last look at the great cypress trees. Captain Ben never forgot those trees with the long streamers of moss dangling from them
and blowing back and forth in the wind like ancient webs of incredible spiders.

Beyond Chapultepec they followed the mountain road upward past
Tlálpam on the slope of the extinct volcano, Mount Ajusco. After
Tlálpam, the road climbed even higher until they reached Tres Cum-
bres, the Three Peaks. From here they looked back for their last view
of the Valley of Mexico, and ahead they saw the Valley of Cuernavaca.

Captain Ben wrote nothing at all about the beauty of Cuernavaca,
where Aztec emperors once had their summer homes and where
Cortés had built his palace. When the Richardsons passed through
this beautiful city with its temperate climate they were riding hard
to catch up to their party. And Captain Ben had a very good reason

to hurry, as he was carrying $1,200 in gold dollars inside his horse's feedbag.

They rode through the present State of Morelos, and somewhere just inside the State of Guerrero they caught up to the party at a small *poblado*. "How glad was I," Captain Ben wrote, "when we reached the village & found our party waiting for us." [42] And no small wonder, for the country between Cuernavaca and Acapulco was *ladrón* land. Worse yet, the *ladrones* in this region were as interested in murder as they were in plunder. Mexican bandits were out for revenge against *gringos*, and riding with them were deserters from General Scott's invading troopers who were noted for their hatred of their former countrymen.

Yet *ladrones* also had their bad days, and Richardson saw what happened to these highwaymen whenever they were captured. In one stretch of his trip, in an area on the plains where it was too warm to ride except in the early morning hours and at night, he saw ". . . a robber hanging to the branch of a tree over a rock & the fat dripping out of him on the rocks below from the scorching sun & not the least smell. . . ." [43]

But *ladrones* and heat were only two of the many experiences the Argonauts had on the China Road. Between Cuernavaca and Acapulco they crossed the Río Mezcala—one of Mexico's largest—and this was done ". . . on a raft of reeds laced together on top of gourds." [44] Not far beyond the river crossing, the trail followed the dry creek bed of Zopilote or Vulture Canyon, where gold seekers saw ". . . beautiful varieties of Cactus and some of immense growth." [45] After the canyon the trail led up an easy grade to the *poblado* of Zumpango. Ten miles south of Zumpango the trail wound upward into the Sierra Madre del Sur for over another 1,000 feet, and the gold seekers entered the only city other than Cuernavaca that they ever seemed to remember with any joy on their ride from Mexico City to Acapulco. This was Chilpancingo, and many Argonauts remembered it as a decent city in a fine valley.

When Albert G. Osbun rode through Chilpancingo in January of 1851 he was on his way back from California and the South Seas. He and his party had just climbed up the hot and humid Pacific slopes on the jungle trail, and Chilpancingo was a breath of fresh air and a city of pleasure compared to the poor Indian *poblados* they had stayed in along their way. Osbun thought it was a city of wealth, and he estimated that it had a population of between 15,000 and 20,000. The houses were in considerable contrast to the grass and reed huts of Acapulco, as they were usually two stories in height and were built of adobe or stone.

We find here [he wrote] quite a large plaza, with a fountain of pure mountain water conducted from the neighboring mountains. . . . The streets & sidewalks are well paved & kept very clean. We find here on the sidewalks surrounding the plaza, a fine market of milk, tortillas, with trinkets & finery of every kind worn by them. They have also large stores of dry goods [hard] ware & groceries.[46]

Chilpancingo was the last place of pleasure on the ten- to fifteen-day trip between Mexico City and Acapulco. From there to the Pacific Ocean the mule trail worked its way down the western slopes of the Sierra Madre del Sur, climbed in and out of *barrancas*, followed the path that had been hacked through a living wall of jungle growth, passed through poor *poblados* where food and lodging were extremely primitive, crossed the Río Papagayo, and, just when there seemed to be no end to the journey, the gold seekers topped a last ridge and caught their first view of the bay. And to all who saw it for the first time, it was like seeing some incredible sea-level lake that was sheltered from the world by a wall of mountains and sheered-off cliffs. As one sea voyager wrote about the bay, it was as though it had ". . . suddenly burst upon our view." [47] And to the Argonauts this harbor where the Spanish had built and launched Manila galleons that carried cargoes of silver, Spanish and Mexican wines, fabric from Saltillo and Puebla, Oaxacan cloth and other items to the Philippine Islands and even to China and India to trade for fine silks, porcelain, spices, and marble was much more than the historical past. For most Argonauts didn't know about Acapulco's time of glory. What they knew, and what counted most to them, was that this tropical seaport was the last of their Mexico crossing. All that remained was to endure the stifling heat, and put up with the conditions of this small waterfront town of about 3,000 people, primarily made up of local Indians, mestizos, mulattos, and Chinese.

While the gold seekers feasted on tropical fruits, swam in the deep bay, and looked at the graceful coconut palms, the steep cliffs lining the shore, and the flights of parrots and other colorful birds, these men of the trail hoped the next ship that put in would have

271

# THE EL DORADO TRAIL

passenger space to take them away from this town of grass and reed huts, of mosquitoes, and of fever. All they wanted was to take one last look, bid farewell to Mexico, board a ship and sail northward from this southern *playa* to the land of gold.

## ACAPULCO: THE SOUTHERN PLAYA

The origin of the name is lost in the ruins of pre-Columbian civilization, but is thought to mean "... *the place of large reeds or the place of large cane.*" [48] And this name was very close to the truth, for as the Argonauts of the gold rush and other travelers saw it, Acapulco was a town of "... huts built ... of reeds in a kind of basket work...." [49] Of the substantial buildings in this beach town, one was star-shaped Fort San Diego, built on a bluff to the northeast of the town. It had a long history of holding off English and Dutch pirates and of protecting the rich cargoes sailing in and out of the port on Manila galleons. The only other building that appeared as though it were made by man and wasn't another tropical plant was the church. It stood in the plaza. As one 1849 traveler wrote:

> The interior is as plain as it can possibly be; but on *fête* days, it is customary to ornament it with palm-branches and flowers. Observing a miniature ship suspended from the ceiling, I inquired ... and was informed that it had been placed there in compliment to the sailors, of whom great numbers frequent the town, the port being one of the chief recruiting places for whalers.[50]

But as simple as the town looked to men who came in from the sea, its avenues lined with tall coconut palms and broadleafed banana trees were a welcome sight to Captain Ben Richardson and the men he had been traveling with, for theirs had been a hard-luck party. By the time they had dropped down the last stretches of the China Road and felt the stifling warm air of this boxed-in harbor, they had buried ten companions alongside the trail. All these men had died of fever in a hot land. They had been delirious, and chilled. They had vomited, had been unable to control their bowels, and had wasted

272

away. As the survivors rode into Acapulco they knew that one more man was nearing the end of his string. Before the party's first day in port ended the eleventh man died, and they buried him in a clearing overlooking the bay.

Still there was no guarantee that more of the men wouldn't perish as they waited for space on a passing ship. True enough, ships stopped, all right. They sailed in through the narrow harbor openings to the southwest separated by Isla de la Roqueta, where one entrance was about a mile and a half wide and known as Boca Grande, or Big Mouth, and the other about 260 yards wide, and known as Boca Chica, or Small Mouth. But it didn't matter which mouth a ship sailed through. As far as beached Argonauts were concerned few ships had any passenger space. It wasn't even a question of money. No man already aboard a northbound vessel would sell his space.

Yet luck ran with Captain Ben and his son. They were in Acapulco but a short time when the steamer *California* sailed into port, and she was short of hands. Captain Ben signed on as first cook, and Joseph signed on as a seaman. The gold dollars Richardson had carried across Mexico didn't even have to be spent, as he and his son worked their way from Acapulco to San Francisco.

Other gold seekers were not so lucky as the Richardsons. They waited a long time before they caught an empty berth on a northbound ship. In some cases men gave up the wait. They rode back over the China Road, and headed for San Blas or Mazatlán. But while they were at Acapulco they saw other men come ashore to stretch their sea legs on land, to buy fresh food, and to look over this southern Mexico seaport. When these days took place, when a ship appeared in the harbor and dropped anchor for a few days, it was almost as though sleepy Acapulco had suddenly awakened and remembered the old times of the *feria*, or fair.

The *feria* in Acapulco's past had been a time for couriers to be sent along the China Road to Mexico City to notify all traders that Manila galleons were in port with a cargo to sell. During these times the population of Acapulco jumped overnight from three or four thousand to twelve thousand. The atmosphere became one of bartering, of stories about faraway places, of strange names, of new faces from the Orient, of *fandangos* night after night, of fights over women, over cards, or over long-time grudges that had been held in check for the long months at sea, and there were always secret deals to avoid the high colonial taxes. As a result of these taxes and because of the temptation for bigger profits after weary months at sea and long waits at home, Acapulco ". . . became a source of graft on a grand scale, through smuggling." [51]

During the gold-rush years, something of the spirit of the *feria* returned to Acapulco. While merchants didn't come from Mexico City any more, local businesses flourished. Boys dove into the harbor for coins tossed by laughing *gringos*. Gamblers operated monte games around the clock. *Cantinas, fondas,* and *mesones* jacked their prices, and grafters drifted back into the old pattern left over from a heritage of smuggling and outwitting the law.

*And what was it like? Hear the voices of the past:*

"My name is Luther Schaeffer. On my way back from the Mother Lode our ship stopped for a time in Acapulco. It was late August, and the air was hot and sticky. When we dropped anchor the natives came out to our ship in rowboats, dugouts, or anything else that would float. They sold us fresh tropical fruit, fresh eggs and milk, and for a price they offered to take us ashore.

"Just in front of the fort I enjoyed a fine bath in the ocean every day that I remained here. The rocks were so worn by the repeated washings of the tide that in some places they formed excellent substitutes for bathing tubs; and I had capital sport in watching the tide coming in and dashing its briny spray over me." [52]

"Just call me Letts, J. M. Letts. On our way up the coast the steamer dropped anchor practically on the shore. We were happy to get ashore and stretch our legs. We ate fresh fruit, strolled about the town, and then took a bath.

"Just back of this town is a stream of the purest water from springs on the mountainside; this is the bathing place of the inhabitants, and a more inviting one could not be imagined; the stream is so limpid, and of such a congenial temperature, that one feels that he could repose in its bosom forever. In taking a bath it was difficult to rid ourself of the presence of a half-dozen *señoritas* who would come to the bank, towel in hand, offering to prepare you for your clothes, for the moderate sum of sixpence. They were all beautiful, but I preferred seeing them under other circumstances. This want of modesty, as it will be termed, is a characteristic of Spanish America, and although it may show a want of refined delicacy according to the frigid laws of the States, they are entirely unconscious of impropriety." [53]

*But it wasn't always that pleasant. There were bad times, too. There must have been some bad times.*

"Let me tell you, there were bad times all right. My name is Walter Griffith Pigman, and I was on my way home. I paid $100 to sail on the steamship *Republic* from San Francisco to Panama. We stopped over in Acapulco on February 11, 1851, after a ten-day voyage down the coast."

*But you mentioned trouble, Mr. Pigman. What did you mean by that?*

"Our passengers got into serious trouble with the citizens on shore; many of them were shot at and one man was wounded severely by a bayonet. Many did not get aboard until midnight and three of our men were caught by the Mexicans and put in the calaboose and it was with difficulty the captain got them released at $10 each." [54]

*Wasn't there any recourse? Didn't the United States government help these men?*

"My name is N. A. McClure, and I was the United States Consul at Acapulco in 1851. Believe me, there was more than difficulty with Mexican officials. I wrote to the Honorable Daniel Webster, who was Secretary of State. I told him that there were between 3,000 and 5,000 of our citizens visiting this port each month. Many of these people were short of money. Some were sick, and some were the victims of scoundrels who sold them passage on an unseaworthy ship."

*But the other cases, what about the men who were thrown into a cell at Fort San Diego without any trial and for a crime they may or may not have committed?*

"I can tell you about that. My name is Francis W. Rice. In 1852 I held the position vacated by Mr. McClure. I can assure you, sir, that we did indeed have a good deal of trouble with corrupt Mexican officials. I kept the Honorable Daniel Webster fully informed, and I requested that the United States send a gunboat to Acapulco."

*It was* that *bad?*

"Indeed it was, sir. I suggest that you glance over my correspondence for the details. I think you'll find very little missing. For in point of fact, sir, outrages were committed on a daily basis."

And very little was missing from Mr. Francis W. Rice's letters to the Secretary of State. And Mr. Rice had more than one complaint, as outrages against Americans were almost a daily affair.

OUTRAGE: ". . . one *Wilson*, an American citizen, was sentenced to labor in the *chain-gang* three hundred days, at 50 cents per day, to pay a debt of one hundred and fifty dollars, which debt could not be, or was not, proved. . . ." [55]

OUTRAGE: "An American negro, named George Boon, had been ten weeks confined in the castle at this place, on the most baseless charge of murder, without trial." [56]

OUTRAGE: "William H. Taylor, of Iowa . . . came on shore in company with seven or eight of his comrades in a small boat. On landing, the boatman demanded as fare 50 cents each, which is double the usual price. . . . Mr. Taylor objected . . . offered the usual price . . . which was refused. After a short conversation, he proffered the amount first demanded . . . which was also refused, the boatman then demanding five dollars. On Mr. Taylor's refusing . . . he was violently seized by the guard of the 'captain of the port' and made fast, with a heavy chain about his leg, to a large anchor in the vestibule of the guard-house; while in this position he was struck a violent blow in the face by one of the guard, the officers taking not the least notice of the assault.

"Knowing the full circumstances of the case, I immediately demanded his release from the 'captain of the port,' who is also an *alcalde.* . . .

"He positively refused . . . and told me I must pay, within fifteen minutes, fifty dollars for Mr. Taylor's release, or he would send him to the filthy dungeon of the castle of the town. . . . I warned him against this course. . . . His reply was, that he cared neither for the United States nor her power; his *word* was *law.* . . . He then went to the commander of the naval and military forces . . . obtained a guard of soldiers and marched Mr. Taylor to prison, where he is now immured." [57]

Acapulco had not got over its old ways. A *peso* was a *peso*, what did it matter how a man got it? The thing to do was to get it, and the *gringo* was an easy mark. It was just like old times once again.

Acapulco, the place of reeds; the harbor of myths; the southern *playa* for the golden dream was back in business, if only in a limited way and for a short time. But it was good to hear the old talk again, good to carry out the small graft, and good to know that once again men were sailing out Boca Grande and Boca Chica, that they were heading north into the coast of secrecy to a land called El Dorado.

# EPILOGUE

## THE DEATH OF EL DORADO

It had been a time for believing. In a way it was the last act of faith in the drama of the New World. There had been the Fountain of Youth, and men had searched. They proved it did not exist, and they died in the swamplands of Florida in the proving. There had been the Seven Cities of Cíbola, and men had searched. They proved that no such cities existed, and they died of thirst in the vast deserts of the Southwest in the proving. There had been the tale of *el hombre dorado*, and men had searched. They proved the gilded man existed but that he had to buy his gold, and they died in the South American jungle and in the high country of the Andes in the proving. Then, as it appeared all over, as the old illusions were vanishing, as men began to accept the notion that there would never again be anything like the golden fortunes found by Cortés and Pizarro, the land called El Dorado was discovered. The true believers polished their gear, listened to the old tales once again, and struck out for that undiscovered fortune in a mood of golden madness.

From all walks of life, from all parts of the country, from all the far corners of the earth men with gold fever struck out on the quest for El Dorado. During those first two wild years when maps and guidebooks were often tailored to fit the wish, men followed as many paths to California as were sold by sellers of the dream. And the El Dorado Trail across Mexico offered these companies of gold seekers what they thought would be an easier trek to California.

# THE EL DORADO TRAIL

How many made this journey is an easy question to ask in our Age of Computers, our Society of Record Keepers. But in 1849 and 1850 even the boundary between the United States and Mexico had not been marked off. So, to men who took the northern branch of the El Dorado Trail, they were in Mexico once they left Texas, and were in California once they crossed the Río Colorado. According to the rough count made by the United States troopers stationed at the Colorado Crossing, 10,000 gold seekers a year entered California at the confluence of the Gila and Colorado rivers.

Argonauts who selected the Central Mexico Crossing were also hard to count. Some came across the Río Grande after landing at one of the Texas seaports on the northern curve of the Gulf of Mexico. Some came across from Tampico, or landed at Vera Cruz and made the trip to Mexico City and then up the Central Plateau. A very conservative estimate for this branch of the trail would be some 4,000 per year.

The southern branch of the trail, the one to Acapulco, drew the smallest amount of traffic, and some of these men gave up their wait for passenger space on northbound ships. They either returned home or trekked northward to San Blas or Mazatlán. Even so, it would not be out of line to say that five hundred to a thousand men per year came this way.

In the game of numbers, a conservative estimate of the total for the El Dorado Trail came to about 15,000 gold seekers per year for 1849 and 1850. Then the word about the difficulties of this trail got back to the States, and for the rest of the gold-rush years the Mexico crossing saw fewer and fewer Argonauts.

In the long run, though, numbers really don't mean too much. What finally counts is the experience of the individual. And the experiences of men who took any branch of the El Dorado Trail were automatically different. They crossed another nation, got boxed in by a strange language, and faced a way of life they usually didn't understand. Some events were often the same as they were for other trails to California. Men died of cholera, of yellow fever, of accidents, of thirst, and of violence among themselves. But in Mexico there were many ways to die. If the land didn't kill the Argonauts, the *ladrones* and the Indians were willing to oblige. Other gold seekers on other trails faced many dangers, but they never knew the whistle of a *ladrón's* bullet, the whir of an Apache arrow, or the final thud of a Comanche lance.

# Epilogue

And when it was all over, when the search for gold had ended, and the Mexico crossing was a memory scrawled in a faded journal or dictated to a disinterested granddaughter, few men of the El Dorado Trail had hit anything vaguely resembling a bonanza. Some came all the way only to cash in their chips. Josiah Gregg, worn out and exhausted, fell off his horse as he and his companions from the Trinity River mines were trying to work their way south after having discovered Humboldt Bay as a port for this northwestern mining area in the Pacific Coast range. On February 25, 1850, the great Santa Fé trader was buried in an unmarked and lost grave near Clear Lake, about 200 miles northwest of San Francisco. John Stevens, Audubon's close friend, sailed for home aboard the *Central America* with a major portfolio of Audubon's sketches, but Stevens never made it. His ship went to the bottom of the sea in a storm off Cape Hatteras in 1851.

Most of the Argonauts remained in California for a short time, grew discouraged and left. Some men, such as artists John Woodhouse Audubon and H. M. T. Powell, had come only to see the action, and they caught an early ship home. Daniel Wadsworth Coit returned to his family home in Norwich, Connecticut, with a new stake he had made by selling coins in coinless California and with a great collection of Mexico and California sketches. And here he died in his eighty-ninth year in 1876—twenty-seven years after the big rush of 1849.

But other emigrants remained in California and made their mark in ways other than mining. John H. Tone, of the Audubon Party, tied up a considerable tract of fine farming land in the San Joaquin Valley near Stockton. To this day it is possible to drive along the Jack Tone Road. Dr. Lewis Gunn and William Perkins did very well for themselves in the Tuolumne County area of the Southern Mother Lode. Dr. Gunn practiced as a physician in Jamestown (my hometown) and Sonora. He also published the Sonora *Herald* for two years. His original adobe home still stands, and it is now a much better *mesón* than the good doctor ever found in Mexico. William Perkins ran a successful store in Sonora, but ultimately became a prominent citizen of Argentina. John Strentzel also was in Tuolumne County for a time, and he and his wife ran a hotel and ferry at La Grange. However, Strentzel is best remembered for his later years at Martínez about thirty-five miles east of San Francisco. Here Strentzel established the Alhambra Vineyards and became the father-in-law of John Muir. The incredible Parker H. French was a California politician for a time, newspaper editor, District Attorney of San Luis Obispo County, one of William Walker's compatriots in the Nicaraguan adventure, a Civil War spy, and finally a legendary character who was last seen in Washington, D.C., as an alcoholic who enjoyed a chloroform booster with his whiskey. Dr. Oliver M. Wozencraft returned to the Colorado Desert with the idea of irrigating the region that became the Imperial Valley. Boat-Wagon Harris had a career in Sacramento that included being sheriff of the county, mayor of the city, and Deputy Secretary of the State of California. Texas Ranger John Coffee Hays became Sheriff of San Francisco, and was the commanding officer in the war against Nevada's Paiute Indians during the second Battle of Pyramid Lake in 1860.

Other gold seekers who made the Mexico crossing were not always as colorful in their later years, but they also had their memories. And when nobody was interested any more about what it had been like to have been in on the gold rush, these men never forgot. They knew all of it deep inside, way past the ache of arthritic knuckles and joints, way past the strongly etched vision of another day of hard traveling, another day of watching the horizon. They knew they had been in on the last great quest in the New World. Other gold strikes were made, and men gave the name El Dorado to saloons, mines, camps, towns, and counties. But the land called El Dorado was gone. The dream was dead and buried. There had been a time to travel to El Dorado. That time had passed.

# NOTES

## PROLOGUE

1. Christopher Columbus, *Journals and Other Documents on the Life and Voyages of Christopher Columbus*, trans. and ed. by Samuel Eliot Morison (New York: The Heritage Press, 1963), p. 67. Quotation taken from The Limited Editions Club edition of *Journals and Other Documents on the Life and Voyages of Christopher Columbus* by permission of The George Macy Companies, Inc.

## CHAPTER I

1. Rodman W. Paul, ed., *The California Gold Discovery: Sources, Documents, Accounts and Memoirs Relating to the Discovery of Gold at Sutter's Mill* (Georgetown, California: The Talisman Press, 1966), p. 80.
2. William T. Sherman, *Memoirs of General William T. Sherman* (New York: D. Appleton & Co., 1875), Vol. I, p. 58.
3. George P. Hammond, ed., *The Larkin Papers*, Vol. VII (Berkeley: University of California Press, 1960), p. 303.
4. Commodore Thomas ap Catesby Jones, "Letters to the Secretary of the Navy, November 4, 1847–August 26, 1850"; The United States Navy Department, The National Archives Record Group 45, No. 24, p. 88.
5. *Ibid.*, No. 25; p. 92.
6. Marie Beale, *Decatur House and Its Inhabitants* (Washington, D.C.: National Trust for Historic Preservation, 1954), p. 77.
7. *Ibid.*, p. 77.
8. Stephen Bonsal, *Edward Fitzgerald Beale* (New York: G. P. Putnam's Sons, 1912), p. 43.
9. —— Forbes, *A Trip to Mexico, or Recollections of a Ten Months' Ramble in 1849–1850 By a Barrister* (London: Smith, Elder, & Co., 1851), p. 64.
10. Daniel Wadsworth Coit, *Digging for Gold—Without a Shovel: The Letters of Daniel Wadsworth Coit From Mexico City to San Francisco 1848–1851*, ed. by George P. Hammond (Denver: Old West Publishing Co., 1967), pp. 48–49.
11. Forbes, *op. cit.*, p. 57.
12. *Ibid.*, p. 59.
13. Bonsal, *op cit.*, p. 45.

14. J. A. Perry, *Thrilling Adventures of a New Englander* (Boston: Redding & Co., 1853), p. 19.
15. A. C. Ferris, "To California in 1849 through Mexico," *Century*, XLII (1891), p. 673.
16. Bernard DeVoto, *The Year of Decision, 1846* (Boston: Little, Brown & Co., 1943), p. 472.
17. Forbes, *op. cit.*, p. 43.
18. *Ibid.*, p. 39.
19. Reprinted by permission of the publishers, The Arthur H. Clark Company, from *Southern Trails to California in 1849*, Ralph Bieber, ed. (Glendale, California: 1937), p. 96.
20. U.S. Congress, House. *House Executive Documents*, No. 1, 30th Cong., 2d sess., 1848, p. 10.
21. Beale, *op. cit*, p. 79.
22. *Ibid.*, p. 79.

CHAPTER II

1. George P. Hammond, ed., *The Larkin Papers*, Vol. VII (Berkeley: University of California Press, 1960), p. x.
2. *Ibid.*, p. xiii.
3. *Ibid.*, p. xiii.
4. Reprinted by permission of the publishers, The Arthur H. Clark Company, from *Southern Trails to California in 1849*, Ralph Bieber, ed. (Glendale, California: 1937), p. 127.
5. *Ibid.*, p. 138.
6. *Ibid.*, p. 138.
7. *Corpus Christi: A History and Guide* (Corpus Christi, Texas: The Corpus Christi *Caller-Times*, 1942), pp. 86–87.
8. *Ibid.*, pp. 86–87.
9. Josiah Gregg, *Commerce of the Prairies* (New York: Henry G. Langley, 1844), Vol. II, p. 79.
10. *Ibid.*, p. 79.
11. Ray A. Billington, "Books That Won the West," *The American West*, IV, No. 3 (August, 1967), p. 26.
12. Lansford W. Hastings, *A New History of Oregon and California* (Cincinnati: Published by George Conclin, 1849), p. 138.
13. Billington, *op. cit.*, p. 28.
14. Joseph Ware, *The Emigrants' Guide to California* (St. Louis: 1849), p. 1.
15. John Walton Caughey, *Gold Is the Cornerstone* (Berkeley: University of California Press, 1948), p. 54.
16. Odie B. Faulk, *Too Far North . . . Too Far South* (Los Angeles: Westernlore Press, 1967), p. 58.
17. The first gold-rush song was written in November, 1848, by John Nichols, who was aboard ship and bound for California. He called it "Oh, California," and arranged it to be sung to the tune of Stephen Foster's "Oh! Susanna."
18. David Lavender, *Climax at Buena Vista* (New York: J. P. Lippincott Company, 1966), p. 60.
19. *Corpus Christi: A History and Guide, op. cit.*, p. 85.

# Notes

20. *Ibid.*, pp. 86–87.
21. Joseph Wyatt McGaffey, "Across Mexico in the Days of '49," *Touring Topics,* XXI (Copyright May, 1929, Automobile Club of Southern California), p. 20.
22. Michael Baldridge, *A Reminiscence of the Parker H. French Expedition through Texas and Mexico to California in the Spring of 1850* (Los Angeles: John B. Goodman III, 1959), p. 1.
23. *Ibid.*, p. 2.
24. Edward McGowan, *The Strange Eventful History of Parker H. French, with Introduction, Notes and Comments* by Kenneth M. Johnson (Los Angeles: Dawson's Book Shop, 1958), p. 6.
25. Baldridge, *op. cit.*, p. 2.
26. McGowan, *op. cit.;* see fold-out broadside.

CHAPTER III

1. George R. Stewart, *The California Trail* (New York: McGraw-Hill Book Company, 1962), p. 217.
2. John Theophil Strentzel, *Autobiography,* MS., 1890, Bancroft Library, University of California, Berkeley, p. 6.
3. Stewart, *op. cit.*, p. 232.

CHAPTER IV

1. John Woodhouse Audubon, "Illustrated Notes of an Expedition through Mexico and California, 1849–50," *Magazine of History,* XI, Extra Number 41 (1936), p. 7.
2. Alexander B. Adams, *John James Audubon* (New York: G. P. Putnam's Sons, 1966), p. 467.
3. Audubon, *op. cit.*, p. 8.
4. A. B. Clarke, *Travels in Mexico and California* (Boston: 1852), p. 11.
5. *Ibid.*, p. 12.
6. Audubon, *op. cit.*, p. 11.
7. Clarke, *op. cit.*, p. 11.
8. *Ibid.*, p. 14.
9. John B. Goodman III, "Introduction," *Personal Recollections of Harvey Wood* (Pasadena, California: John B. Goodman III, 1955), p. xii.
10. Harvey Wood, *Personal Recollections of Harvey Wood* (Pasadena, California: John B. Goodman III, 1955), p. 2.
11. George W. B. Evans, *Mexican Gold Trail: The Journal of a Forty-Niner,* ed. by Glenn S. Dumke, Preface by Robert Glass Cleland (San Marino, California: The Huntington Library, 1945), p. 15.
12. Thomas B. Eastland, "To California through Texas and Mexico," *Quarterly,* California Historical Society, XVIII (1939), p. 101.
13. Audubon, *op. cit.*, p. 16.
14. *Ibid.*, p. 18.
15. *Ibid.*, p. 40.
16. John E. Durivage, "Through Mexico to California: Letters and Journal of John E. Durivage"; reprinted by permission of the publishers, The Arthur H. Clark Company, from *Southern Trails to California in 1849,* Ralph Bieber, ed. (Glendale, California: 1937), p. 162.

17. *Ibid.*, p. 165.
18. *Ibid.*, p. 166.
19. *Ibid.*, p. 166.
20. Audubon, *op. cit.*, p. 43.
21. John W. Audubon, *Audubon's Western Journal: 1849–1850.* Reprinted by permission of the publishers, The Arthur H. Clark Company, ed. by Frank Heywood Hodder (Glendale, California: 1906), p. 87.
22. Clarke, *op. cit.*, p. 25.
23. Audubon, "Illustrated Notes," *op. cit.*, p. 49.
24. Clarke, *op. cit.*, p. 28.
25. Durivage, *op. cit.*, p. 178.
26. Audubon, "Illustrated Notes," *op. cit.*, p. 49.
27. *Ibid.*, p. 50.
28. *Ibid.*, p. 50.
29. Clarke, *op. cit.*, p. 30.
30. Durivage, *op. cit.*, p. 180.
31. Audubon, "Illustrated Notes," *op. cit.*, p. 52.
32. Audubon, *Western Journal, op. cit.*, pp. 99–100.
33. Audubon, "Illustrated Notes," *op. cit.*, p. 62.
34. *Ibid.*, p. 62.
35. *Ibid.*, p. 66.
36. *Ibid.*, p. 68.
37. Audubon, *Western Journal, op. cit.*, pp. 116–117.
38. *Ibid.*, p. 136.
39. *Ibid.*, p. 139.
40. *Ibid.*, p. 143.

CHAPTER V

1. Marc Simmons, trans. and ed., *Border Comanches* (Santa Fe: Stagecoach Press, 1967), p. 15.
2. *Corpus Christi: A History and Guide* (Corpus Christi, Texas: The Corpus Christi *Caller-Times*, 1942), p. 89.
3. Oliver M. Wozencraft, "Through Northern Mexico in '49," *The Californian*, VI (November 1882), p. 423.
4. George W. B. Evans, *Mexico Gold Trail: The Journal of a Forty-Niner*, ed. by Glenn S. Dumke, Preface by Robert Glass Cleland (San Marino, California: The Huntington Library, 1945), p. 104.
5. Ralph J. Smith, "The Scalphunter in the Borderlands, 1835–1850," *Arizona and the West: A Quarterly Journal of History*, VI (Spring, 1964), p. 17.
6. *A Perrysburg 49's Trip to California* (Toledo, Ohio: 1903), p. 10.
7. Smith, *op. cit.*, p. 22.
8. A. B. Clarke, *Travels in Mexico and California* (Boston: 1852), p. 43.
9. *Ibid.*, p. 46.
10. *Ibid.*, p. 46.
11. *Ibid.*, p. 49.
12. *Ibid.*, p. 49.
13. *Ibid.*, p. 51.
14. *Ibid.*, pp. 50–51.
15. Harvey Wood, *Personal Recollections of Harvey Wood* (Pasadena, California: John B. Goodman III, 1955), p. 11.

# Notes

16. John E. Durivage, "Through Mexico to California: Letters and Journal of John E. Durivage"; reprinted by permission of the publishers, The Arthur H. Clark Company, from *Southern Trails to California in 1849,* Ralph Bieber, ed. (Glendale, California: 1937), pp. 189–190.
17. Wozencraft, *op. cit.,* p. 426.
18. Evans, *op. cit.,* p. 121.
19. *Ibid.,* p. 102.
20. *Ibid.,* p. 103.
21. *Ibid.,* p. 103.
22. *Ibid.,* p. 100.
23. Thomas B. Eastland, "To California through Texas and Mexico," *Quarterly,* California Historical Society, XVIII (1939), p. 235.
24. *Ibid.,* p. 231.
25. Evans, *op. cit.,* p. 135.
26. Wood, *op. cit.,* p. 11.
27. Durivage, *op. cit.,* p. 201.
28. Clarke, *op. cit.,* p. 67.
29. *Ibid.,* p. 72.

CHAPTER VI

1. Mary A. Maverick and George Madison Maverick, *Memoirs of Mary A. Maverick,* ed. by Rena Maverick Green (San Antonio: 1921), p. 102.
2. *Ibid.,* p. 102.
3. John Theophil Strentzel, *Autobiography,* MS., 1890, Bancroft Library, University of California, Berkeley, p. 7.
4. *Ibid.,* p. 8.
5. *Ibid.,* p. 12.
6. *Ibid.,* p. 13.
7. *Ibid.,* p. 14.
8. *Ibid.,* p. 15.
9. Nicolas De Lafora, *The Frontiers of New Spain: Nicolas De Lafora's Description 1766–1768,* ed. by Lawrence Kinnaird (Berkeley: The Quivira Society, 1958), p. 83.
10. Josiah Gregg, *Commerce of the Prairies* (New York: Henry G. Langley, 1844), Vol. II, p. 76.
11. Aurora Hunt, "Overland by Boat to California in 1849," *Quarterly,* Southern California Historical Society, XXXI (1949), p. 214.
12. Augustus W. Knapp, "An Old Californian's Pioneer Story," *The Overland Monthly,* X, 2d Series (October, 1887), p. 392.
13. *Ibid.,* p. 393.
14. *Ibid.,* p. 394.
15. In 1890, "The Great Western" and 158 Army men were moved from the Fort Yuma cemetery to the Presidio in San Francisco, California. She is buried there under a headstone that is engraved SARAH A. BOWMAN.
16. Joseph Pownall, "From Louisiana to Mariposa," ed. by Robert Glass Cleland, *Rushing for Gold,* ed. by John Walton Caughey (Berkeley: University of California Press, 1949), p. 26.
17. *Ibid.,* p. 26.
18. *Ibid.,* p. 27.
19. Michael Baldridge, *A Reminiscence of the Parker H. French Expedition*

# THE EL DORADO TRAIL

*Through Texas and Mexico to California in the Spring of 1850* (Los Angeles: John B. Goodman III, 1959), p. 7.

20. *Ibid.*, p. 7.
21. *Ibid.*, p. 19.
22. Charles Cardinell, "Adventures on the Plain," *Courier* (1856), reprinted *Quarterly*, California Historical Society, I (July, 1922), p. 57.
23. Baldridge, *op. cit.*, p. 31.
24. Frances Fuller Victor, "On the Mexican Border," *The Overland Monthly*, VI (May, 1875), p. 467.
25. Cave Johnson Couts, *Hepah, California! The Journal of Cave Johnson Couts from Monterey, Nuevo León, Mexico, to Los Angeles, California, during the Years 1848–1849*, ed. by Henry F. Dobyns (Tucson: Arizona Pioneers' Historical Society, 1961), pp. 50–51.
26. *Ibid.*, p. 51.
27. *Ibid.*, p. 51.
28. Robert Watson Noble, "Diary of a Journey from Chihuahua, Mexico, to the Pueblo de San Jose, California, April 10–August 1, 1849," MS.; *Parkman Family Papers*, Bancroft Library, University of California, Berkeley, p. 4.
29. John E. Durivage, "Through Mexico to California: Letters and Journal of John E. Durivage"; reprinted by permission of the publishers, The Arthur H. Clark Company, from *Southern Trails to California in 1849*, Ralph Bieber, ed. (Glendale, California: 1937), p. 203.
30. A. B. Clarke, *Travels in Mexico and California* (Boston: 1852), p. 73.
31. *Ibid.*, p. 74.
32. George W. B. Evans, *Mexican Gold Trail: The Journal of a Forty-Niner*, ed. by Glenn S. Dumke, Preface by Robert Glass Cleland (San Marino, California: The Huntington Library, 1945), p. 143.
33. Charles Pancoast, *A Quaker Forty-Niner: The Adventures of Charles Edward Pancoast on the American Frontier*, ed. by Anna Paschall Hannum (Philadelphia: University of Pennsylvania Press, 1930), pp. 231–232.
34. H. M. T. Powell, *The Santa Fé Trail to California 1849–1852, The Journal and Drawings of H. M. T. Powell*, ed. by Douglas S. Watson (San Francisco: The Book Club of California, 1931), p. 123.
35. *Ibid.*, p. 124.
36. *Ibid.*, p. 127.
37. John Robert Forsyth, *John Robert Forsyth's Journal of a Trip from Peoria, Illinois, to California on the Pacific in 1849*, Typed transcript in Peoria, Illinois Public Library, Transcript copy, Bancroft Library, University of California, Berkeley, p. 66.
38. Agua Prieta is one of the tributaries of the Río Sonora. It is across the border from Douglas, Arizona.
39. Durivage, *op. cit.*, p. 208.
40. Casper S. Ricks, *Diary of an Overland Journey from Albuquerque to Santa Cruz, New Mexico, 1849*, MS., Bancroft Library, University of California, Berkeley, p. 30.
41. "Arkansas State Gazette and Democrat, April 26, 1850"; reprinted by permission of the publishers, The Arthur H. Clark Company, from *Southern Trails to California in 1849*, Ralph Bieber, ed. (Glendale, California: 1937), p. 319.

# Notes

42. Forsyth, *op. cit.*, p. 71.
43. *Ibid.*, p. 70.
44. *Ibid.*, p. 73.
45. Lafora, *op. cit.*, p. 109.
46. Powell, *op. cit.*, p. 142.
47. Forsyth, *op. cit.*, p. 75.
48. Durivage, *op. cit.*, p. 210.
49. Forsyth, *op. cit.*, p. 78.
50. José Francisco Velasco, *Sonora: Its Extent, Population, Natural Productions, Indian Tribes, Mines, Mineral Lands, etc.*, trans. by William F. Nye (San Francisco: H. H. Bancroft & Co., 1861), p. 74.
51. *Ibid.*, p. 74.
52. Clarke, *op. cit.*, p. 87.
53. Noble, *op. cit.*, p. 9.
54. Durivage, *op. cit.*, p. 218.
55. Both men became famous in California. Eugene was a lawyer who was killed in the Pyramid Lake War of 1860 between Virginia City miners and Nevada's Paiute Indians. Myron lived until 1911, and achieved fame as a California and Nevada historian and newspaper editor.
56. Pancoast, *op. cit.*, p. 249.
57. *Ibid.*, p. 250.
58. Powell, *op. cit.*, p. 159.
59. Couts, *op. cit.*, p. 86.
60. Evans, *op. cit.*, p. 160.
61. Lt. William H. Emory, "Report on the United States and Mexican Boundary Survey," U.S. Congress, Senate. *Senate Executive Document*, 108, 34th Cong., 1st Session, Vol. I, p. 131.
62. Cave Johnson Couts, *From San Diego to the Colorado in 1849: The Journal and Maps of Cave J. (Johnson) Couts*, ed. by William McPherson (Los Angeles: Zamorano Club, 1932), p. 48.

## CHAPTER VII

1. William Watkin Winn, *An Autobiography: A Family History* (Including Albert Maver Winn, 1810–1883), MS., Bancroft Library, University of California, Berkeley, p. 4.
2. Joseph Wyatt McGaffey, "Across Mexico in the Days of '49," *Touring Topics*, XXI (Copyright May 1929, Automobile Club of Southern California), p. 21.
3. *Ibid.*, p. 21.
4. Lewis C. Gunn and Elizabeth L. Gunn, *Records of a California Family*, ed. by Anna Lee Marston (San Diego: 1928), p. 40.
5. *Ibid.*, p. 45.
6. Samuel McNeil, *McNeil's Travels in 1849, to, through and from the Gold Regions, in California* (Columbus, Ohio: 1850), p. 16.
7. *Ibid.*, p. 16.
8. William Perkins, *Three Years in California: William Perkins' Journal of Life at Sonora, 1849–1852*, Introduction and Annotations by Dale L. Morgan and James R. Scobie (Berkeley: University of California Press, 1964), p. 79.
9. McNeil, *op. cit.*, p. 18.
10. McGaffey, *op. cit.*, p. 38.

11. *Ibid.*, p. 39.
12. G. F. Von Tempsky, *Mitla,* ed. by J. S. Bell (London: Longman, Brown, Green, Longmans, & Roberts, 1858), p. 43.
13. Gunn, *op. cit.,* pp. 45–46.
14. McNeil, *op. cit.,* p. 18.
15. *Ibid.,* p. 18.
16. Perkins, *op. cit.,* pp. 79–80.
17. *Ibid.,* p. 80.
18. Gunn, *op. cit.,* p. 48.
19. *A Perrysburg 49's Trip to California* (Toledo, Ohio: 1903), p. 11.
20. Thomas B. Eastland, "To California through Texas and Mexico," *Quarterly,* California Historical Society, XVIII (1939), p. 241.
21. Michael Baldridge, *A Reminiscence of the Parker H. French Expedition through Texas and Mexico to California in the Spring of 1850* (Los Angeles: John B. Goodman III, 1959), p. 43.
22. Tempsky, *op. cit.,* pp. 38–39.
23. Perkins, *op. cit.,* p. 80.
24. Gunn, *op. cit.,* p. 50.
25. *Ibid.,* p. 51.
26. McGaffey, *op. cit.,* p. 39.
27. Joseph Warren Revere, *A Tour of Duty in California* (New York: C. S. Francis & Co., 1849), p. 22.
28. McGaffey, *op. cit.,* p. 50.
29. Tempsky, *op. cit.,* p. 9.
30. Gunn, *op. cit.,* p. 52.
31. William T. Sayward, *Pioneer Reminiscences, 1882,* MS., Bancroft Library, University of California, Berkeley, p. 3.
32. Tempsky, *op. cit.,* p. 11.
33. William Dunphy, *Statement,* San Francisco 1891, MS., Bancroft Library, University of California, Berkeley, p. 1.
34. Augustus W. Knapp, "An Old Californian's Pioneer Story," *The Overland Monthly,* X, 2d Series (October, 1887), p. 402.
35. H. O. Harper, "To California in '49," *The Overland Monthly,* XXII, 2d Series (1893), p. 328.
36. George S. McKnight, "California 49er . . . Travels from Perrysburg to California, Letter to His Brother," The Perrysburg *Reville* (1849), (Reprint by The Andrews Printing Co., Toledo, Ohio: 1903).
37. *Ibid.*
38. Edward McGowan, *The Strange Eventful History of Parker H. French, with Introduction, Notes and Comments* by Kenneth M. Johnson (Los Angeles: Dawson's Book Shop, 1958), p. 11.
39. *Ibid.,* p. 13.
40. Baldridge, *op. cit.,* p. 47.
41. Daniel B. Woods, *Sixteen Months at the Gold Diggings* (New York: Harper & Brothers, 1851), p. 21.
42. During his career as a journalist, Edwin Allen Sherman had been associated with William Lloyd Garrison's anti-slavery newspaper, the *Emancipator and Free American.* Then, during the Mexican War, Sherman had worked on the United States Army newspaper *American Flag* that was published on captured Mexican presses in Matamoros and Monterrey.

# Notes

43. Edwin Allen Sherman, *Autobiographical Material,* Typescript from original MS., Bancroft Library, University of California, Berkeley, p. 4.
44. Thomas Sayre, *Diary of a Gold-Seeker Who Crossed Mexico from Tampico to Mazatlán in 1849,* MS., Bancroft Library, University of California, Berkeley, p. 5.
45. R. H. Mason, *Pictures of Life in Mexico* (London: Smith, Elder, & Co., 1852), Vol. II, p. 246.
46. Woods, *op. cit.,* p. 22.
47. *Ibid.,* p. 21.
48. Henry Alexander Wise, *Los Gringos: or, An Inside View of Mexico and California, With Wanderings in Peru, Chile, and Polynesia* (New York: Baker and Scribner, 1849), p. 277.
49. *Ibid.,* p. 277.
50. J. A. Perry, *Thrilling Adventures of a New Englander* (Boston: Redding & Co., 1853), p. 47.
51. *Ibid.,* p. 47.
52. *Ibid.,* p. 50.
53. *Ibid.,* p. 53.
54. *Ibid.,* p. 56.
55. Sayre, *op. cit.,* p. 26.
56. Daniel Wadsworth Coit, *Digging for Gold—Without a Shovel: The Letters of Daniel Wadsworth Coit from Mexico City to San Francisco 1848–1851,* ed. by George P. Hammond (Denver: Old West Publishing Co., 1967), p. 71.
57. *Ibid.,* p. 71.
58. *Ibid.,* p. 71.
59. Perry, *op. cit.,* p. 60.
60. Wise, *op. cit.,* p. 232.
61. *Ibid.,* p. 232.
62. J. Disturnell, *The Emigrant's Guide to New Mexico, California, and Oregon; Giving the Different Overland and Sea Routes* (New York: Published by J. Disturnell, 1849), p. 48.
63. Coit, *op. cit.,* p. 72.
64. W. C. Smith, *A Journey to California in 1849* (n.p., n.d.), p. 7.
65. Perry, *op. cit.,* p. 67.
66. Smith, *op. cit.,* p. 8.
67. Coit, *op. cit.,* p. 73.
68. —— Forbes, *A Trip to Mexico, or Recollections of a Ten Months' Ramble in 1849–50 by a Barrister* (London: Smith, Elder, & Co., 1851), p. 201.
69. Smith, *op. cit.,* p. 8.
70. William W. Carpenter, *Travels and Adventures in Mexico* (New York: Harper & Brothers, 1851), p. 290.
71. Perry, *op. cit.,* p. 68.
72. *Ibid.,* p. 68.
73. Forbes, *op. cit.,* pp. 208–209.
74. Smith, *op. cit.,* p. 9.

CHAPTER VIII

1. Bernal Díaz del Castillo, *The Discovery and Conquest of Mexico,* Translated with an Introduction and Notes by A. P. Maudslay, Introduction to

# THE EL DORADO TRAIL

the American edition by Irving A. Leonard (3d ed.; New York: Grove Press, Inc.; Copyright, 1956 by Farrar, Straus & Giroux, Inc.), p. 74.

2. George H. Baker, "Records of a California Journey," *Quarterly*, Society of California Pioneers, VII (1930), p. 219.

3. *Ibid.*, p. 226.

4. J. A. Perry, *Thrilling Adventures of a New Englander* (Boston: Redding & Co., 1853), p. 13.

5. Lesley Byrd Simpson, *Many Mexicos* (4th ed., revised; Berkeley: University of California Press, 1966), p. 94.

6. D. H. Strother, *Illustrated Life of General Winfield Scott* (New York: A. S. Barnes & Co., 1847), p. 140.

7. A. C. Ferris, "To California in 1849 through Mexico," *The Century Illustrated Magazine*, XLII (1891), p. 666.

8. I. I. Murphy, *Life of Colonel Daniel E. Hungerford* (Hartford, Connecticut: Lockwood & Brainard Co., 1891), p. 79.

9. Perry, *op. cit.*, p. 14.

10. *Ibid.*, p. 15.

11. Ferris, *op. cit.*, p. 670.

12. (Lt. Col.) William Preston, *Journal in Mexico* (Paris, France: n.p., n.d.), p. 7.

13. Ferris, *op. cit.*, p. 670.

14. W. C. Smith, *A Journey to California in 1849* (n.p., n.d.), p. 4.

15. Baker, *op. cit.*, p. 230.

16. *Ibid.*, p. 230.

17. Ferris, *op. cit.*, p. 670.

18. Baker, *op. cit.*, p. 232.

19. Ferris, *op. cit.*, pp. 673–674.

20. Rudolf Jordan, "An Autobiography," *Quarterly*, Society of California Pioneers, IV (December, 1927), p. 178.

21. Perry, *op. cit.*, p. 20.

22. *Ibid.*, pp. 20–21.

23. Preston, *op. cit.*, p. 22.

24. *Ibid.*, p. 22.

25. *Ibid.*, p. 28.

26. Perry, *op. cit.*, p. 22.

27. *Ibid.*, p. 22.

28. Preston, *op. cit.*, p. 29.

29. Smith, *op. cit.*, p. 6.

30. Ferris, *op. cit.*, p. 674.

31. *Ibid.*, pp. 674–675.

32. Smith, *op. cit.*, p. 6.

33. Perry, *op. cit.*, p. 27.

34. *Ibid.*, p. 29.

35. *Ibid.*, p. 30.

36. *Ibid.*, p. 32.

37. George P. Hammond, ed., "Introduction," *Digging for Gold—Without a Shovel: The Letters of Daniel Wadsworth Coit From Mexico City to San Francisco 1848–1851* (Denver: Old West Publishing Co., 1967), p. 71.

38. Daniel Wadsworth Coit, *Digging for Gold—Without a Shovel: The Letters of Daniel Wadsworth Coit From Mexico City to San Francisco 1848–1851*,

# Notes

ed. by George P. Hammond (Denver: Old West Publishing Co., 1967), p. 51.
39. *Ibid.*, p. 35.
40. Smith, *op. cit.*, p. 7.
41. Simpson, *op. cit.*, p. 252.
42. Benjamin Richardson, *Mining Experiences* (Letter to A. L. Bancroft, January 23, 1880), MS., Bancroft Library, University of California, Berkeley, p. 3.
43. *Ibid.*, p. 3.
44. William M'Ilvaine, Jr., *Sketches of Scenery and Notes of Personal Adventure in California and Mexico* (Philadelphia, Pennsylvania: 1850), p. 29.
45. Albert G. Osbun, *To California and the South Seas: The Diary of Albert G. Osbun 1849–1851*, ed. by John Haskell Kemble (San Marino, California: The Huntington Library, 1966), p. 187.
46. *Ibid.*, p. 186.
47. Luther M. Schaeffer, *Sketches of Travels in South America, Mexico and California* (New York: James Egbert, Printer, 1860), p. 101.
48. *Brief Sketch of Acapulco, The State of Guerrero, The Republic of Mexico* (Published for the Occasion of the Meeting between President Dwight D. Eisenhower and President Adolfo López Mateos, February 19 and 20, 1959), p. 19.
49. M'Ilvaine, *op. cit.*, p. 25.
50. William Redmond Ryan, *Personal Adventures in Upper and Lower California in 1847–1849* (London: William Shoberl, Publisher, 1850), Vol. II, p. 362.
51. *Brief Sketch of Acapulco, op. cit.*, p. 24.
52. Schaeffer, *op. cit.*, p. 102.
53. J. M. Letts, *California Illustrated: Including a Description of the Panama and Nicaragua Routes* (New York: R. T. Young, 1852), p. 143.
54. Walter Griffith Pigman, *The Journal of Walter Griffith Pigman*, ed. by Ulla Staley Fawkes (Mexico, Missouri: Walter G. Staley, Publisher, 1942), p. 60.
55. U.S. Congress, Senate, "Francis W. Rice to Mr. Webster," *Senate Executive Document*, No. 17, 32d Congress, 2d Session, p. 1.
56. *Ibid.*, p. 1.
57. *Ibid.*, pp. 1–2.

# BIBLIOGRAPHY

## I. PRIMARY SOURCES

MANUSCRIPTS, LETTERS, PAMPHLETS
(*Bancroft Library, University of California, Berkeley*)

Allsopp, J. P. C. *Leaves from My Log Book.*

Beale, Edward Fitzgerald. *Autobiographical Sketch* (1888?).

Demarest, David Durie. *Diary, March 8, 1849–May 1850.*

Dodge, Henry Lee. *Statement.* ca. 1888. (To San Francisco via Vera Cruz and San Blas, 1849.)

Dunphy, William. *Statement.* San Francisco? 1891?

Eastland, Joseph Green. *Dictations.* 1886.

Forsyth, John Robert. *Diary, 1849.* (Typed transcript in Peoria, Illinois, Public Library.)

Hall, Maggie. *Crossing the Plains in 1853.*

Hayes, Benjamin Ignatius. *Diary, 1849–1850.*

Hopkins, Casper Thomas. *Autobiography.* 1885?

Lane, John Lafayette. *Diaries, April 27, 1852–May 14, 1867.*

Lee, Richard Bland. *Letter to Major General George Gibson, 1849.*

Noble, Robert Watson. "Carta de Seguridad," *Parkman Family Papers.*

Noble, Robert Watson. "Diary of a Journey from Chihuahua, Mexico, to the Pueblo de San José, California, April 10–August 1, 1849," *Parkman Family Papers.*

Pierce, Henry Augustus. *Journals of Voyages on the Schooner* Morse *in 1839 and Brig* Maryland *in 1841–1842.*

Richardson, Benjamin. *Mining Experiences.* (As recorded in a letter to A. L. Bancroft.)

# THE EL DORADO TRAIL

Ricks, Casper S. *Diary of an Overland Journey from Albuquerque to Santa Cruz, New Mexico, 1849.*

Romie, Charles Theodore. *Dictation.* 1888?

Sayre, Thomas. *Diary of a Gold-Seeker Who Crossed Mexico from Tampico to Mazatlán in 1849.*

Sayre, Thomas. *Receipt Book, 1849.*

Sayward, William T. *Pioneer Reminiscences.* 1882.

Sherman, Edwin Allen. *Biographical Sketch.* (Typescript from original.)

Sherman, Edwin Allen. *Autobiographical Material.* (Typescript from original.)

Soule, Frank. "Statement of," *Miscellaneous Statements on California History.* 1878.

Steele, Andrew. *Diary, 1850–1851.*

Strentzel, John Theophil. *Autobiography, 1890.*

Winn, William Watkins. *An Autobiography.* 1957. (Grandfather, Albert Maver Winn, crossed Mexico in 1849.)

Wright, John T. *Early Navigation in California Waters.* 1887?

### PERIODICALS

Audubon, John Woodhouse. "Illustrated Notes of an Expedition through Mexico and California, 1849–50." *Magazine of History,* XI, Extra Number 41 (1936).

Bachman, Jacob Henry. "Audubon's Ill-Fated Western Journey: Recalled by the Diary of J. H. Bachman." Ed. by Jeanne Skinner Van Nostrand. *Quarterly,* California Historical Society, XXI (December, 1942).

Bachman, Jacob Henry. "The Diary of a 'Used-Up' Miner." Ed. by Jeanne Skinner Van Nostrand. *Quarterly,* California Historical Society, XXII (March, 1943).

Baker, George H. "Records of a California Journey." *Quarterly,* Society of California Pioneers, VII (1930).

Beattie, George William. "Diary of a Ferryman and Trader at Fort Yuma." *Quarterly,* Southern California Historical Society, XIV (1929).

Bonestell, Louis H. "Autobiography." *Quarterly,* Society of California Pioneers, IV (1927).

Cardinell, Charles. "Adventures on the Plain." *Courier* (1856). Reprinted in *Quarterly,* California Historical Society, I (July, 1922).

Cox, C. C. "From Texas to California in 1849." Edited by Mabelle Eppard Martin. *Southwestern Historical Quarterly,* XXIX (1925).

Eastland, Thomas B. "To California through Texas and Mexico." *Quarterly,* California Historical Society, XVIII (1939).

Ferris, A. C. "To California in 1849 through Mexico." *Century,* XLII (1891).

Harper, H. O. "To California in '49." *The Overland Monthly,* XXII, Series No. 2 (1893).

"The Diary of James D. Hawks." *Quarterly,* Society of California Pioneers, VI, No. 2 (June, 1929).

# Bibliography

Jordan, Rudolf. "An Autobiography." *Quarterly,* Society of California Pioneers, IV (1927).

"Journey from New Orleans to California." *Chambers Journal of Popular Literature,* No. 100 (December, 1855).

Knapp, W. Augustus. "An Old Californian's Pioneer Story." *The Overland Monthly,* X, Series No. 2 (1887).

McClintock, William A. "Journal of a Trip through Texas and Northern Mexico in 1846–1847." *Southwestern Historical Quarterly,* XXXIV (1931).

McGaffey, Joseph Wyatt. "Across Mexico in the Days of '49." *Touring Topics,* XXI, No. 5 (May, 1929).

Stillman, J. D. B. "Cruise of the San Blaseña." (Adventures of Gold-Hunters in 1849), *The Overland Monthly,* XV (September, 1875).

Veeder, Charles H. (a Statement by). "Yuma Indian Depredations on the Colorado in 1850." *Quarterly,* Southern California Historical Society, VII, Nos. 1–2 (1907–1908).

Wozencraft, Oliver M. "Through Northern Mexico in '49." *The Californian,* VI, No. 35 (November, 1882).

GOVERNMENT PUBLICATIONS

Cooke, Philip St. George. "Journal." *Senate Ex. Doc.,* 31st Cong., Special sess., No. 2.

*Despatches from United States Consuls in Acapulco, 1823–1906.* Vol. 1, July 18–December 31, 1853, and Vol. 2, January 10, 1854–December 31, 1855. National Archives, Washington, D.C., 1949.

*Despatches from United States Consuls in Ciudad Juárez (El Paso del Norte), 1850–1906.* Register, 1850–1906. April 10, 1850–December 23, 1869. National Archives, Washington, D.C., 1950.

*Despatches from United States Consuls in Monterrey, Mexico, 1849–1906.* Register, 1849–1906. National Archives, Washington, D.C., 1949.

*Despatches from United States Consuls in Veracruz, 1822–1906.* Vol. 5, January 6, 1844–July 1, 1850. National Archives, Washington, D.C., 1950.

*Diplomatic Instructions of the Department of State, Mexico, 1801–1906.* Vol. XVI, November 10, 1845–April 6, 1854. National Archives, Washington, D.C., 1946.

Emory, William H. (Lt.) "Notes of a Military Reconnaissance from Fort Leavenworth to San Diego, 1846–1847." *House Ex. Doc.,* 30th Cong., 1st sess., No. 41.

Emory, William H. (Lt.) "Report on the United States and Mexican Boundary Survey." *Senate Ex. Doc.,* 34th Cong., 1st sess., No. 108, Vol. 1.

Jones, Thomas ap Catesby (Commodore). "Letters to the Secretary of the Navy, November 4, 1847–August 26, 1850." R. G., 45, National Archives, Washington, D.C.

*Report of the Commissioner of General Land Office, for the Year 1867.* Washington Government Printing Office. Washington, D.C., 1867.

# THE EL DORADO TRAIL

"Francis W. Rice to Mr. Webster." *Senate Ex. Doc.*, 32nd Cong., 2d sess., No. 17.

**BOOKS AND PAMPHLETS**

Aldrich, Lorenzo D. *A Journal of the Overland Route to California! and the Gold Mines.* Lansingburgh, New York: Alex. Kirkpatrick, Printer, 1851.

"Arkansas State Gazette and Democrat, April 26, 1850." *Southern Trails to California in 1849.* Edited by Ralph Bieber. Glendale, California: The Arthur H. Clark Co., 1937.

Audubon, John Woodhouse. *Audubon's Western Journal: 1849–1850.* Edited by Frank Heywood Hodder. Glendale, California: The Arthur H. Clark Co., 1906.

Baldridge, Michael. *A Reminiscence of the Parker H. French Expedition through Texas and Mexico to California in the Spring of 1850.* Introduction by John B. Goodman III. Los Angeles: John B. Goodman III, 1959.

Bartlett, John Russell. *Personal Narrative of Explorations and Incidents in Texas, New Mexico, California, Sonora, and Chihuahua.* New York: D. Appleton & Co., 1854.

Calderón de La Barca, Francis Erskine (Inglis). *Life in Mexico during a Residence of Two Years in That Country.* London: 1843.

Canfield, Chauncey de Leon, ed. *The Diary of a Forty-Niner.* New York: 1906.

Carpenter, William W. *Travels and Adventures in Mexico.* New York: Harper & Brothers, 1851.

Castillo, Bernal Díaz del. *The Discovery and Conquest of Mexico.* Translated with an Introduction and Notes by A. P. Maudslay. Introduction to the American edition by Irving A. Leonard. 3rd ed. New York: Grove Press, Inc., 1956.

Chamberlain, Samuel E. *My Confession.* Introduction and Postscript by Roger Butterfield. New York: Harper & Brothers, 1956.

Clarke, A. B. *Travels in Mexico and California.* Boston: 1852.

Coit, Daniel Wadsworth. *Digging for Gold—Without a Shovel: The Letters of Daniel Wadsworth Coit from Mexico City to San Francisco, 1848–1851.* Edited, with an Introduction by George P. Hammond. Denver, Colorado: Old West Publishing Co., 1967.

Coit, Daniel Wadsworth. *The Drawings and Letters of Daniel Wadsworth Coit: An Artist in El Dorado.* Edited, with a biographical sketch by Edith M. Coulter. San Francisco: The Book Club of California, 1937.

Colton, Joseph Hutchins. *Colton's Map of the United States, Mexico, &c., Showing the Gold Region in California.* New York: 1849.

Columbus, Christopher. *Journals and Other Documents on the Life and Voyages of Christopher Columbus.* Translated and edited by Samuel Eliot Morison. New York: The Heritage Press, 1963.

Cooke, Phlip St. George (Major General). *The Conquest of New Mexico and California: An Historical and Personal Narrative.* New York: G. P. Putnam's Sons, 1878.

# Bibliography

Couts, Cave Johnson. *From San Diego to the Colorado in 1849: The Journal and Maps of Cave J. (Johnson) Couts, 1821–1874.* Edited by William Mc-Pherson. Los Angeles: Zamorano Club, 1932.

Couts, Cave Johnson. *Hepah, California! The Journal of Cave Johnson Couts from Monterey, Nuevo León, Mexico, to Los Angeles, California, during the Years 1848–1849.* Edited by Henry F. Dobyns. Tucson: Arizona Pioneers' Historical Society, 1961.

Creuzbaur, Robert. *Route from the Gulf of Mexico and the Lower Mississippi Valley to California and the Pacific Ocean.* New York: 1849.

Crosby, Elisha Oscar. *Memoirs: Reminiscences of California and Guatemala from 1849 to 1864.* San Marino, California: The Huntington Library, 1945.

Dawson, Nicholas. *Narrative of Nicholas "Cheyenne" Dawson.* Introduction by Charles L. Camp. San Francisco: The Grabhorn Press, 1933.

Delavan, James. *Notes on California and the Placers, How to Get There, and What to Do Afterwards.* New York: H. Long & Brother, 1850.

Disturnell, J. *The Emigrant's Guide to New Mexico, California, and Oregon; Giving the Different Overland and Sea Routes. . . .* New York: J. Disturnell, 1849.

Durivage, John E. "Through Mexico to California: Letters and Journal of John E. Durivage." *Southern Trails to California in 1849.* Edited by Ralph Bieber. Glendale, California: The Arthur H. Clark Co., 1937.

Dye, Job Francis. *Recollections of a Pioneer, 1830–1852.* Los Angeles: Glenn Dawson, 1951.

"Early News of the Gold Discovery." *Southwest Historical Series.* Vol. V. Edited by Ralph P. Bieber and LeRoy R. Hafen. Glendale, California: The Arthur H. Clark Co., 1937.

Eccleston, Robert. *Overland to California on the Southwestern Trail, 1849: Diary of Robert Eccleston.* Edited by George P. Hammond and Edward H. Howes. Berkeley: University of California Press, 1950.

Edwards, Frank S. *A Campaign in New Mexico with Colonel Doniphan.* New York: Carey & Hart, 1847.

Evans, George W. B. *Mexican Gold Trail: The Journal of a Forty-Niner.* Edited by Glenn S. Dumke. Preface by Robert Glass Cleland. San Marino, California: The Huntington Library, 1945.

Farnham, Thomas J. *Mexico: Its Geography—Its People—and Its Institutions. . . .* New York: H. Long & Brother, 1846.

Forbes, ———. *A Trip to Mexico, or Recollections of a Ten Months' Ramble in 1849–50.* London: Smith, Elder, & Co., 1851.

Foster, G. G., ed. *The Gold Regions of California.* New York: Dewitt & Davenport, 1849.

Furber, George C. *The Twelve Months Volunteer; or, Journal of a Private in the Tennessee Regiment of Cavalry in the Campaign in Mexico, 1846–7.* Cincinnati, Ohio: J. A. & U. P. James, 1850.

# THE EL DORADO TRAIL

Grant, Ulysses S. *Personal Memoirs*. New York: Charles L. Webster & Co., 1885.

Gregg, Josiah. *Commerce of the Prairies*. New York: Henry G. Langley, 1844.

Gregg, Josiah, *Diary and Letters of Josiah Gregg*. Edited by Maurice Garland Fulton. Introduction by Paul Horgan. Norman, Oklahoma: University of Oklahoma Press, 1944.

Gunn, Lewis C. and Elizabeth L. *Records of a California Family*. Edited by Anna Lee Marston. San Diego: 1928.

Hammond, George P., ed. *The Larkin Papers*. Vols. VII and VIII. Berkeley: University of California Press, 1960 and 1962.

Hammond, George P., ed. *Letters of the Gold Discovery*. San Francisco: The Book Club of California, 1948.

Harris, Benjamin Butler. *The Gila Trail: The Texas Argonauts and the California Gold Rush*. Edited and annotated by Richard H. Dillon. Norman, Oklahoma: University of Oklahoma Press, 1960.

Hastings, Lansford W. *A New History of Oregon and California Containing Descriptions of Those Countries Together with the Oregon Treaty and Correspondence*. Cincinnati, Ohio: Published by George Conclin, 1849.

Hayes, Benjamin Ignatius. *Pioneer Notes from the Diaries of Judge Benjamin Hayes*. Edited by Marjorie Tisdale Walcott. Los Angeles: Published by the editor, 1929.

Henry, W. S. *Campaign Sketches of the War with Mexico*. New York: Harper & Brothers, 1847.

Hitchcock, Ethan Allen. *Fifty Years in Camp, Diary of General Hitchcock*. New York: G. P. Putnam's Sons, 1909.

Klarwill, Victor von, ed. *The Fugger News-Letters*. Translated by Pauline de Chary. New York: G. P. Putnam's Sons, 1924.

Lafora, Nicolas de. *The Frontiers of New Spain, Nicolas de Lafora's Description, 1766–1768*. Edited by Lawrence Kinnaird. Berkeley: The Quivira Society, 1958.

Lamar, Mirabeau Buonaparte. *The Papers of Mirabeau Buonaparte Lamar*. Edited by Charles A. Gulick, Jr., and Katherine Elliot. Austin, Texas: A. C. Baldwin Sons, 1922–1926.

Letts, J. M. *California Illustrated: Including a Description of the Panama and Nicaragua Routes*. New York: R. T. Young, 1852.

Magoffin, Susan Shelby. *Down the Santa Fé Trail and Into Mexico: The Diary of Susan Shelby Magoffin*. Edited by Stella Drumm. New Haven, Connecticut: Yale University Press, 1926.

Mason, R. H. *Pictures of Life in Mexico*. London: Smith, Elder, & Co., 1852.

Maverick, Mary A., and George Madison Maverick. *Memoirs of Mary A. Maverick*. Edited by Rena Maverick Green. San Antonio, Texas: 1921.

McCoy, Alexander W., John, and Samuel Finley McCoy. *Pioneering on the Plains, Journey to Mexico in 1848, the Overland Trip to California*. Kaukauna, Wisconsin: 1924.

# Bibliography

M'Collum, William S. *California As I Saw It.* Edited by Dale L. Morgan. Los Gatos, California: The Talisman Press, 1960.

McGowan, Edward. *The Strange Eventful History of Parker H. French, with Introduction, Notes and Comments* by Kenneth M. Johnson. Los Angeles: Dawson's Book Shop, 1958.

M'Ilvaine, William, Jr. *Sketches of Scenery and Notes of Personal Adventure in California and Mexico.* Philadelphia: 1850.

McKnight, George S. "California 49er . . . Travels from Perrysburg to California, Letter to His Brother." The Perrysburg *Reville*, 1849. Toledo, Ohio: Reprint edition, The Andrews Printing Co., 1903.

McNeil, Samuel. *McNeil's Travels in 1849, to, through and from the Gold Regions, in California.* Columbus, Ohio: 1850.

Miles, William. *Journal of the Suffering and Hardships of Capt. Parker H. French's Overland Expedition to California, Which Left New York City, May 13, 1850, and Arrived at San Francisco, Dec. 14.* Chambersburg, Pennsylvania: 1851.

Osbun, Albert G. *To California and the South Seas: The Diary of Albert G. Osbun, 1849–1851.* Edited by John Haskell Kemble. San Marino, California: The Huntington Library, 1966.

Pancoast, Charles. *A Quaker Forty-Niner: The Adventures of Charles Edward Pancoast on the American Frontier.* Edited by Anna Paschall Hannum. Philadelphia: University of Pennsylvania Press, 1930.

Patterson, Lawson B. *Twelve Years in the Mines of California.* Cambridge, Massachusetts: Miles and Dillingham, 1862.

Perkins, William. *Three Years in California: Journal of Life at Sonora, 1849–1852.* Introduction and Annotations by Dale L. Morgan and James R. Scobie. Berkeley: University of California Press, 1964.

Perry, J. A. *Thrilling Adventures of a New Englander.* Boston: Redding & Co., 1853.

*A Perrysburg 49's Trip to California.* Toledo, Ohio: 1903.

Pigman, Walter Griffith. *The Journal of Walter Griffith Pigman.* Edited by Ulla Staley Fawkes. Mexico, Missouri: Walter G. Staley, Publisher, 1942.

Powell, H. M. T. *The Santa Fé Trail to California, 1849–1852: The Journal and Drawings of H. M. T. Powell.* Edited by Douglas S. Watson. San Francisco: The Book Club of California, 1931.

Pownall, Joseph. "From Louisiana to Mariposa." Edited by Robert Glass Cleland. *Rushing for Gold.* Edited by John Walton Caughey. Berkeley: University of California Press, 1949.

Preston, William (Lt. Col.). *Journal in Mexico.* Paris, France: Privately printed, n.d.

Revere, Joseph Warren. *A Tour of Duty in California.* New York: C. S. Francis & Co., 1849.

Robinson, Fayette. *California and Its Gold Regions.* New York: Stringer & Townsend, 1849.

# THE EL DORADO TRAIL

Ryan, William. *Personal Adventures in Upper and Lower California in 1847–49*. London: 1850.

Sartorius, Christian. *Mexico: Landscapes and Popular Sketches*. London: Trübner & Co., 1859.

Schaeffer, Luther M. *Sketches of Travels in South America, Mexico and California*. New York: James Egbert, 1860.

Sherman, William T. *Memoirs of General William T. Sherman*. New York: D. Appleton & Co., 1875.

Sherwood, J. Ely. *The Pocket Guide to California*. New York: Published by author, 1849.

Smith, George Winston, and Charles Judah, eds. *Chronicles of the Gringos: The U.S. Army in the Mexican War, 1846–1848, Accounts of Eyewitnesses & Combatants*. Albuquerque: The University of New Mexico Press, 1968.

Smith, W. C. *A Journey to California in 1849*. n.p., n.d.

Swan, John Alfred. *A Trip to the Gold Mines of California in 1848*. Edited by John A. Hussey. San Francisco: The Book Club of California, 1960.

Taylor, Bayard. *Eldorado: Being a True Facsimile of the Whole of the First 1850 Edition, Including the Original Color Plates*. "A Biographical Introduction" by Richard H. Dillon. Palo Alto: Lewis Osborne, 1968.

Tempsky, G. F. von. *Mitla*. Edited by J. S. Bell. London: Longman, Brown, Green, Longmans, & Roberts, 1858.

Turner, Henry Smith. *The Original Journals of Henry Smith Turner: With Stephen Watts Kearny to New Mexico and California, 1846*. Edited and with an Introduction by Dwight L. Clarke. Norman, Oklahoma: University of Oklahoma Press, 1966.

Tyson, James L., M.D. *Diary of a Physician in California*. Foreword by Joseph A. Sullivan. Oakland: Biobooks, 1955.

Ware, Joseph. *The Emigrants' Guide to California, Containing Every Point of Information for the Emigrant*. St. Louis: 1849.

Webber, Charles Wilkins. *The Gold Mines of the Gila*. New York: Dewitt & Davenport, 1849.

Wheat, Marvin (Cincinnatus). *Travels on the Western Slope of the Mexican Cordillera*. San Francisco: Whitton, Towne & Co., 1857.

White, Philo. *Narrative of a Cruize in the Pacific to South America and California on the U.S. Sloop-of-War "Dale" 1841–1843*. Edited by Charles L. Camp. Denver, Colorado: Old West Publishing Co., 1965.

Wise, Henry Alexander, *Los Gringos: or, An Inside View of Mexico and California, with Wanderings in Peru, Chile, and Polynesia*. New York: Baker & Scribner, 1849.

Wood, Harvey. *Personal Recollections of Harvey Wood*. Introduction by John B. Goodman III. Pasadena, California: John B. Goodman III, 1955.

Woods, Daniel B. *Sixteen Months at the Gold Diggings*. New York: Harper & Brothers, 1851.

Woodward, Arthur, ed. *Journal of Lieutenant Thomas W. Sweeny, 1849–1853*. Los Angeles: Westernlore Press, 1956.

# Bibliography

## II. SECONDARY SOURCES

BOOKS AND PAMPHLETS

Adams, Alexander B. *John James Audubon.* New York: G. P. Putnam's Sons, 1966.

Alvaréz, José J., and Rafael Durán. *Itinerarios y Derroteros de la Republica Mexicana.* Mexico: 1856.

Bandelier, Adolph, F. A. *The Gilded Man.* Reprint of the 1893 edition. Chicago: The Rio Grande Press, Inc., 1962.

Eeale, Marie. *Decatur House and Its Inhabitants.* Washington, D.C.: National Trust for Historic Preservation, 1954.

Benítez, Fernando. *In the Footsteps of Cortez.* New York: Pantheon Books, Inc., 1952.

Berthold, Victor M. *The Pioneer Steamer California.* New York: Houghton Mifflin Co., 1932.

Bieber, Ralph, ed. *Southern Trails to California in 1849.* Glendale, California: The Arthur H. Clark Co., 1937.

Bieber, Ralph and LeRoy R. Hafen. *The Southwest Historical Series.* Glendale, California: The Arthur H. Clark Co., 1943.

Bonsal, Stephen. *Edward Fitzgerald Beale.* New York: G. P. Putnam's Sons, 1912.

*Brief Sketch of Acapulco, The State of Guerrero, the Republic of Mexico.* Mexico: 1959.

Caughey, John Walton. *Gold Is the Cornerstone.* Berkeley: University of California Press, 1948.

Caughey, John Walton, ed. *Rushing for Gold.* Berkeley: University of California Press, 1949.

Chapman, Walker. *The Golden Dream: Seekers of El Dorado.* New York: The Bobbs-Merrill Co., Inc., 1967.

Clarke, Dwight L. *Stephen Watts Kearny: Soldier of the West.* Norman, Oklahoma: University of Oklahoma Press, 1961.

*Corpus Christi: A History and Guide.* Corpus Christi, Texas: Corpus Christi Caller-Times, 1942.

DeVoto, Bernard. *The Year of Decision, 1846.* Boston: Little, Brown & Co., 1943.

Dillon, Richard. *Fool's Gold: The Decline and Fall of Captain John Sutter of California.* New York: Coward-McCann, Inc., 1967.

Dunbier, Roger. *The Sonoran Desert: Its Geography, Economy, and People.* Tucson: The University of Arizona Press, 1968.

# THE EL DORADO TRAIL

Faulk, Odie B. *Too Far North . . . Too Far South.* Los Angeles: Westernlore Press, 1967.

Foreman, Grant. *The Adventures of James Collier: First Collector of the Port of San Francisco.* Chicago: Black Cat Press, 1937.

Foreman, Grant. *Marcy and the Gold Seekers.* Norman, Oklahoma: University of Oklahoma Press, 1939.

Gilman, William C. *A Memoir of Daniel Wadsworth Coit, 1787–1876.* Cambridge, Massachusetts: Privately printed, 1908.

Heitman, Francis B. *Historical Register and Dictionary of the United States Army, 1789–1903.* Washington, D.C.: Government Printing Office, 1903.

Hine, Robert V. *Bartlett's West: Drawing the Mexican Boundary.* New Haven and London: Yale University Press, 1968.

Hollon, W. Eugene. *Beyond the Cross Timbers: The Travels of Randolph B. Marcy, 1812–1887.* Norman, Oklahoma: University of Oklahoma Press, 1955.

Howe, Octavius Thorndike. *Argonauts of '49.* Cambridge, Massachusetts: Harvard University Press, 1923.

Jaeger, Edmund C. *The California Deserts.* 3rd. ed. ,Stanford, California: Stanford University Press, 1955.

James, George Wharton. *Wonders of the Colorado Desert.* Boston: Little, Brown & Co., 1906.

Knight, Oliver. *Fort Worth: Outpost on the Trinity.* Norman, Oklahoma: University of Oklahoma Press, 1953.

Kroeber, Alfred L. *Cultural and Natural Areas of Native North America.* Berkeley: University of California Press, 1939.

Lavender, David. *Climax at Buena Vista.* New York: J. B. Lippincott Co., 1966.

Lewis, Oscar. *Sea Routes to the Gold Fields.* New York: Alfred A. Knopf, Inc., 1949.

Lister, Florence C. and Robert H. Lister. *Chihuahua: Storehouse of Storms.* Albuquerque: The University of New Mexico Press, 1966.

McCampbell, Coleman. *Saga of a Frontier Seaport.* Dallas: Southwest Press, 1934.

Moorhead, Max L. *The Apache Frontier.* Norman, Oklahoma: University of Oklahoma Press, 1968.

Murphy, I. I. *Life of Colonel Daniel E. Hungerford.* Hartford, Connecticut: Lockwood & Brainard Co., 1891.

Paul, Rodman W. *The California Gold Discovery: Sources, Documents, Accounts and Memoirs Relating to the Discovery of Gold at Sutter's Mill.* Georgetown, California: The Talisman Press, 1966.

Paul, Rodman W. *Mining Frontiers of the Far West, 1848–1880.* New York: Holt, Rinehart and Winston, Inc., 1963.

Pomfret, John E., ed. *California Gold Voyages, 1848–1849.* San Marino, California: The Huntington Library, 1954.

Richardson, Rupert Norval. *The Comanche Barrier to South Plains Settlement:*

# Bibliography

*A Century and a Half of Savage Resistance to the Advancing White Frontier.* Glendale, California: The Arthur H. Clark Co., 1933.

Schurz, William Lytle. *The Manila Galleon.* New York: E. P. Dutton & Co., Inc., 1959.

Sconnichsen, C. L. *Pass of the North: Four Centuries on the Río Grande.* El Paso: Texas Western Press, 1968.

Scott, Florence Johnson. *Old Rough and Ready on the Río Grande.* San Antonio, Texas: Naylor Co., 1935.

Simmons, Marc, trans. and ed. *Border Comanches.* Santa Fé: Stagecoach Press, 1967.

Simpson, Lesley Byrd. *Many Mexicos.* 4th ed., revised. Berkeley: University of California Press, 1966.

Smith, Arthur D. Howden. *Old Fuss and Feathers.* New York: The Greystone Press, 1937.

Stewart, George R. *The California Trail.* New York: McGraw-Hill Book Company, Inc., 1962.

Strother, D. H. *Illustrated Life of General Winfield Scott.* New York: A. S. Barnes & Co., 1847.

Taylor, Paul Schuster. *An American-Mexican Frontier: Nueces County, Texas.* Chapel Hill, North Carolina: University of North Carolina Press, 1934.

Thrapp, Dan L. *The Conquest of Apachería.* Norman,. Oklahoma: University of Oklahoma Press, 1967.

Thurman, Michael E. *The Naval Department of San Blas: New Spain's Bastion for Alta California and Nootka, 1767 to 1798.* Glendale, California: The Arthur H. Clark Co., 1967.

Velasco, José Francisco. *Noticias Estadísticas del Estado Sonora, Mexico.* Sonora, Mexico: 1850.

Velasco, José Francisco. *Sonora: Its Extent, Population, Natural Productions, Indian Tribes, Mines, Mineral Lands, etc.* Translated by William F. Nye. San Francisco: H. H. Bancroft & Co., 1861.

Wallace, Ernest, and E. Adamson Hoebel. *The Comanches: Lords of the South Plains.* Norman, Oklahoma: University of Oklahoma Press, 1952.

Webb, Walter Prescott, ed. *The Handbook of Texas.* Austin: Texas State Historical Association, 1952.

Wiltsee, Ernest Abram. *Gold Rush Steamers of the Pacific.* San Francisco: The Grabhorn Press, 1938.

Woodward, W. E. *Meet General Grant.* New York: Garden City Publishing Co., 1928.

PERIODICALS

Benjamin, Theodosia. "The Audubon Party—New York to California, 1849." *The Pacific Historian,* Vol. 12, No. 4 (Fall, 1968).

Billington, Ray A. "Books That Won the West." *The American West,* IV, No. 3 (August, 1967).

# THE EL DORADO TRAIL

Brandes, Ray. "A Guide to the History of the U.S. Army Installations in Arizona, 1849–1886." *Arizona and the West: A Quarterly Journal of History*, I, No. 1 (Spring, 1959).

Donohue, J. Augustine, S.J. "The Unlucky Jesuit Mission of Bac." *Arizona and the West: A Quarterly Journal of History*, II, No. 2 (Summer, 1960).

Eckhart, George B. "A Guide to the History of the Missions of Sonora." *Arizona and the West: A Quarterly Journal of History*, II, No. 2 (Summer, 1960).

Faulk, Odie B. "The Controversial Boundary Survey and the Gadsden Treaty." *Arizona and the West: A Quarterly Journal of History*, IV, No. 3 (Autumn, 1962).

Guinn, J. M. "The Sonoran Migration." *Quarterly*, Southern California Historical Society, VIII, Nos. 1 & 2 (1909–1910).

Guinn, J. M. "Yuma Indian Depredations and the Glanton War." *Quarterly*, Southern California Historical Society, VI, No. 1 (1903).

Hunt, Aurora. "Overland by Boat to California in 1849." *Quarterly*, Southern California Historical Society, XXXI, No. 3 (1949).

Keene, Tom A. "Corpus Christi: A City of Destiny." *Epic Century Magazine*, V, No. 2 (March, 1938).

Lamb, Taze and Jessie. "Dream of a Desert Paradise." *Desert* (June, 1939).

Martin, Mabelle Eppard. "California Emigrant Roads through Texas." *Southwestern Historical Quarterly*, XXVIII, No. 4 (April, 1925).

Park, Joseph F. "The Apaches in Mexican American Relations, 1848–1861." *Arizona and the West: A Quarterly Journal of History*, III, No. 2 (Summer, 1961).

Park, Joseph F. "Spanish Indian Policy in Northern Mexico, 1765–1810." *Arizona and the West: A Quarterly Journal of History*, IV, No. 4 (Winter, 1962).

Roske, Ralph J. "The World Impact of the California Gold Rush, 1849–1857." *Arizona and the West: A Quarterly Journal of History*, V, No. 3 (Autumn, 1963).

Smith, Ralph J. "The Scalphunter in the Borderlands, 1835–1850." *Arizona and the West: A Quarterly Journal of History*, VI, No. 1 (Spring, 1964).

Stevens, Robert C. "The Apache Menace in Sonora, 1831–1849." *Arizona and the West: A Quarterly Journal of History*, VI, No. 3 (Autumn, 1964).

Victor, Frances Fuller. "On the Mexican Border." *The Overland Monthly* (May, 1871).

### DISSERTATIONS AND THESES

Holliday, J. S. "The California Gold Rush in Myth and Reality." Unpublished Ph.D. dissertation, University of California at Berkeley, 1959.

Kemble, John Haskell. "The Genesis of the Pacific Mail Steamship Company." Unpublished M.A. thesis, University of California at Berkeley, 1934.

Tate, Vernon Dale. "The Founding of the Port of San Blas." Unpublished Ph.D. dissertation, University of California at Berkeley, 1934.

# INDEX

# Index

Cundinamarca, El Dorado, gilded man of, 2–4

Daily Missouri Republican, 23
Davis, Jefferson, 38, 173
Defiance (Ohio) Gold Hunter's Expedition, 63
Democratic Telegraph and Texas Register, 31
Diseases, tropical, 244–245, 269
  See also Cholera epidemic
Disturnell's guidebook, 35–36, 219
Doniphan, Col. Alexander W., 94, 101–103
Donner Party disaster, 33, 52
Drusina, William de, 263–264
Dunphy, William, 93, 200–201
Durango, Mexico, 29, 40, 55, 74–75, 135, 182–188
  mule trail to Mazatlán, 188–195
  road from Parras, 178–182
Durivage, John E., 68, 72, 76, 90–91, 98, 104–105, 128–129, 143–144, 148, 150, 154–155, 158, 162
Duval, Capt. Isaac H., 118, 126–130, 153, 167
Duval Company, 153, 167

Eagle Pass, Texas, 177
Eastland, Joseph, 117–118, 171, 191
Eastland, Thomas B., 63, 100, 101, 116–118, 171, 191–192, 200
Edward, Mary, 25.
Edwards, Tom, 129–130
El Carmen, Mexican village, 92
El Dorado, myths about, 2–4, 111, 167, 279
El Dorado (Van Heuvel), 3–4
El Galeana, Mexico, 104, 129
El Paso del Norte, Mexico, 31–32, 55, 67, 87, 94, 100, 109, 110, 111, 113, 114–137
  frontier crossroads, 114–124
  road to Janos, 124–137
El Poso, Mexico, 77
El Salto, Mexico, 192
El Valle, Mexico, 79
Emory, Maj. William H., 164
Essex Company, 175–176
Estevánico, giant Negro slave, 3, 157
Evans, George W.B., 63, 91–92, 98–99, 104, 144, 163

Fandangos, 230, 273–274
Fees, for passage to California, 33, 35, 44, 50, 54, 231

route around Cape Horn, 50–51
Feria or fair, 273–274
Feris, A.C., 248–249, 251–252, 257–258
Finefrock, B.F., 183
First Missouri Volunteers, 94, 101–103
Flim-flam promoters, 36, 41–45, 130–131
Florida, expedition to conquer, 3
Flotte, Lewis, 128, 136
Folsom, Capt. Joseph, 8
Fondas, 200, 230, 246, 260
Food and wines, 14, 18–19, 21, 35, 74, 76, 97, 99, 115, 118, 120, 147, 185, 228, 246, 252
Foote, Senator, 21–22, 24
Forsyth, John Robert, 146, 150–154, 156
Fort Hall, 52
Fort Kearny, 51
Fort Laramie, 52
Fort San Carlos, 253–254
Fort Yuma, 161
Forty-Niners, 36, 118–119, 123
  companies of, 40
  See also under names of companies
Fourth of July celebration, 81–82
Franklin, Texas, 134
Fremont, John C., 33, 49–50
French, Parker H., 42–45, 130–137, 171, 193, 282
  flim-flam man, 202–203
  Overland Expedition to California, 131–137

Galveston, Texas, 53, 63–64, 177
Gila, Expedition, 166
Gila River, 31, 134
  confluence with Colorado River, 40, 43, 75, 161, 165
Gila Trail, 60, 111, 135, 156–160
Glanton, John, 92–93, 123, 165–166
Glover, William R., 177
Gold fever, 1–3, 23–24, 62, 68, 165, 236–237, 279–280
  mass hysteria, 49–50
  number of seekers, 280
Gold strike, 7–25, 30
Gómez, Apache chief, 92
Graham, Maj. Lawrence P., 67, 88, 123, 138–139, 162
Grand Society (Mexico City hotel), 16, 263
Grant, Ulysses S., 16, 37
Great Basin, 33, 35, 52–53
Great Salt Lake, 52
"Great Western, The," 122–123, 171

# Index

# Index